Marriage Migration, Family and Citizenship in Asia

Amidst the increasing global trend of cross-border marriage migration, this book offers timely theoretical and empirical insights into contemporary debates about migration and citizenship. Extant scholarship on marriage migration and citizenship have concentrated on East-West inter-cultural marriages and tended to approach citizenship as an individual-centred concept linked to the nation-state, thus fading the family into the background.

Focusing on cross-border marriages within Asia, a region where collectivist and familistic values are still prevalent, this book points to the importance of going beyond the state-individual nexus to conceptualise and foreground the family as a strategic site where citizenship is mediated, negotiated and experienced. Through six critical and in-depth case studies on cross-border marriages between East, Southeast, and South Asia, this book reveals how nation-states mobilize patriarchal notions of the family for its citizenship project; how formal frameworks of citizenship structure the trajectory and circumstances of cross-border families; how the repercussions of marriage migrants' citizenship are experienced and negotiated across generations; and how the tensions between the individual, the family and the state are produced along gender, class, race/ethnic, religious, cultural, geographical and generational boundaries. Collectively, this book calls for a rethinking of citizenship from an individual-centred proposition to a family-level concept.

Its wealth of case studies and examples make it an essential resource for students, academics and researchers of Sociology, Geography, Anthropology, Politics, International Development Studies and Asian Studies. The chapters in this book were originally published as a special issue of *Citizenship Studies*.

Tuen Yi Chiu is Assistant Professor at the Department of Sociology and Social Policy, Lingnan University, Hong Kong. She is a sociologist specialising in migration, gender, family, and ageing. Her research focuses on cross-border marriage migration, transnational ageing, intimate partner violence, and intergenerational relations.

Brenda S.A. Yeoh is Raffles Professor of Social Sciences, National University of Singapore (NUS) and Research Leader, Asian Migration Cluster, at NUS' Asia Research Institute. Her research interests in Asian migrations span themes including social reproduction and care migration; skilled migration and cosmopolitanism; and marriage migrants and cultural politics.

Marriage Migration, Family and Citizenship in Asia

Edited by
Tuen Yi Chiu and Brenda S.A. Yeoh

Routledge
Taylor & Francis Group

LONDON AND NEW YORK

First published 2023
by Routledge
4 Park Square, Milton Park, Abingdon, Oxon OX14 4RN

and by Routledge
605 Third Avenue, New York, NY 10158

Routledge is an imprint of the Taylor & Francis Group, an informa business

British Library Cataloguing in Publication Data
A catalogue record for this book is available from the British Library

ISBN13: 978-1-032-49016-8 (hbk)
ISBN13: 978-1-032-49017-5 (pbk)
ISBN13: 978-1-003-39186-9 (ebk)

DOI: 10.4324/9781003391869

Typeset in Minion Pro
by Newgen Publishing UK

Publisher's Note
The publisher accepts responsibility for any inconsistencies that may have arisen during the conversion of this book from journal articles to book chapters, namely the inclusion of journal terminology.

Disclaimer
Every effort has been made to contact copyright holders for their permission to reprint material in this book. The publishers would be grateful to hear from any copyright holder who is not here acknowledged and will undertake to rectify any errors or omissions in future editions of this book.

Contents

Citation Information

The chapters in this book were originally published in the journal *Citizenship Studies*, volume 25, issue 7 (2021). When citing this material, please use the original page numbering for each article, as follows:

Introduction

Marriage migration, family and citizenship in Asia
Tuen Yi Chiu and Brenda S.A. Yeoh
Citizenship Studies, volume 25, issue 7 (2021), pp. 879–897

Chapter 1

Transnational marriage migration and the negotiation of precarious pathways beyond partial citizenship in Singapore
Brenda S.A. Yeoh, Heng Leng Chee, Rohini Anant and Theodora Lam
Citizenship Studies, volume 25, issue 7 (2021), pp. 898–917

Chapter 2

Penalizing 'runaway' migrant wives: commercial cross-border marriages and home space as confinement
Sohoon Yi
Citizenship Studies, volume 25, issue 7 (2021), pp. 918–935

Chapter 3

Discretionary maternal citizenship: state hegemony and resistance of single marriage migrant mothers from mainland China to Hong Kong
Tuen Yi Chiu
Citizenship Studies, volume 25, issue 7 (2021), pp. 936–954

Chapter 4

From 'social problems' to 'social assets': geopolitics, discursive shifts in children of Southeast Asian marriage migrants, and mother-child dyadic citizenship in Taiwan
Hsiao-Chuan Hsia
Citizenship Studies, volume 25, issue 7 (2021), pp. 955–974

Chapter 5

Chapter 6

Afterword

For any permission-related enquiries please visit:
www.tandfonline.com/page/help/permissions

Notes on Contributors

Rohini Anant obtained her Master of Social Sciences (Research) degree in Geography from the National University of Singapore. She is a qualitative researcher interested in labour geographies and migration studies. Currently, she is working as Research Assistant in the Asian Migration Cluster at the Asia Research Institute, National University of Singapore.

Katharine Charsley is Professor of Migration Studies at the School for Sociology, Politics and International Studies at the University of Bristol. Her research focusses on issues of family, gender and migration, and in particular on marriage-related migration.

Heng Leng Chee carried out research on marriage migration in Malaysia and Singapore while she was a senior research fellow at the Asia Research Institute, NUS, 2003–2012.

Isabelle Cheng is Senior Lecturer in East Asian and International Development Studies at the School of Area Studies, History, Politics and Literature, University of Portsmouth, Portsmouth, UK. Her research interests include marriage migration, citizenship, citizenship legislation, national identity, in-betweenness, multiculturalism, Overseas Chinese Studies, migration in East Asia, Taiwan Studies, and women's political participation.

Tuen Yi Chiu is Assistant Professor at the Department of Sociology and Social Policy, Lingnan University, Hong Kong. She is a sociologist specialising in migration, gender, family, and ageing. Her research focuses on cross-border marriage migration, transnational ageing, intimate partner violence, and intergenerational relations.

Hsiao-Chuan Hsia Professor at the Graduate Institute of Social Work, National Chengchi University, Taiwan, the first scholar studying marriage migration issues in Taiwan. Her publications analyze issues of immigrants, migrant workers, citizenship, empowerment and social movement. Hsia is a praxis-oriented researcher striving for the empowerment of immigrant women and the making of im/migrant movements. She initiated the Chinese programs for marriage migrants in 1995, leading to the establishment of TransAsia Sisters Association of Taiwan, spearheading the movement for marriage migrants' rights and welfare in Taiwan.

Masako Kudo is Professor of Cultural Anthropology at the College of Arts and Sciences, J.F. Oberlin University, Japan. Her research interests are in migration, transnationalism, and social integration, with a focus on gender, family, and identity. Her work has been published in Asian Anthropology and Critical Asian Studies among other journals. She is co-author of Marriage Migration in Asia: Emerging Minorities at the Frontiers of Nation-States (2016).

Theodora Lam is Research Fellow in Asia Research Institute, National University of Singapore (NUS). She obtained her PhD in Geography from NUS and her dissertation focused on understanding changing gender subjectivities, webs of care and relationships within the family in the wake of transnational labour migration. Her research interests cover transnational migration, children's geographies and gender studies.

Brenda S.A. Yeoh is Raffles Professor of Social Sciences, National University of Singapore (NUS) and Research Leader, Asian Migration Cluster, at NUS' Asia Research Institute. Her research interests in Asian migrations span themes including social reproduction and care migration; skilled migration and cosmopolitanism; and marriage migrants and cultural politics.

Sohoon Yi is Assistant Professor in Sociology at Kyungpook National University. Her research interest is migrant subjectivity at the intersection of gender, immigration laws, precarious labor, and the informal market. She is currently developing a book manuscript on temporariness, borders, and ethno-kinship migration programs in South Korea.

Introduction: Marriage migration, family and citizenship in Asia

Tuen Yi Chiu and Brenda S.A. Yeoh ⓘ

ABSTRACT

Despite the burgeoning scholarship on marriage migration and citizenship, extant studies have tended to approach citizenship as an individual-centred concept linked to the nation-state, thus fading the family domain into the background. Focusing on cross-border marriages within Asia, this special issue points to the importance of going beyond the state-individual nexus to conceptualise the family as a strategic site where citizenship is mediated, negotiated and experienced. In this Introduction, we draw attention to the gendered mode of familial citizenship and explicate how it operates locally and transnationally to limit the rights and agency of marriage migrants. We then illustrate how the link between marriage migration and citizenship is mediated through the family as a significant site of negotiation and contestation, and as an important lens for understanding the intergenerationality of citizenship. Collectively, this special issue calls for a rethinking of citizenship from an individual-centred proposition to a family-level concept.

Migrations and challenges to citizenship in Asia

The challenges that contemporary migrations pose to meanings and practices of citizenship in Asia need to be contextualised within the historical development of nation-states in the region. When large-scale migrations within the region (mainly in the form of low-waged labour migration to the Middle East) started in the 1970s, many Asian countries – including several which had only recently severed their colonial apron strings – were still in the process of consolidating projects of nation-state building (Asis and Battisella 2012, 31). These nation-building developments in Asia differ from both the European model of supposedly homogeneous and insular states, as well as multiculturalist versions prominent in the North American and Australasian settler colonies that privilege 'white' subjects as the core of the nation. Instead, Southeast Asian postcolonial nation-states such as Indonesia, Malaysia and Singapore strained towards welding together a nation-state from 'an *already existing* plurality' rooted in the diasporas and people movements of colonial times, while postwar East Asian polities such as Japan and South Korea constructed a sense of nationhood on the basis of idealised narratives of ethnic homogeneity that denied the presence of ethnically-different others (Collins, Lai, and Yeoh 2013, 15).

In the struggle for territorial legitimacy and social coherence, nation-states in Asia exercise the power of sovereignty in determining borders and terms of membership by wielding citizenship rules as a legal instrument of exclusion that sharply separates citizens as insiders from those deemed outsiders. For the vast majority of Asian nation-states, the perspective that citizenship describes a one-to-one umbilical relationship – one that allocates persons to states and confers specific bundles of rights and responsibilities tied to national territory – is seldom challenged in policy discourses. In this context, the migration regime that emerged in Asia was premised on keeping migration temporary, and apart from creating a privileged pathway for highly skilled migrants to gain residency and citizenship, most Asian receiving nation-states 'rule[d] out settlement, family reunification and long-term integration, including acquisition of citizenship, for less skilled migrants' (Asis and Battisella 2012, 32). In other words, the migration system that developed in Asia was one that minimised challenges to the fragile imaginary of the nation-state in the making, by rendering migrants as transient sojourners whose place in host societies is to sell their labour but make no claims on the receiving nation-state (Yeoh et al. 2020).

In most Asian countries, citizenship is inherited and ascribed primarily through 'blood' descent (Asis and Battisella 2012). While many countries in the region also allow for (but not necessarily encourage) naturalisation, and some extend special consideration to long-term residents (as exemplified by the longstanding Korean community in Japan), the requirements for naturalisation usually favour those with substantial economic capital or possess high levels of skills which are in demand. Apart from the citizenship pathways exclusively paved for those who possess talent or capital, the other available route to legal citizenship in Asia – one ridden with far more uncertainty and risk – lies through entering into marriage unions with citizens of the host nation-state. In recent decades, East Asian industrialised economies such as Taiwan, South Korea, Japan, Singapore and Hong Kong have experienced a significant increase in the rate of non-marriage and delayed marriage, partly as a result of the growing mismatch in marriage expectations between the two largest groups of singles: on the one hand, independent-minded, financially well-resourced graduate women with sophisticated expectations of marriage partners, and on the other, less educated men in lowly paid jobs with a preference for women willing to uphold traditional gender roles and values. Following the logic of the 'marriage gradient' (Constable 2005), these men who find themselves marginalised in the local marriage market turn to less developed countries in the region for sources of brides, and this growing dynamic creates the impetus for intra-regional marriage migration. The turn of the 21st century saw the flow of Southeast Asian women to the more developed economies in the region such as Japan, South Korea, Taiwan and Singapore reaching new levels, although the peak in the early years of the new century seems to have passed in some polities (Chung, Kim, and Piper 2016).

In this context, by giving rise to a fraught terrain for negotiating citizenship, marriage migration and the rise of cross-border families have the potential to challenge the substance, meanings and boundaries of citizenship. Training the analytical lens on marriage migration not only foregrounds questions of gender, ethnicity, nationality and class in negotiating citizenship, it also addresses Turner's (2008) earlier critique – in the pages of *Citizenship Studies* – that the literature on citizenship tends to lack systematic consideration of familial relations. It is also important to note that while 'mixed marriage' in the traditional Western-centric literature tends to be seen as a 'facilitator of integration' as marital unions potentially provide 'privileged access to residence and citizenship status for family members of citizens' (De Hart 2015, 171), this is not the case with contemporary marriage migration in Asia. In contradistinction, the scholarly literature on cross-national marriages based on the Asian experience emphasises that accessing legal citizenship status through familial incorporation often presents the migrant with a rocky road towards residency and citizenship, complete with U-turns and detours (Yeoh, Chee, and Vu 2013). As opposed to the claim that marriage to host country nationals serves as a privileged pathway to citizenship rights, the Asian literature shows that the links between marriage migration and citizenship tend to be constrained by gendered notions that limit women's roles to being domestic caregivers and biological and social reproducers. In this sense, marriage migrants straddle the ambivalent position of being both 'insiders' and 'outsiders' within the state and family – entitled to stay and 'theoretically become new citizens ... [but] not yet [full] members of the society' (Wang and Bélanger 2008, 93).

Scholars have also argued that instead of a static framework of rights and obligations, citizenship should be understood as 'a terrain of struggle' (Stasiulis and Bakan 1997), shaped by state-led ideologies of gender, race and class, and subject to varying degrees of negotiation, contestation and compromise. These forms of negotiation have particular salience in the case of female marriage migrants, as the reach of their citizenship claims is often constrained not only by gendered hierarchies central to the patriarchal family, but also the gendered mode of 'familial citizenship' upheld by many Asian nation-states. Extant studies, however, have tended to approach citizenship as an individual-centred concept vis-à-vis the nation-state (López 2015), thus fading the family into the background, resulting in a relative under-examination of the family in the scholarship of marriage migration and citizenship. This special issue attempts to extend the scholarship by going beyond the state-individual nexus to conceptualise the family as a strategic site where citizenship is mediated, negotiated and experienced. By doing so, it points to the importance of contextualising contemporary debates about marriage, migration and citizenship in the realm of the family, and calls for a rethinking of citizenship from an individual-centred proposition to a family-level concept. In the following, we first introduce the gendered mode of familial citizenship that is common in the Asian marriage migration context. We then expand our arguments by showing how the link between marriage migration and citizenship is mediated through the family as a significant site of negotiation and contestation, and as a lens for understanding intergenerational effects. We conclude the introduction by situating the six substantive papers of this special issue within broader arguments linking marriage migration, family, and citizenship in Asia.

The gendered mode of familial citizenship in Asia

In Asia, marriage migration is a highly gendered phenomenon not only because a substantial proportion of marriage migrants are women (Palriwala and Uberoi 2005; Constable 2005) but also because of the way female marriage migrants are incorporated into host societies. Typically, female marriage migrants gain admission into nation-states as wives and dependents of their citizen-husbands, and as biological and social reproducers of citizen-children (Kim 2013; Yeoh, Chee, and Vu 2013; Wang and Bélanger 2008; Sheu 2007). This mode of incorporation binds female marriage migrants' residency and citizenship rights to their gendered role within the marital family, thus constituting a kind of 'familial citizenship' inextricable from the immigration and citizenship laws governing marriage migrants' entrance and presence in the host societies. This gendered mode of familial citizenship contributes to their limited rights not only within the intimate sphere of the family but also in the context of broader society.

In many countries in Asia, marriage migrants gain admission to host country through a spousal sponsorship scheme which grants them a dependent visa or a temporary social visit pass for family reunification. Under this scheme, marriage migrants have little choice but to depend on their citizen-husbands for the legal right to remain in the country as well as the right to apply for permanent residency status (Coté, Kérisit, and Coté 2001; Liversage 2012; Wang and Bélanger 2008). The resultant marital union reflects a serious power imbalance between the marriage migrant and the citizen spouse (Kim, Park, and Shukhertei 2017; Chiu 2017; Friedman 2010). In some host societies such as Taiwan, marriage migrants also need to go through 'authenticity' checks (Friedman 2015). Female marriage migrants, and sometimes their citizen-husbands, would be interrogated by border officials or immigration bureaucrats at entry points. They have to prove the authenticity of their marriage to local citizens by demonstrating that the marriage is built on genuine intimacy, which is thought to be detectable by examining their caregiving commitment and/or childbirth intention. The absence of childbirth intentions may lead to suspicion on the part of the immigration authority that the marriage is fake or deceptive; conversely, proof of childbirth intentions enables marriage migrants to 'assert marital authenticity in the eyes of the state and to gain preferential treatment that helps them to acquire residency or citizenship sooner' (Lan 2019, 322; Friedman 2015). In Singapore, although not explicitly stated, female marriage migrants' pathway to longer-term residency is believed to be partly predicated on reproducing citizen-children from the marriage (Yeoh et al. 2021, this issue), alluding to the importance of procreation in progressing the pathway to citizenship. Immigration procedures for marriage migrants from the start are hence undergirded by state-led and socially embedded gendered ideologies around procreation and caregiving, which confirm gendered hierarchies that are central to the patriarchal family.

After passing through the first stage of immigration clearance, female marriage migrants under their husbands' sponsorship are usually not granted long-term residency immediately. For cross-border couples, many nation-states require a minimum number of years of marriage before full residency/citizenship rights are granted to the marriage migrant. For instance, in South Korea, marriage migrants are required to have a stable married life for at least 2 years before they can apply for naturalization; yet the process usually takes about 4 years and only about one-third of female marriage migrants successfully acquire citizenship (Kim, Park, and Shukhertei 2017). Taiwan used to require mainland Chinese spouses to wait for 2 years before obtaining residency and another 8 years before applying for citizenship[1] (Friedman 2016). Hong Kong sets similar rules for marriage migrants from mainland China, who used to have to wait for up to 10 years to qualify for ordinary residency (this has since been shortened to 4 years from 2009[2]), after which they need to wait for another seven years before applying for permanent residency (Chiu 2020).

While waiting, marriage migrants are subject to a probationary period during which they may lose their right to stay if the marriage dissolves before they obtained permanent residency. This waiting period reflects deep-seated suspicion that marriage migration is an illicit pathway to gain entry into the nation-state, resulting in sham marriages with local men in order to take advantage of the resources, opportunities, and social rights available in host society (Chiu 2020; Constable 2005; Hsia 2007). The notion that a probation period is necessary as a litmus test of authenticity also reflects ethno-nationalist and patriarchal views that marriage migrants are only provisional rather than full members of the family and the state (Kim 2013). In Singapore, marriage migrants' rights to residency papers are inextricably tied to their husbands' status, as the income level and willingness of their husbands to sponsor appear to be critical factors in enabling marriage migrants to secure longer-term residency (Yeoh, Chee, and Vu 2013). These measures deliver considerable authority into the hands of citizen-husbands over their foreign wives, positioning the latter in a subordinate position within the marriage (Quah 2020). This patriarchal mode of citizenship has been criticised for enforcing inescapable dependency of female marriage migrants on their citizen husbands (Coté, Kérisit, and Coté 2001; Liversage 2012; Wang and Bélanger 2008), as well as for putting female marriage migrants in positions of heightened risk of experiencing and enduring spousal violence (Chiu 2017; Chaudhuri, Morash, and Yingling 2014; Williams and Yu 2006). The extension of state sovereignty via citizen-husbands results in what Jongwilaiwan and Thompson (2013) call 'a distinctive system of transnational patriarchy'.

Alongside an increasingly restrictive migration regime with the rise of xenophobia and economic nationalism, this gendered mode of familial citizenship further constricts marriage migrants' spheres of autonomy in the post-arrival context. For instance, scholars have argued that the limited access to citizenship rights, particularly in the first few years of arrival, significantly reduces marriage migrants' capacity to gain financial independence apart from citizen-husbands, undermining their ability to support themselves and their natal families (Chiu 2017; Friedman 2010). Familial citizenship as a mode of incorporation into host society also prioritises the women's prescribed reproductive role in the family, which impacts their access to paid work and social subsidies (Yeoh, Chee, and Vu 2013; Wang and Bélanger 2008; Wang 2007). Within the family realm, the structural inequalities between citizen and non-citizen spouses further reduces non-citizen marriage migrants' bargaining and decision-making power, which may result in domestic confinement, economic deprivation, and infringement of individual human rights (Sheu 2007). In other words, when female marriage migrants enter the host state, they are rarely seen as subjects entitled to residency and citizenship rights on their own terms. Instead, pathways to citizenship are littered with multiple obstacles at both the entry and post-arrival stages, a fraught process requiring marriage migrants to prove their deservingness at every turn.

As accounted above, the emerging scholarship on marriage migration in the Asian context has focused primarily on how restrictive immigration systems and citizenship laws have shaped the vulnerability of marriage migrants and limited their access to social rights in host society. What is less visible in the literature is the ways in which the family – the primary realm of incorporation confronting marriage migrants – mediates such vulnerability and access, while also playing a key role in shaping and modulating the effects of restrictive policies on other citizen and non-citizen members of the family across genera-tion. Against this background, this special issue goes beyond conceptualizing citizenship as a relationship between the individual and the state and instead foregrounds the impor-tance of including the inter-scalar sphere of the family in understanding citizenship negotiation in the case of marriage migration and cross-national families.

The family as a site of citizenship negotiation and contestation

Although marriage and reproduction are seemingly private decisions within the intimate sphere, nation-states have particular interests in regulating intimate unions which are also cross-border for several reasons. First, as cross-border marriages involve the entry of individuals of a different nationality, the very existence of marriage migrants challenges the host state's boundaries of citizenship and sovereignty. Cross-border marriage there-fore concerns not only the relationship between two individuals but also implicates the relationship between the state and the individuals (Toyota 2008). Second, female mar-riage migrants in particular are often seen by nation-states as 'breeding subjects' of the nation who bear future citizens of the nation (Turner 2008). Especially when nation-states are facing ultra-low fertility and population ageing, female marriage migrants' reproductive capacity may have significant impact on population dynamics and social development (Lee 2012). In this context, female marriage migrants' contribution to the host nation-state is often valorised through reproduction and caregiving, which in turn potentially provide legitimate grounds for claiming citizenship entitlements from the state (Turner 2008; Chee, Lu and Yeoh 2014; Yi 2019). Marriage migration policies therefore function as a *de facto* social (re)production system for nation-states in tackling population issues (Kim and Kilkey 2016). Nation-states have keen interests in regulating cross-border unions so as to shape the contours of the nation, simultaneously asserting sovereignty while also ensuring national reproduction (Friedman 2015). It is within this context that notions of motherhood and citizenship intersect as women's procreation and care work become vital to the reproduction of the nation (Longman, De Graeve, and Brouckaert 2013; Roseneil et al. 2013; Yuval-Davis 1996; Anthias and Yuval-Davis 1989).

Reproductive assimilation and marriage migrants as ethnicized maternal citizens

Incorporated into the nation-state as national reproducers, female marriage migrants continue to straddle the ambivalent position of being 'new citizens' and social 'outsiders' at the same time (Wang and Bélanger 2008, 93). Coming from countries occupying the lower socio-economic ranks in the global hierarchy of nation-states, female marriage migrants are often stereotyped as 'social liabilities' who depend on and drain social welfare, 'deficit' mothers who lack human and cultural capital to nurture their citizen-children, and ultimately, an insidious threat to the nation's population quality (Lan 2019; Cheng 2013; Hsia 2007). Without adequate knowledge of local language, culture, and history, marriage migrants are often thought to be limited and handicapped in raising their children as 'full and authentic' citizens (Chiu and Choi 2019). With the rising tide of xenophobia and anti-immigrant sentiment, effective control over marriage migrants and their offspring has become socially and politically crucial for extending state governance (Chiu 2020).

To ensure the quality of the nation's population and the next generation, host states often resort to implementing various programmes targeted at facilitating female marriage migrants' social and cultural assimilation into host society so that they are equipped to assume their reproductive familial roles. Examples include 'Mother's Class' in Japan (Faier 2008), 'Family Life Education' in Hong Kong (Newendorp 2008), 'Life Adjustment' courses in Taiwan (Lan 2019; Wang and Bélanger 2008), and the 'Grand Plan' (Lee 2008) and later, the 'Multicultural Family Support Programme' in South Korea (Kim 2013). All of these programmes explicitly or implicitly target female marriage migrants, especially those coming from Southeast Asia or mainland China. The key goals are to teach marriage migrants local languages and customs, caregiving, mothering and culinary skills, as well as traditional feminine and familial virtues, so that they would be able to take on the mantle of dutiful wives, mothers, and daughters-in-law in accordance with local standards and dominant cultural values. Here, motherhood is considered 'an essential pathway for [marriage migrants] to achieve social and cultural integration' (Lan 2019, 322). What is also implied in these examples is that 'the links between marriage migration and citizenship are not only based on but constrained by notions of the patriarchal family, and of women as domestic caregivers and biological and social reproducers' (Yeoh, Chee, and Vu 2013, 141). Through such 'reproductive assimilation' programmes, nation-states attempt to manage, and where possible reduce, the potential risks that female marriage migrants may bring to population quality (Lan 2019, 318). In the case of South Korea, producing what Kim (2013) calls 'ethnicized maternal citizens' may begin prior to arrival with the implementation of 'pre-migration orientation' classes sponsored by the Korean government to prepare Vietnamese marriage migrants to take up their roles by assimilating them into Korean culture. As a step-up measure, middle-class Korean citizen women have also been mobilised to become 'maternal guardians' of marriage migrants to guide the latter in performing maternal roles according to local ideals of motherhood (Choo 2017).

While useful steps in assisting marriage migrants' adaptation to their new lives in host society, the limited choices offered by these reproductive assimilation programmes have been criticised for treating female marriage migrants as partial citizens who are expected to prioritize and fulfil feminized roles within the private realm of the family, rather than as full citizens who should be equipped with the wherewithal to exercise all-rounded political, economic, and civil rights (Cheng 2013; Friedman 2010; Wang and Bélanger 2008; Hsia 2007). Furthermore, while these programmes driven by assimilationist imperatives may be successful in turning marriage migrants into 'qualified' maternal citizens, they also do so by accentuating their ethnic, class, and cultural differences (Lan 2019; Choo 2017; Kim 2013; Newendorp 2008). In effect, the fashioning of 'reproductive' or 'maternal' citizens also relegates marriage migrants to the category of 'ethnic others' (Kim 2013) who are treated as 'inferior, helpless, and [as an] underclass' (Wang and Bélanger 2008, 103). Such constructions reinforce negative stereotypes and stigmatisation of marriage migrants while serving directly or indirectly to boost the superiority of host culture and national identity (Wang and Bélanger 2008); and in the long run, they also justify and perpetuate the social hierarchy between citizens and immigrants along gendered, ethnicized and classed lines (Choo 2017).

Patriarchal bargains and marriage migrants' agency

Rather than defining citizenship within a static framework of rights and obligations, scholars have contended that citizenship should be conceptualized as a set of processes shaped by ideologies of gender, ethnicity/race, and class, and negotiated on an everyday basis within public and private spheres (Stasiulis and Bakan 1997; Turner 2008). In this light, the hegemony of the gendered mode of familial citizenship prevalent in Asia is 'never fully achieved – it is always negotiated and contested' (Wang 2007, 724). The agency of female marriage migrants in seeking overt and covert spaces for negotiating degrees of autonomy and mounting acts of resistance should not be overlooked (Wang 2007, see also Constable 2005).

Instead of being passive recipients caught in the nettle of familial citizenship, a growing body of studies has emerged to point out that female marriage migrants are involved in 'the dual dynamics of citizenship as self-making and being made' (Ong 1996, 737). By drawing on – as opposed to denying – their roles within the family, marriage migrants may become active agents who are capable of utilising their 'resourcefulness, creativity and adaptability' (Quah 2020, 4) to deploy various tactics in order to resist or negotiate the state's hegemonic citizenship project. For instance, focusing on Filipina marriage migrants in South Korea, Kim (2013) found that some female marriage migrants strategically appropriate their motherhood to apply for naturalisation and to enhance their social and legal rights (Kim 2013; see also Fresnoza-Flot 2018 for a discussion on a similar tactic employed by Filipino and Thai migrant mothers in Belgium). Even as they claim legal membership of the host nation-state, they emotionally resist Korean identity and actively seek ways to 'disrupt, subvert, or resist the patriarchal and ethno-nationalist principles' (Kim 2013, 473), such as emphasising their Philippine identity and cultural traditions in their mothering practices, developing physical and financial autonomy outside the ambit of their in-laws' households, or refusing to conform to traditional ideals of Korean womanhood/motherhood.

In Taiwan, Wang (2007) found that although Vietnamese wives tend to adhere to their prescribed role of 'a good daughter in-law, a good wife, and a good mother', they may covertly network with the Vietnamese community through mobile phones or by going to Vietnamese restaurants where their co-ethnics frequent. Ironically, some Vietnamese female marriage migrants appropriate the reproductive assimilation programmes offered by the host state in order to make friends with co-ethnics, even though the classes are designed to discipline them into docile, feminine bodies. These classes become the hidden spaces of resistance where female marriage migrants could find temporary refuge from the conjugal family's surveillance and control as well as from the state's hegemonic and patriarchal citizenship assimilation project.

In the Mainland China–Hong Kong cross-border family context, some female marriage migrants have rebelled against the patriarchal system by seeking alternative family arrangements, such as by remaining in their original place of residence or opting for a split household arrangement to avoid conflict with, or escape the control of, their husbands and/or parents-in-law, and by refusing to change their legal status to maintain personal freedom and autonomy (Chiu and Choi 2019). Some Vietnamese female marriage migrants in Singapore also turned away from Singapore citizenship after acquiring permanent residency so as to retain their Vietnamese nationality and maintain emotional bonding and instrumental linkage with their natal family (Yeoh, Chee, and Vu 2013). In South Korea and Taiwan, female marriage migrants used the threat of divorce (Freeman 2005) or threat to leave (Wang 2007) to bargain with their husbands and in-laws for personal autonomy, financial independence, or paid employment opportunities outside the home. From this vantage point, marriage migrants' ambivalent position in the family may be a source of both domination and resistance.

Crucially, these examples illustrate female marriage migrants' resilience and situated agency in making strategic negotiations and patriarchal bargains (Chaudhuri, Morash, and Yingling 2014) within the gendered mode of familial citizenship imposed by host states. No matter how mundane these citizenship practices may seem, they manifest the intricate and subtle ways in which citizenship becomes 'a terrain of struggle' (Stasiulis and Bakan 1997) that is negotiated on a quotidian basis within the intimate sphere of the family. As an interlocking scale within the citizenship framework, the family denotes both an ideological realm as well as a sphere of practical action, and in order to negotiate with the state, female marriage migrants must also negotiate the substance, meanings, and boundaries of citizenship within the family. In other words, as marriage migrants negotiate their roles, relationships, identity and care practices within the family, they are simultaneously resisting the top-down familial citizenship framework imposed by host states. In this light, marriage migrants' agency in resisting the patriarchal family should also be understood and conceptualised as citizenship acts that counter state governmentality. Whilst the examples above underscore the importance of contextualising citizenship struggles, everyday contestation, and hidden resistance within the family, they also reveal the blurring of the public–private dichotomy. Notably, in the hidden spaces of resistance within the family, female marriage migrants' citizenship practices and negotiation strategies might simultaneously affirm and challenge state and patriarchal domination through selective compliance with the prescribed gender and familial norms (Yeoh and Ramdas 2014), thus demonstrating the paradoxical effects of the gendered mode of familial citizenship in Asia.

Intergenerationality of citizenship

As seen so far, for marriage migrants, the family is an important and strategic site where citizenship – its meanings and practices – is experienced, mediated and negotiated, with salient implications for the individual-state nexus in understanding citizenship. The family's significance as a site of negotiation and mediation, however, cannot be fully understood without also examining the intergenerational link in the citizenship framework. Given that individuals are interconnected and interdependent in the family system, what happens to an individual member may have profound impact on other members intragenerationally and intergenerationally. An understanding of the link between marriage migration and citizenship therefore needs to go beyond the individual-state nexus by including and conceptualising family-level intergenerational experience. In this section, we put forth the concept of the 'intergenerationality of citizenship' as a starting point for examining both the positive and negative spillover effects of non- or partial citizenship across generations, such as between marriage-migrant mothers and their citizen-children.

Families formed out of cross-border marriages are typically 'mixed-status families' – that is, families that contain a mix of both citizens and non-citizens (Fix and Zimmermann 2001) – especially at the initial stage of family formation due to the delayed granting of residency to the marriage-migrant family member (Chiu 2020). As a result, cross-border marriages, at least at first, may involve family separation rather than reunification through migration (Beck-Gernsheim 2007; Charsley and Shaw 2006). In places where marriage migrants are required to wait for several years before obtaining residency and citizenship, this may bring profound impact not only on the marriage migrants but also their family members. Previous studies on 'mixed-status families' in the West have suggested that even when immigration and citizenship laws target non-citizen migrants, their effects are likely to spill over to other members in the family, citizen and non-citizen alike (Enchautegui and Menjivar 2015; Fix and Zimmermann 2001). For instance, the precariousness brought about by the unauthorised legal status of the mother may lead to unintended but chilling effects on her citizen-children's use of public benefits (Fix and Zimmermann 2001), constituting a kind of 'multigenerational punishment' (Enriquez 2015) that jeopardises the wellbeing not only of the mother but also her children. Similar spillover effects have been found in families formed out of cross-border marriages, where the precarious legal status of the marriage-migrant mother has not only limited her presence in host society but also crippled her capacity to perform caregiving duties and gain economic and social protection (Chiu 2020). This has in turn adversely affected the functioning of the family as well as the well-being of the citizen-children, pointing to an intergenerational diffusion of legal precarity. As seen in the emerging scholarship, it is unrealistic to assume that state laws and regulations could target non-citizen family members without harming other citizen members in the same family (López, 2015; Schueths 2015).

Negative intergenerational diffusion of citizenship is not only evident among marriage migrant mothers with precarious legal status but also those who are constructed and stigmatised as inferior, second-class citizens with questionable parenting and social reproduction skills. In Asia, the negative perception of marriage migrants is widespread, as documented in host societies such as Japan (Nakamatsu 2005), South Korea (Sheu 2007), Taiwan (Lan 2019; Hsia 2007), and Hong Kong (Chiu and Choi 2018). In the case of Taiwan, as mentioned previously, Southeast Asian female marriage migrants were considered unfit national reproducers ('risky mothers', in the words of Lan 2019) due to their imagined racial otherness, low socio-economic status, unfamiliarity with local languages and the lack of cultural knowledge (Cheng 2013; Lan 2008; Wang and Bélanger 2008; Hsia 2007). Such stigmatised images of marriage-migrant mothers often percolate down to encompass their children who are viewed, by association, as having a higher risk of biological defect or developmental delay, thus posing a potential threat to the nation's population quality (Hsia 2021, this issue; Lan 2019). As a consequence, the children of Southeast Asian marriage migrants become a source of public anxiety and the target of state monitoring. Similarly, in the Mainland China-Hong Kong migration context, Mainland Chinese immigrants are stereotyped as dirty, greedy, and uncultivated by Hong Kong residents (Newendorp 2008) and have long been stigmatised as unproductive free riders who take advantage of Hong Kong resources (Chiu and Choi 2020; Chiu 2017). The broader anti-immigrant climate which has intensified in recent years also adversely affect marriage migrants from Mainland China, as well as their children, who are often considered inauthentic 'half' citizens as they are thought to lack the ability to speak, dress, act, and interact like a local even though they are born in Hong Kong and have acquired citizenship there (Chiu and Choi 2018). Given the salient rhetoric of cultural membership, legal citizenship is no longer a sufficient condition for claiming legitimate membership in society; instead, 'migrants and their descendants may only become "real" Hong Kong citizens when they are fully assimilated into local values and are able to demonstrate their cultural competence with ease' (Chiu and Choi 2018, 4). In response, these marriage migrant mothers devised proactive mothering strategies to help their children become accepted as full and legitimate members of host society, by equipping them with local cultural practices and knowledge in early childhood and by drawing identity boundaries between themselves and other mainland immigrants and tourists (Chiu and Choi 2018). These studies indicate the salience of the intergenerational diffusion of (non)citizenship meanings from the marriage-migrant mothers to their citizen-children, which underscores the importance of attention to intergenerational relations in understanding the conditions for practicing, negotiating, and gaining recognition in citizenship matters.

While intergenerational diffusive effects of citizenship might spill from marriage migrant mothers to their children, they may also diffuse in the reverse direction from citizen-children to their migrant mothers in a positive light. In this regard, the recent discursive shift in marriage migrants and their children in Taiwan represents an intriguing case. The 'New Southbound Policy' launched in 2016 is a crucial economic and trade strategy put forth by the Taiwanese state to gain a foothold in the thriving Southeast Asian market through building stronger alliances with ASEAN countries as 'a bulwark against the political and economic threats posed by China' (Lan 2019, 329). Strategically adopting the rhetoric of multiculturalism, the cultural and ethnic differences that mark the second generation with Southeast Asian marriage-migrant mothers were recalibrated as a valuable market asset for national development (Cheng 2021, this issue; Hsia 2021, this issue; Lan 2019). As these children are reframed as 'multicultural children' and the 'vanguards of the New Southbound Policy', state discourses and public attitudes toward Southeast Asian marriage migrants have also changed considerably, taking a positive turn. Parallel to the discursive shift in how their children are perceived, Southeast Asian marriage migrants' linguistic and cultural differences are no longer framed as a deficit quality but elevated to a marketable form of multicultural capital they could inculcate in their citizen-children so as to prepare the latter as 'new southbound soldiers' (Lan 2019, 327). While revealing the reverse intergenerational diffusion of citizenship from the younger to the older generation, this example also signifies that the intergenerational diffusion of citizenship does not necessarily only generate detrimental effects, as suggested by previous studies on mixed-status families, but also positive and conducive effects at the family and national levels.

Taken together, the examples of both positive and negative intergenerational diffusion of citizenship point to the fact that female marriage migrants' mothering is often a critical site and potential resource for negotiating citizenship meanings and practices within cross-border families. The family, as a nurturing ground for biological and social reproduction, becomes an important arena where citizenship is perceived, experienced, constructed, mediated, and reframed. These biopolitical realities underpinning conceptions of social and cultural reproduction indicate the significance of examining the intergenerationality of citizenship, especially in the marriage migration context. Collectively, the cases also demonstrate that neither marriage migrants nor their children are situated in relation to the state as individuals; instead, applying the family lens as a prism to examine citizenship allows us to discern the significance of the inter-connected and inter-dependent relationalities in unpacking citizenship. The fact that citizenship carries family-level connotations and effects implies that approaching citizenship as an individual-centred concept is no longer adequate (see also López, 2015). As the effects of citizenship may spill over to other citizen family members, a re-conceptualisation of citizenship from an individual-centred concept to include family-level experience is warranted. Indeed, some countries have started to consider taking policy measures to prevent detrimental effects of intergenerational diffusion of (the lack of) citizenship within migrant families. For instance, in the European Union, residency is granted to a non-citizen migrant mother of citizen-children so that the children can effectively claim and benefit from their citizenship rights (van Walsum 2016). Future studies should consider adopting the lens of intergenerationality to illuminate the varied and nuanced mechanisms in which citizenship is mediated through the intergenerational link within the family realm. Policy makers should also recognise that citizenship is a family-level experience and that children cannot exercise their rights effectively without the company and support of their parents. Proactive measures need to be delineated to prevent possible intergenerational diffusion of legal precarity among cross-border and migrant families.

The special issue

Marriage migration within Asia is an important area of investigation for citizenship scholars that has been given less attention in the literature compared to East-West cross-cultural marriages. Focusing on families formed out of cross-border marriages, articles in this special issue examine the following issues: how nation-states mobilise notions of the family for its citizenship project; how citizenship structures the trajectory and circumstances of different types of families formed out of cross-border marriages; how the repercussions of marriage migrants' citizenship are experienced and negotiated across generations; and how the tensions between the individual, the family and the state are produced along gender, class, race/ethnic, cultural, religious, and geographical boundaries. The six articles included in this special issue originate from an international workshop held at the Asia Research Institute, National University of Singapore in 2019. They provide a critical and in-depth analysis of cross-border marriages and families in five major receiving countries/cities in Asia, including Singapore, Taiwan, South Korea, Hong Kong, and Japan. These families involve marriage migrants from popular sending countries such as Vietnam, China, India, and Pakistan. This range of empirical case studies provides a good representation of the phenomenon of cross-border marriage migration in Asia, which aptly illustrates how the intricate nexus between marriage migration, family and citizenship emerges and develops in the context of inter-regional marriage migration within Asia. The focus on marriage migration within Asia, a region with predominant collectivist and familistic norms, helps us to grasp the consequences of applying state-led citizenship frameworks formulated along gendered and generational hierarchies to marriage migrants and cross-border families.

Adopting the family as an analytical lens, the first three articles in this special issue give attention to the experiences of female marriage migrants in negotiating their citizenship claims vis-à-vis the nation-state with the family sphere posing as facilitator, mediator and impediment. Through examining female marriage migrants' struggle for long-term residency and/or full citizenship, Yeoh et al. (2021, this issue), Chiu (2021, this issue), and Yi (2021, this issue) show that, when female marriage migrants enter the host state, they are rarely seen as individuals deserving residency and citizenship rights on their own. Instead, their marital and reproductive roles in the family is seen as the only legitimate way for them to be incorporated as members of the host society. By positioning marriage migrants as wives of citizens and biological and social reproducers of the nation, female marriage migrants' personal rights and entitlements are essentially tied to their legal and continuous marital relation with their citizen-husbands as well as their commitment to the prescribed reproductive roles in the conjugal family. These three articles further examine what happened when female marriage migrants attempt to resist or refract the implications of the state-sanctioned, gendered mode of familial citizenship for their everyday lives.

Focusing on Southeast Asian women marrying Singaporean men, Yeoh et al. (2021, this issue), illustrate how the host nation-state's hierarchical control interacts with family processes in producing marriage migrants as partial citizens with limited rights to work, residency and citizenship. They also show how the family as a sphere of ideology and practical action features in the way marriage migrants find leverage in negotiating the paradox of being responsible affinal subjects of the family and partial citizens of the nation-state. Yi (2021, this issue) and Chiu (2021, this issue) extend the discussion of the gendered mode of familial citizenship by focusing on relatively less explored situations when marriage migrants run away from their conjugal family and when marriage migrants lose their eligibility for residency/citizenship due to marital dissolution, respectively. Using the case of South Korea (Yi) and Hong Kong (Chiu), both authors separately illuminate how the hegemonic, patriarchal marriage migration regime has put female marriage migrants in a legally precarious position, which has hampered the wellbeing of not only the marriage migrants but also their citizen-children, resulting in a form of intergenerational diffusion of legal precarity. Conceptualising home space as confinement, Yi (this issue) further elucidates how the rigid ideologies of marriage and family of the South Korean state have led to the criminalisation of migrant wives who left their conjugal homes to escape unhappy and abusive marriage and/or unreasonable control of the in-laws. Irrespective of the reasons for their departure from home, judicial and executive authorities penalise marriage migrants because their actions display disloyal to and betrayal of their conjugal family, signalling a divergence from their prescribed reproductive role stipulated in the state's gendered framework of familial citizenship.

Turning to an under-studied group of single marriage migrants who are widowed, divorced and separated from their citizen husbands, Chiu (2021, this issue) elucidates how the Hong Kong state idealises and institutionalises certain types of cross-border families that are intact and normative while delegitimizing those that do not fit its hegemonic definitions of the marriage and family through a hegemonic 'marrytocracy-based' immigration system that recognises marriage migrants exclusively by their legal and continuous marital relationship with a citizen. Interestingly, while having a citizen child enables married marriage migrants to increase their chance of acquiring residency or citizenship sooner in other East Asian contexts, it is not recognised as a sufficient reason for marriage migrants to obtain residency in Hong Kong when the marriage migrants become single. Nonetheless, the single marriage migrant mothers unremittingly mobilised a rhetoric of rights to family and politics of intergenerational care to claim maternal citizenship through discretion of the state. This strategic mobilisation shows that the reproductive role is not only used by the state to regulate the existence and behaviours of female marriage migrants, but it may also be used by marriage migrants as a feminized weapon to confront the state and make citizenship claims, underscoring the paradoxical effects of the gendered mode of familial citizenship and the family as a site of both domination and resistance.

The other three articles in this special issue shift the spotlight from female marriage migrants to also cover children of cross-border marriages. Focusing on the discursive shift of Southeast Asian marriage migrants and their children in Taiwan, Hsia (2021, this issue) and Cheng (2021, this issue) illustrate how the citizenship of marriage migrants and their children are inter-related and mutually constitutive. Both studies show how globalised economic and political developments have significant impacts on the public perception of Southeast Asian marriage migrants and their children. In this context, they discuss how political entities mobilise notions of 'the multicultural family' for citizenship projects. Depending on how state policies (re)frame the link between their multicultural heritage and their positions as partial or new citizens, the marriage migrants and their children's life chances and wellbeing could undergo considerable change.

To highlight the intergenerationality of citizenship, Hsia (2021, this issue) develops the concept of 'mother-child dyadic citizenship' to show how the Taiwanese state formulates laws and policies concerning marriage migration based on the mother-child dyad rather than treat marriage migrants and their children as separate entities deserving rights and entitlements on their own merits. This can be seen from the parallel positive shifts in the discourses surrounding Southeast Asian marriage migrants and their children. As the children are reframed from being 'social problems' to 'social assets' who possess Southeast Asian cultures and language necessary for expanding the Southeast Asian market as a leverage against the threat from China, their marriage migrant mothers are correspondingly celebrated as cultural reproducers of the 'seeds of the New Southbound'. Yet, as Hsia remarks, the positive discursive shift has not been matched with correspondent law and policy changes regarding marriage migration; instead, immigration laws concerning Southeast Asian marriage migrants have become even more classist and discriminatory, leading to a paradoxical incongruence between immigration discourse and laws.

Building on the positive discursive shift of Southeast Asian marriage migrants and their children, Cheng (2021, this issue) further examines the acts of citizenship of Vietnamese marriage migrant activists in Taiwan. She reveals how the marriage migrants' activism is motivated by their motherhood and enabled by their multicultural capital inherited from their origin, both of which have empowered them to advocate for the rights of their children and other co-ethnic marriage migrants and migrant workers in the public sphere. However, as the Vietnamese marriage migrant activists criticised, although the 'New Southbound Policy' offers Southeast Asian marriage migrants new opportunities for gaining financial independence and autonomy by working as language tutors and tour guides in the public domain, the Taiwanese state has overlooked the patriarchal suppression that the women experienced at home as the job opportunities offered contradict the women's maternal role as expected by their husbands and in-laws. The gender-blindness in the policy, therefore, has limited the extent to which the marriage migrants can exercise their agency and citizenship within and beyond the family.

While extant studies tend to examine how female marriage migrants exercise their agency in citizenship negotiation, the last article in this special issue turns attention to the agency of children of mixed parentage. Through a longitudinal study of cross-border families in Japan, Kudo (2021, this issue) features the intersectional nature of citizenship and unravels the citizenship negotiation experiences of daughters of Japanese-Pakistani parentage. Given the traditional emphasis on patrilineality in Japan, daughters with a migrant father experience a disjuncture between full citizenship and their sense of belonging. Apart from being treated as ethnic others at schools and in local communities, these daughters also feel deprived of freedom due to their migrant fathers' patriarchal control based on their Islamic ideals of femininity. Kudo shows that, as the young women struggle for rights and freedom to study, work, and marry, they reconfigure their Muslim selves as a form of citizenship negotiation. This points to the fact that citizenship is not merely a legal status granted by the state, but a set of negotiation processes shaped by ideologies of gender, ethnicity/race, class, as well as culture and religion. More importantly, Kudo reveals that citizenship negotiation and identity formation of the daughters are interwoven with power dynamics between their citizen mothers and migrant fathers, who, as their life cycle progresses, reposition themselves in the family and local and transnational communities. Such repositioning signifies the intergenerational and transformative nature of citizenship.

Collectively, the articles in this special issue extend existing scholarship on marriage migration and citizenship by going beyond the state-individual nexus to conceptualise the family as the strategic site where citizenship is perceived, experienced, mediated, and negotiated. As a whole, this special issue addresses an important gap in the existing literature by pointing to the significance of contextualising contemporary debates about migration and citizenship in the realm of the family. It also opens new inquiry about the dynamics between the norms and forms of both domination and resistance in relation to citizenship and calls for a reframing of citizenship from an individual status to include a careful consideration of the power relations and gender dynamics at play in the family sphere.

Notes

1. This rule only applied to mainland Chinese spouses but not other foreign spouses such as those from Southeast Asia. Since 2009, mainland Chinese spouses are granted residency upon first arrival and the citizenship wait for them has been reduced to six years (Friedman 2010).
2. Similar to Taiwan, this probationary rule only applies to marriage migrants from mainland China, foreign spouses from other countries normally can obtain ordinary residency at a much faster pace. The seven-year residence requirement is the same for all migrants.

Disclosure statement

No potential conflict of interest was reported by the author(s).

Funding

The articles included in this special issue originate from an international workshop supported by the Asia Research Institute, National University of Singapore.

ORCID

Brenda S.A. Yeoh iD http://orcid.org/0000-0002-0240-3175

References

Anthias, F., and N. Yuval-Davis. 1989. *Woman-Nation-State*. New York: Palgrave Macmillan.

Asis, M. M. B., and G. Battisella. 2012. "Multicultural Realities and Membership: States, Migrations and Citizenship in Asia." In *Migration and Diversity in Asian Contexts*, edited by L. A. Eng, F. L. Collins, and B. S. A. Yeoh, 31–55. Singapore: Institute of Southeast Asian Studies.

Beck-Gernsheim, E. 2007. "Transnational Lives, Transnational Marriages: A Review of the Evidence from Migrant Communities in Europe." *Global Networks* 7 (3): 271–288. doi:10.1111/j.1471-0374.2007.00169.x.

Charsley, K., and A. Shaw. 2006. "South Asian Transnational Marriages in Comparative Perspective." *Global Networks* 6 (4): 331–344. doi:10.1111/j.1471-0374.2006.00147.x.

Chaudhuri, S., M. Morash, and J. Yingling. 2014. "Marriage Migration, Patriarchal Bargains, and Wife Abuse: A Study of South Asian Women." *Violence against Women* 20 (2): 141–161. doi:10.1177/1077801214521326.

Chee, H. L., M. C. Lu, and B. S. A. Yeoh. 2014. "Ethnicity, Citizenship and Reproduction: Taiwanese Wives Making Citizenship Claims in Malaysia." *Citizenship Studies* 18 (8): 823–838. doi:10.1080/13621025.2014.964545

Cheng, I. 2013. "Making Foreign Women the Mother of Our Nation: The Exclusion and Assimilation of Immigrant Women in Taiwan." *Asian Ethnicity* 14 (2): 157–179. doi:10.1080/14631369.2012.759749.

Cheng, I. 2021. "Motherhood, Empowerment and the New Southbound Policy: The Act of Citizenship of Vietnamese Immigrant Activists in Taiwan" *Citizenship Studies*. Advance online publication.

Chiu, T. Y. 2017. "Marriage Migration as A Multifaceted System: Intersectionality of Intimate Partner Violence in Cross-Border Marriages." *Violence Against Women* 23 (11): 1293–1313. doi:10.1177/1077801216659940.

Chiu, T. Y., and S. Y. P. Choi. 2019. *"Frequent Border-Crossing Children and Cultural Membership." Population, Space and Place* 25 (3): e2153.

Chiu, T. Y. 2020. "Everyday Mixed Status: Spillover Effects of State Power in Cross-Border Families." *Gender, Place and Culture* 27: (5),:643–659. doi:10.1080/0966369X.2019.1615411.

Chiu, T. Y. 2021. "Discretionary Maternal Citizenship: State hegemony and Bottom-up Resistance of Single Marriage Migrant Mothers from Mainland China to Hong Kong." *Citizenship Studies*. Advance online publication. 10.1080/13621025.2021.1968685.

Chiu, T. Y., and S. Y. P. Choi. 2020. "The Decoupling of the Legal Migration and Spatial Migration of Female Marriage Migrants". *Journal of Ethnic and Migration Studies* 46 (14): 2997–3013. doi:10.1080/1369183X.2019.1585018.

Choo, H. Y. 2017. "Maternal Guardians: Intimate Labor and the Pursuit of Gendered Citizenship among South Korean Volunteers for Migrant Women." *Sexualities* 20 (4): 497–514. doi:10.1177/1363460716651416.

Chung, C., K. Kim, and N. Piper. 2016. "Marriage Migration in Southeast and East Asia Revisited through a Migration-Development Nexus Lens." *Critical Asian Studies* 48 (4): 463–472. doi:10.1080/14672715.2016.1226600.

Collins, F. L., A. E. Lai, and B. S. A. Yeoh. 2013. "Introduction: Approaching Migration and Diversity in Asian Contexts." In *Migration and Diversity in Asian Contexts*, edited by L. A. Eng, F. L. Collins, and B. S. A. Yeoh, 1–28. Singapore: Institute of Southeast Asian Studies.

Constable, N. 2005. *Cross-border Marriages: Gender and Mobility in Transnational Asia.* Philadelphia: University of Pennsylvania Press.

Coté, A., M. Kérisit, and M. L. Coté. 2001. *Sponsorship-for Better or for Worse: The Impact of Sponsorship on the Equality Rights of Immigrant Women.* Ottawa: Status of Women Canada.

De Hart, B. 2015. "Regulating Mixed Marriages through Acquisition and Loss of Citizenship." *The Annals of the American Academy of Political and Social Science* 662 (1): 170–187. doi:10.1177/0002716215595390.

Enchautegui, M., and C. Menjivar. 2015. "Paradoxes of Family Immigration Policy: Separation, Reorganization, and Reunification of Families under Current Immigration Laws." *Law & Policy* 37 (1–2): 32–60. doi:10.1111/lapo.12030.

Enriquez, L. 2015. "Multigenerational Punishment: Shared Experiences of Undocumented Immigration Status within Mixed-Status Families." *Journal of Marriage and Family* 77 (4): 939–953. doi:10.1111/jomf.12196.

Faier, L. 2008. "Runaway Stories: The Underground Micromovements of Filipina Oyomesan in Rural Japan." *Cultural Anthropology* 23 (4): 630–659. doi:10.1111/j.1548-1360.2008.00021.x.

Fix, M., and W. Zimmermann. 2001. "All under One Roof: Mixed-Status Families in an Era of Reform." *International Migration Review* 35 (2): 397–419. doi:10.1111/j.1747-7379.2001.tb00023.x.

Freeman, C. 2005. "Marrying up and Marrying Down: The Paradoxes of Marital Mobility for Chosonjok Brides in South Korea." In *Cross-border Marriages: Gender and Mobility in Transnational Asia*, edited by N. Constable, 80–100. Philadelphia: University of Pennsylvania Press.

Fresnoza-Flot, A. 2018. "Raising Citizens in 'Mixed'family Setting: Mothering Techniques of Filipino and Thai Migrants in Belgium." *Citizenship Studies* 22 (3): 278–293. doi:10.1080/13621025.2018.1449807.

Friedman, S. L. 2010. "Marital Immigration and Graduated Citizenship: Post-Naturalization Restrictions on Mainland Chinese Spouses in Taiwan." *Pacific Affairs* 83 (1): 73–93. doi:10.5509/201083173.

Friedman, S. L. 2015. "Regulating Cross-Border Intimacy: Authenticity Paradigms and the Specter of Illegality among Chinese Marital Immigrants to Taiwan." In *Migrant Encounters: Intimate Labor, the State, and Mobility across Asia*, edited by S. Friedman and P. Mahdavi, 206–230. Philadelphia: University of Pennsylvania Press.

Friedman, S. L. 2016. "The Right to Family: Chinese Marriage Immigrants, Chinese Children, and Graduated Citizenship in Taiwan." In *Gender and Citizenship in Historical and Transnational Perspective, edited by A. R. Epstein and R. G. Fuchs*, 211–231. London: Palgrave

Hsia, H. C. 2007. "Imaged and Imagined Threat to the Nation: The Media Construction of the 'Foreign Brides' Phenomenon' as Social Problems in Taiwan." *Inter-Asia Cultural Studies* 8 (1): 55–85. doi:10.1080/14649370601119006.

Hsia, H. C. 2021. "From 'Social Problems' to 'Social Assets': Geopolitics, Discursive Shifts in Children of Southeast Asian Marriage Migrants, and the Mother-Child Dyadic Citizenship in Taiwan." *Citizenship Studies*. Advance online publication.

Jongwilaiwan, R., and E. C. Thompson. 2013. "Thai Wives in Singapore and Transnational Patriarchy." *Gender, Place & Culture* 20 (3): 363–381. doi:10.1080/0966369X.2011.624588.

Kim, G., and M. Kilkey. 2016. "Marriage Migration Policy as a Social Reproduction System: The South Korean Experience." In *Family Life in an Age of Migration and Mobility*, edited by M. Kilkey and E. Palenga-Möllenbeck, 137–161. London: Palgrave Macmillan.

Kim, H. M., S. Park, and A. Shukhertei. 2017. "Returning Home: Marriage Migrants' Legal Precarity and the Experience of Divorce." *Critical Asian Studies* 49 (1): 8–53. doi:10.1080/14672715.2016.1266679.

Kim, M. 2013. "Citizenship Projects for Marriage Migrants in South Korea: Intersecting Motherhood with Ethnicity and Class." *Social Politics* 20 (4): 455–481. doi:10.1093/sp/jxt015.

Kudo, M. 2021. "Negotiating Citizenship and Reforging Muslim Identities: The Case of Young Women of Japanese-Pakistani Parentage." *Citizenship Studies*. Advance online publication.

Lan, P. C. 2008. "Migrant Women's Bodies as Boundary Markers: Reproductive Crisis and Sexual Control in the Ethnic Frontiers of Taiwan." *Signs: Journal of Women in Culture and Society* 33 (4): 833–861. doi:10.1086/528876.

Lan, P. C. 2019. "From Reproductive Assimilation to Neoliberal Multiculturalism: Framing and Regulating Immigrant Mothers and Children in Taiwan." *Journal of Intercultural Studies* 40 (3): 318–333. doi:10.1080/07256868.2019.1598952.

Lee, H. 2012. "Political Economy of Cross-Border Marriage: Economic Development and Social Reproduction in Korea." *Feminist Economics* 18 (2): 177–200. doi:10.1080/13545701.2012.688139.

Lee, H. K. 2008. "International Marriage and the State in South Korea: Focusing on Governmental Policy." *Citizenship Studies* 12 (1): 107–123. doi:10.1080/13621020701794240.

Liversage, A. 2012. "Transnational Families Breaking Up: Divorce among Turkish Immigrants in Denmark." In *Transnational Marriage: New Perspectives from Europe and Beyond*, edited by K. Charsley, 145–160. New York: Routledge.

Longman, C., K. De Graeve, and T. Brouckaert. 2013. "Mothering as a Citizenship Practice: An Intersectional Analysis of 'Carework' and 'Culturework' in Non-Normative Mother–Child Identities." *Citizenship Studies* 17 (3–4): 385–399. doi:10.1080/13621025.2013.791540.

López, J. L. 2015. "'Impossible Families': Mixed-Citizenship Status Couples and the Law."*Law & Policy* 37 (1–2): 93–118. doi:10.1111/lapo.12032

Nakamatsu, T. 2005. "Faces of 'Asian Brides': Gender, Race, and Class in the Representations of Immigrant Women in Japan." *Women's Studies International Forum* 28 (5): 405–417. doi:10.1016/j.wsif.2005.05.003.

Newendorp, N. D. 2008. *Uneasy Reunions: Immigration, Citizenship, and Family Life in Post-1997 Hong Kong*. Stanford, California: Stanford University Press.

Ong, A. 1996. "Cultural Citizenship as Subject-Making: Immigrants Negotiate Racial and Cultural Boundaries in the United States." *Current Anthropology* 37 (5): 737–762. doi:10.1086/204560.

Palriwala, R., and P. Uberoi. 2005. "Marriage and Migration in Asia Gender Issues." *Indian Journal of Gender Studies* 12 (2–3): 5–29. doi:10.1177/097152150501200201.

Quah, S. E. L. 2020. "Transnational Divorces in Singapore: Experiences of Low-income Divorced Marriage Migrant Women." *Journal of Ethnic and Migration Studies* 46 (14): 3040–3058. doi:10.1080/1369183X.2019.1585023.

Roseneil, S., I. Crowhurst, A. C. Santos, and M. Stoilova. 2013. "Reproduction and Citizenship/Reproducing Citizens: Editorial Introduction." *Citizenship Studies* 17 (8): 901–911. doi:10.1080/13621025.2013.851067.

Schueths, A. M. 2015. "Barriers to Interracial Marriage? Examining Policy Issues Concerning US Citizens Married to Undocumented Latino/A Immigrants." *Journal of Social Issues* 71 (4): 804–820. doi:10.1111/josi.12150.

Sheu, Y. 2007. "Full Responsibility with Partial Citizenship: Immigrant Wives in Taiwan." *Social Policy & Administration* 41 (2): 179–196

Shin, J. 2019. "The Vortex of Multiculturalism in South Korea: A Critical Discourse Analysis of the Characterization of 'Multicultural Children' in Three Newspapers." *Communication and Critical/Cultural Studies* 16 (1): 61–81. doi:10.1080/14791420.2019.1590612.

Stasiulis, D., and A. B. Bakan. 1997. "Negotiating Citizenship: The Case of Foreign Domestic Workers in Canada." *Feminist Review* 57 (1): 112–139. doi:10.1080/014177897339687.

Toyota, M. 2008. "Editorial Introduction: International Marriage, Rights and the State in East and Southeast Asia." *Citizenship Studies* 12 (1): 1–7. doi:10.1080/13621020701794083.

Turner, B. 2008. "Citizenship, Reproduction and the State: International Marriage and Human Rights." *Citizenship Studies* 12 (1): 45–54. doi:10.1080/13621020701794166.

van Walsum, S. 2016. "The Contested Meaning of Care in Migration Law." In *Family Life in an Age of Migration and Mobility: Global Perspectives through the Life Course*, edited by M. Kilkey and E. Palenga-Möllenbeck, 313–335. London: Palgrave Macmillan.

Wang, H. Z. 2007. "Hidden Spaces of Resistance of the Subordinated: Case Studies from Vietnamese Female Migrant Partners in Taiwan." *International Migration Review* 41 (3): 706–727. doi:10.1111/j.1747-7379.2007.00091.x.

Wang, H. Z., and D. Bélanger. 2008. "Taiwanizing Female Immigrant Spouses and Materializing Differential Citizenship." *Citizenship Studies* 12 (1): 91–106. doi:10.1080/13621020701794224.

Williams, L., and M. K. Yu. 2006. "Domestic Violence in Cross-Border Marriage: A Case Study from Taiwan." *International Journal of Migration, Health and Social Care* 2 (3/4): 58–69. doi:10.1108/17479894200600032.

Yeoh, B. S. A., and K. Ramdas. 2014. "Gender, Migration, Mobility and Transnationalism." *Gender, Place & Culture* 21 (10): 1197–1213. doi:10.1080/0966369X.2014.969686

Yeoh, B. S. A., B. C. Somaiah, T. Lam, and K. F. Acedera. 2020. "Doing Family in 'Times of Migration': Care Temporalities and Gender Politics in Southeast Asia." *Annals of the American Association of Geographers* 110 (6): 1709–1725. doi:10.1080/24694452.2020.1723397.

Yeoh, B. S. A., H. L. Chee, R. Anant, and T. Lam. 2021 . "Transnational Marriage Migration and the Negotiation of Precarious Pathways Beyond Partial Citizenship in Singapore." *Citizenship Studies*. Advance online publication.

Yeoh, B. S. A., L. H. Chee, and T. K. D. Vu. 2013. "Commercially Arranged Marriage and the Negotiation of Citizenship Rights among Vietnamese Marriage Migrants in Multiracial Singapore." *Asian Ethnicity* 14 (2): 139–156. doi:10.1080/14631369.2012.759746.

Yi, S. 2019. "Suspicious Mothering: Maternal Labor and Marriage Migration in South Korea." *Social Politics: International Studies in Gender, State & Society* 28 (1): 71–93. doi:10.1093/sp/jxz018.

Yi, S. 2021. "Penalizing 'Runaway' Migrant Wives: Commercial Cross-Border Marriages and Home Space as Confinement." *Citizenship Studies*. Advance online publication.

Yuval-Davis, N. 1996. "Women and the Biological Reproduction of 'The Nation'." *Women's Studies International Forum* 19 (1–2): 17–24. doi:10.1016/0277-5395(95)00075-5.

Transnational marriage migration and the negotiation of precarious pathways beyond partial citizenship in Singapore

Brenda S.A. Yeoh ⓘ, Heng Leng Chee ⓘ, Rohini Anant ⓘ and Theodora Lam ⓘ

ABSTRACT

While mixed marriage can act as a 'facilitator of integration' for migrants, feminist scholars have argued that in Asia, pathways to citizenship for marriage migrants are precariously ridden with negotiations around gender, ethnicity, nationality and class. In this context, the family sphere lies between the individual migrant and the state, and features as a strategic site where citizenship categories take effect on migrant lives on the one hand, and where citizenship claims are mediated, negotiated and contested on the other. Drawing on two ethnographic studies of Southeast Asian women marrying Singaporean men belonging to lower socio-economic strata, we show how the host nation-state's hierarchical control interacts with family processes in producing marriage migrants as partial citizens with limited rights to work, residency and citizenship. We also demonstrate how marriage migrants find leverage in negotiating the paradox of being responsible affinal subjects of the family and partial citizens of the nation-state.

Introduction

In a world that has grown accustomed to routinised cross-border mobility and transnational lifestyles, the notion of citizenship as a fixed form of belonging bounded by the nation-state is increasingly out of step with lived reality. Within the sphere of intimate relations, rising international marriage trends have exacerbated this disjuncture between legal citizenship tied to a single nation-state on the one hand, and the human capacity for multiple senses of belonging – experienced simultaneously or over the life-course – on the other. In Asia, international marriage has become a significant mechanism for family formation (Douglass 2006), and this growing phenomenon has spawned families constituted by members holding different citizenship and residency statuses that confer differential rights. In these mixed-status families, individual members often confront divergent contexts of opportunities and constraints, further complicating the pursuit of family aspirations and mobility projects (López 2015). Writ large, this can lead to an increasing disjuncture between the lived realities of the social reproduction of families and the boundary-making work of the nation-state on managing its population.

In recent decades, scholars interested in migration, nationalism and citizenship have begun giving attention to citizenship regimes in Asia, highlighting the effects of nation-building policies on institutionalizing citizen-noncitizen hierarchies in the distribution of socio-political rights and welfare entitlements (Chung 2020). This is an important step towards rebalancing the global scope of citizenship studies, as extant scholarship has tended to focus on immigration to Europe, North America and Oceania (Bloemraad and Sheares 2017). While Western-centric literature has yielded considerable insights into the ways state policies and non-state practices work to reify notions of who is deserving or not in the allocation of differential rights to citizens and migrants, most of this work has considered questions of access to citizenship rights at the individual level. Training the analytical spotlight on Asian countries with deep roots in systematic patriarchy and familialism brings to the foreground the significance of the family as a key social organization for the consideration of citizenship rights. In these contexts, the mobilization of individual rights often cannot be divorced from embeddedness in the primary relations of the family.

Using a case study of capital-poor female marriage migrants who navigate precarious and tenuous pathways towards residency and citizenship rights in Singapore, this paper examines how the nation-state's graduated citizenship regime works out at the level of the family. Focusing on marriage migrants allows us to give attention to the tensions that ensue when familial membership based on affect, intimacy and social obligation is out of alignment with national non- (or partial) membership based on limited rights to welfare, productive work and residency. In this light, the paper is interested in unpacking the disjuncture between the intimate incorporation of marriage migrants into the work of reproducing the family on the one hand, and their enforced partial citizenship (Sheu 2007) vis-à-vis the nation-state on the other.

To accomplish this aim, our paper first draws critically on the literature on international marriage, migration and citizenship to highlight the family as a strategic site where citizenship claims are mediated, negotiated and contested. Next, we explain Singapore's citizenship regime as it applies to migrant spouses, and outline our methodological route in gathering interview data for the paper. In the penultimate two sections, we discuss, respectively, two interrelated questions: First, how does the institutionalization of hierarchical control as part of citizenship and nation-building policies interact with family processes in (re)producing marriage migrants as partial citizens? Second, how do marriage migrants as responsibilised[1] familial subjects cum partial citizens find leverage in negotiating precarious life-paths and asserting their capacity for claims-making? Finally, we reflect on the conceptual contributions of the research.

Marriage migrants, pathways to citizenship, and the family as the locus of struggle

In most Asian countries where citizenship is inherited and ascribed primarily through 'blood' descent (Asis and Battisella 2012), the main route for marriage migrants to gain access to citizenship is through legal application ('naturalization'). For transnational inter-ethnic marriage migrants originating in countries lower down the socio-economic development ladder, pathways towards naturalization in destination countries are often slippery and ambiguous. From the host nation's perspective, their lack of social, economic and (sometimes) linguistic capital is seen not only as an obstacle to integration (Charsley, Bolognani, and Spencer 2017) but also as negative assets that would weigh down national safety nets for welfare provision. In this light, access to citizenship is contingent on demonstrating legitimacy in the face of widespread suspicion that marriage migration is a morally suspect, opportunistic channel exploited by those seeking citizenship, work or material gain (Cheng and Choo 2015). For marriage migrants, the terrain of struggle for citizenship rights at destination countries is markedly uneven, and inextricably entangled with the inequalities of class, gender and ethno-racial background.

As Bloemraad and Sheares (2017, 839) point out, 'paying attention to race, class, and other status markers shifts our conceptual attention from citizenship as legal status to its social construction as privileged membership'. Conceiving of citizenship as *both* fixed legal status and social practice has, in turn, brought to light gaps between legal status and on-the-ground practices around rights, participation and identity. Exploring these gaps has opened up space for 'a claims-making approach to citizenship, one that is a relational process of recognition, includes actors outside the individual/state dyad, and focuses on claims to legitimate membership' (Bloemraad and Sheares 2017, 823). Such an approach takes into account the relational capacity to act on the part of both the state and the migrant, while also opening up conceptual space for considering other interdependent actors such as the family.

More than a decade ago, Turner (2008) observed that the literature on citizenship pathways is marked by an 'absence of any systematic thinking about familial relations, reproduction and citizenship'. The fact that the majority of the world's population are 'born into citizenship' suggests that 'the family is an important but often implicit facet of political identity and membership' (*ibid*). Focusing on the complex arena of transnational marriage migration allows us to draw explicit attention to the myriad ways the locus of struggle for citizenship impinges on the sphere of the family. For marriage migrants, citizenship matters, as both status and practice, in shaping family relationships and functioning; and at the same time, the family sphere is an important site that mediates, limits or aggravates the effects of the state's categorical control and the efficacy of the migrant's claims-making. Attending to marriage migrants' pathways to citizenship hence requires scholars to go beyond the state-individual nexus and foregrounds the family as a contested arena for citizenship claims.

In this emerging scholarship, attention has mainly focused on the nation-state's control of marriage migrants' citizenship pathways, showing how the accordance of citizenship and legal status results in deepening their socio-economic disadvantage and precarity, effectively entrenching them as marginal or partial citizens. As Sheu (2007) argues, Taiwan's spousal sponsorship regime exemplifies the increased vulnerability of immigrant spouses and infringements of their human rights by leaving them entirely dependent on and highly controlled by the dictates of their husbands. Similarly, in the context of cross-Straits political tensions, Friedman (2010) argues that Taiwanese state policies 'create a second-class citizenship status for naturalized Chinese spouses'. In contradistinction to the view sometimes found in Western-centric literature that 'mixed marriage' is a 'facilitator of integration' that enables 'privileged access to residence and citizenship status for family members of citizens' (de Hart 2015, 171), the literature on Asia is more inclined to view marriage migrants' pathways to citizenship as precariously ridden with negotiations around gender, ethnicity, nationality and class (Cheng 2013; Kim 2013).

A related dimension of this literature points out that 'the status of citizen is analytically important, not just as a legal status to access rights, but also as a membership concept of identity, legitimacy, and participation' that shapes roles and relations (Bloemraad and Sheares 2017, 855). Feminist and other critical scholars have shown that marriage migrants who are denied full citizenship rights are further compelled to attain and legitimize membership of the marital family by fitting into retrogressive gender-specific roles. Scholars studying marriage migration in Korea, for example, point out that the creation of the marriage migrant visa that is derivative of the citizen-spouse's status 'established the blueprint for [female marriage migrants'] contingent incorporation into Korean society as wives, mothers, and daughters-in-law' (Chung 2020, 12). By inducting female marriage migrants into the nation-state to play social and biological reproductive roles, Korea's 'multicultural family' policy framework provides a means of securing reproductive capacity in a nation-state experiencing ultra-low fertility among its citizen population (Kim and Kilkey 2018). Immigrant wives are hence expected to fashion themselves as 'ethnicized maternal citizens' within state projects that 'paradoxically promote cultural assimilation while relegating marriage migrants as gendered dependents and ethnic others' (Kim 2013, 455; see also Kim-Bossard 2017). These ideas also echo Turner's (2008) observation of the concept of reproductive citizenship which underscores the significance of parenthood as a key determining factor used by states to allocate citizenship and its related entitlements to prospective citizens.

With some important exceptions (e.g. Kim and Vang 2020), the scholarship on marriage migration and citizenship in the Asian context is largely focused on the policy effects of restricting citizenship gains and has given less attention to how marriage migrants negotiate the paradox of being admitted into gender-specific (and often maternal) membership of the family vis-à-vis non- or partial membership of the nation-state. While there is a broader literature on migration, motherhood and citizenship (mainly situated in western contexts) that foregrounds migrant mothers' agentic capacity to disrupt hegemonic notions of citizenship and group belonging through their 'carework' and 'culturework' (Erel 2013; Longman, De Graeve, and Brouckaert 2013), the literature drawing on marriage migration in Asia tends to focus on women's constrained roles within the family and limited purchase in making citizenship gains. As Kim (2010, 723) summarized, studies on marriage migration in Asia tend to 'connect women's agency and sources of empowerment mainly to paid work or community activities, while reducing women's reproductive labor [within the marital family] to a site of confinement'. Women participating in marriage migration are co-opted into the marital family through a 'transnational patriarchal bargain' whereby they submit to relative disempowerment while men 'parlay citizenship rights into patriarchal privileges within the conjugal relationship' (Jongwilaiwan and Thompson 2013, 365). The outcome of this form of bargaining with patriarchy does not guarantee upward social mobility for women in line with 'global hypergamy' (Constable 2005) but may have the opposite effect (Kim 2010; Zhang, Lu, and Yeoh 2015). In this context, the family sphere has featured more prominently as a site of gender and generational oppression, while marriage migrants' citizenship claims-making and activism occur outside the family and kinship-based power through civil society organization and co-ethnic networking (Wang and Belanger 2008; Hsia 2012).

More recently, emerging scholarship on marriage migration and citizenship has highlighted the significance of the family as a terrain against which marriage migrants negotiate the boundaries of citizenship practices (Kim 2013). In building upon this lead, this paper foregrounds the family as a site of struggle for citizenship as a complex formulation of both legal status and substantive practice. Creating the marriage migrant as a category of partial citizenship is dependent on the interaction between the state's hierarchical control of citizenship rights, and family processes in shaping familial roles and relations. In turn, these family processes condition differential access and claims-making to gain citizenship rights. At the intersection of nation-state and family, marriage migrants are not passive victims but constantly finding leverage to negotiate new positions within the paradox of being responsible affinal subjects of the family while being partial citizens of the nation-state.

The rocky road to partial citizenship for marriage migrants

In Singapore, the changing context for marriage decision-making has seen a widening gap in marriage expectations between the two largest groups of singles – financially-independent graduate Singaporean women with general expectations of hypergamy as compared to working-class Singaporean men with low levels of education and a preference for women willing to uphold traditional gender roles and values (Yeoh, Chee, and Vu 2013). Facilitated by increased cross-border mobility, this mismatch in expectations has led to the expansion of the regional marriage market as Singaporean men turn to 'foreign brides' from less developed economies in Southeast Asia as alternative spousal choices (Cheng 2012). This phenomenon is exemplified by the rising proportion of transnational marriages involving non-citizen spouses, from about 15% of all marriages in the mid-1980s to a peak of around 41% during the mid-2000s, subsequently stabilizing at around 35% in recent years (Singapore Department of Statistics 2020). In 2019, women constituted about 70% of the total number of foreign spouses, and were overwhelmingly (over 95%) from the Asian region (National Population and Talent Division, Strategy Group, Prime Minister's Office, Singapore Department of Statistics, Ministry of Home Affairs, Immigration & Checkpoints Authority, and Ministry of Manpower 2020). This phenomenon is not unique to Singapore as similar demographic trends are observed in other Asian countries, most notably Taiwan and South Korea.

Marriage to a Singaporean does not automatically qualify a foreigner for long-term stay and employment in Singapore[2] (Figure 1). The tenuous pathway begins when marriage migrants – especially those who are capital-poor – typically enter Singapore first on a one-month social visit pass (SVP) that does not permit them to work and is renewable for another 90 days. If the renewal is rejected, applicants must exit the country for at least five days before being allowed to re-enter on another SVP. To stay in Singapore for up to three years, foreign spouses of citizens may apply for a long-term visit pass (LTVP) or an enhanced LTVP+ if eligible (introduced in April 2012) which will take at least six months to process. In the early 2000s, around 14,500 LTVP applications were processed each year.[3]

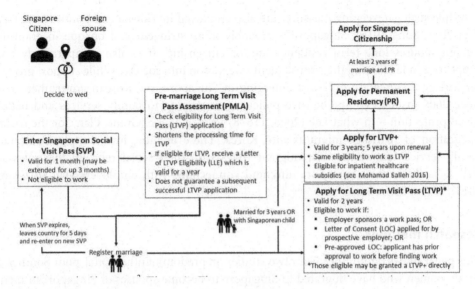

Figure 1. Citizenship pathways for foreign spouses Singaporeans.

From 2015, prospective foreign spouses of Singaporeans have the option of undergoing a pre-marriage long-term visit pass assessment (PMLA) which provides greater clarity on their eligibility for an LTVP before registering their marriage (Tham 2019). This does not guarantee a positive outcome but significantly shortens the processing time for a subsequent LTVP application from six months to six weeks.[4]

Until recently, foreign spouses on the LTVP scheme faced considerable obstacles to access work rights as they must first secure a job offer from a prospective employer willing to sponsor a work pass or a letter of consent (LOC) from the Ministry of Manpower. These conditions were liberalized following the introduction of pre-approval for foreign spouses on an LTVP (from 2015) or LTVP+ (from 2012) to take up employment in Singapore without needing to seek prospective employers' sponsorship.[5]

For foreign spouses, access to permanent residency (PR) and Singapore citizenship (SC) is fraught with further uncertainty. From 2009 to 2015, only half of about 8,000 PR applications from foreign spouses were approved.[6] While it is generally known that much depends on factors such as 'the ability of the sponsor to support his or her foreign spouse financially, whether the marriage is legally in order and [the] good conduct records of both applicant and sponsor' (Tan 2011), specific criteria for a successful application are deliberately kept opaque in order to 'prevent attempts to game the system' (according to the Immigration and Checkpoints Authority [ICA]) and as a safeguard against sham marriages (Tham 2019). Given the obscure and tenuous nature of citizenship pathways, immigrant wives are highly dependent upon citizen-husbands (who in turn have to demonstrate productive citizenship) to secure their rights to stay and build a family in Singapore. As observed by a feminist NGO, without secure residency rights, the state seems to expect that 'the couple should choose not to marry, to live elsewhere, or to accept a compromised family life in Singapore ... effectively penalis[ing] them for exercising their right to enter a marriage of their choosing'.[7]

While such gatekeeping measures are also employed in Taiwan and South Korea (see Tsai 2011; Song 2015), Singapore is arguably more stringent and opaque in granting foreign spouses long-term residency and/or citizenship. It is also comparatively less supportive in facilitating their subsequent integration into society. While support groups for foreign spouses are only just emerging in Singapore, the Korean government has since 2006 instated comprehensive policies – pertaining to family services and better social protection – in what Lee (2008, 116–8) termed as the 'Grand Plan' for the social integration of marriage migrants into Korea. These include, for example, dedicated family service centres to assist migrant wives with their social reproductive roles as well as facilitate their career training and connections with employers (see also Kim 2013).

Research methods

This paper draws on findings from two studies on predominantly capital-poor Southeast Asian women who have migrated to Singapore to become spouses of Singaporean men. The earlier study (2008–2011) focused on Vietnamese women who married Singaporean men through commercial matchmaking agencies and informal brokers. The more recent study (2018–2019) widened the focus to Southeast Asian women who met their Singaporean husbands through personal encounters and social networks, although a small minority were commercially matched.[8]

In the pre-2011 project, we interviewed 26 Vietnamese wives and 22 Singaporean husbands, of which 18 were paired couples (interviewed separately to obtain independent viewpoints). The wives were aged between 18 and 40, with the majority in their twenties and early thirties, while the husbands' ages ranged from 30 to late fifties. Most of the couples had been married between a few months and five years at the time of the interviews, and had between one to three children from the marriage, although a few were then childless. The couples communicated in Mandarin, as the Vietnamese picked up the language quickly, and most of them lived in the lower range of public housing, which is indicative of a generally lower socioeconomic status (SES). The majority (18) were on a SVP or the one-year LTVP, while seven had been granted PR and one had SC. While the migrant wives were mostly housewives (even though they were previously working in Vietnam) and financially dependent on their husbands, the men were mainly in service work (e.g. taxi driver, salesman), the construction industry (e.g. crane driver), self-employed (e.g. hardware business, hawker stall) or insecure work (e.g. odd-job labourer).

In the post-2018 study, 26 migrant wives and 14 Singaporean husbands were interviewed; 14 were paired interviews. Among the migrant wives, the majority were Vietnamese (14) but the study also included Indonesian (4), Filipino (2) and Thai (6) women. The duration of the marriage ranged more widely from 2 to 36 years compared to the earlier study, and the women were mainly in their late twenties to early forties, while the men were in their late thirties to late fifties. Eleven of the migrant wives were 25 and younger when they married. The majority have children from the current marriage (only three of the migrant wives had no children). Two were on the LTVP, five had been granted the LTVP+, 13 were PRs and six were SCs. The increased numbers of wives holding long-term visas in the post-2018 study is possibly reflective of their length of stay in Singapore as well as policy changes in the last decade. As with the earlier study, the men's occupations ranged from blue-collar jobs, service work, to running small businesses. What was distinctly different is the women's job status[9]: the majority (18) were engaged in paid work outside the home – from factory work, service work, to running food stalls, while four were actively engaged as 'assistants' in their husbands' businesses or volunteering in the community. Only four of the migrant wives considered themselves full-time homemakers.

While we encountered considerable difficulty recruiting Vietnamese marriage migrants and their husbands in the earlier study primarily because of the stigma of commercial matchmaking (see Yeoh, Chee, and Vu 2014 for details), our fieldwork a decade later threw up fewer issues of access. Nonetheless, the study's analysis on citizenship negotiations is limited by the difficulties in recruiting respondents who are navigating a failed marriage. We first drew on personal contacts (including some of our student-assistants who knew of or were from mixed-nationality families) and snowballed from these initial leads. We also frequented food centres and shopping malls in Singapore where migrant wives have found work. It also helped that the majority of the migrant wives were now working women with greater confidence in interacting beyond the family circle, and had some grasp of English and Mandarin, languages commonly spoken in Singapore. Working with a research team comprising members of different ethnicities, ages, and language capabilities, we tried to ensure that prospective participants were approached by team members they were most likely to be comfortable with.

In both projects, the interview guide covered the different phases of, and critical junctures in, the respondents' migration journeys (for the wives) and married lives (for both wives and husbands), the difficulties and opportunities encountered, and their plans and aspirations for themselves and their children. All the collected material was transcribed, translated, anonymised, and analysed through inductive thematic scrutiny to highlight different cases reflecting the range of lived experiences and family situations, and focusing on the relationship between family processes and migrant wives' citizenship considerations.

The interaction of state and family processes in the making of partial citizens

In the terrain of struggle for legal status and substantive rights, the right to remain in Singapore often features as the first hurdle for migrant wives, particularly those married to lower SES men. For those accorded SVPs of a few months or the one-year LTVP, their continued residency status is solely dependent on their husbands' willingness to sponsor residency applications, as well as financial and family circumstances. In the case of Dau (twenties, Vietnamese, LTVP, pre-2011 interviewee) who was pregnant at the time of the interview, her relationship with her husband had deteriorated to the point when he had asked her to abort the child and 'sign for legal separation'. While Dau had few illusions left in the marriage and was prepared to go through with both the abortion and legal separation, she was apprehensive that her bid for PR would come to nought and she would have to leave Singapore. Even in marriages which, on the surface, appeared intact, wives fear that their citizen-husbands may withhold support for their PR applications. Ten months into her marriage, Thach (20-year-old Vietnamese, LTVP, pre-2011 interviewee) realised that her husband (55-year-old widowed truck driver) was dragging his feet when it came to applying for PR for her: she had asked him 'many times' but he 'doesn't want to'. According to the commercial matchmaking agent whom we interviewed separately, Thach's husband had 'no long term plans' for the marriage, and was dating another woman even after marrying Thach.

Among our interviewees, Dau's and Thach's cases – where their desire for more stable residency status was thwarted by their husbands – were in the minority. Most Singaporean husbands were willing to support their migrant wives' application for PR, but in several cases, they did not have the financial wherewithal to meet the general criteria for a successful bid.[10] In one case, the couple had been married for over two years, but Lieu (34-year-old, Vietnamese, pre-2011 interviewee) was still on a short-term SVP that needed constant renewal. Her husband, Soon (54-year-old hawker), speculated that her LTVP and PR applications had failed because the income he reported as a taxpayer was too low; he hoped to increase the reported amount, as well as his contributions to the Central Provident Fund, in order to enhance the chances of success in the next round of applications.

Like Soon, Aaron (35-year-old cook, post-2018 interviewee) struggled to secure an LTVP for his wife Betty (36-year-old Thai) who had been granted a month-long SVP upon marriage. Renewing the SVP monthly was not only a 'headache' but costly (the S$40 per renewal was substantial as Aaron only earned about S$60–70 a day). Multiple attempts to secure an LTVP culminated in a fracas with immigration officers when Aaron tried to assert his 'right' to a family, to no avail:

> They told me, okay, if you want to extend [Betty's SVP], you need to pay a sum of money. If [you] have no money to pay . . . they said, cannot extend . . . I don't know what the charge is for. I [only] want to help my wife extend her visa. Why can't it be done? I [want to] use my right . . . I'm fighting for my wife!

For over a year, the precarious nature of Betty's residency status became a significant source of tension for the couple, and soon they were considering divorce should the situation not improve. The turning point only came when the couple heeded an immigration officer's advice to increase their chances of securing the LTVP by producing a child from the marriage. Aaron expressed disbelief ('That ICA officer told me one thing, "*eh*, you try to make a baby *lah*". Really? Must do a baby, then we can have the Long Term Pass or the PR? *Huh*? . . . Like this, you are forcing me!'), but the couple complied and Betty received her LTVP+ soon after their son's birth.

Echoing Kim's (2013, 455) concept of 'ethnicized maternal citizenship', the pathway to longer-term residency for marriage migrants in Singapore is partly predicated on producing citizen-children from the marriage. Betty already has a non-Singaporean child from her first marriage in Thailand (as well as a Singaporean step-child from Aaron's first marriage), but these would not facilitate moving up a rung in the citizenship ladder. Conjoined to notions of maternal citizenship which reduces marriage migrants' rights to claims-making based solely on motherhood, Singapore's marriage-migration-citizenship regime further illustrates a sort of 'fecundity [bargain] for citizenship' wherein pathways to residency are also made more accessible through the biological reproduction of citizen-subjects.

The pathway to conditional 'reproductive citizenship' (Turner 2008), however, is ridden with other pitfalls. Compelled to produce a citizen-child to secure the migrant mother's residency, Aaron and Betty found themselves struggling with the added costs of raising a child:

Aaron: Singapore's [cost of living] pressure ... [is] crazy. If you don't believe, ask my wife. Everything requires money. ... With no [better paying] work, how to have money? And the child, he needs milk. Nobody helps ... I've to help myself.

Betty: We live paycheck to paycheck. We've to raise a child. We've debts, have to send money [remittances to support her natal family in Thailand], and whatever we get, we don't get to keep. We pay this bill, pay that bill, and our child has to drink milk. Every month, [expenditure is] about S$2,000+.

In this case, the lack of extended family support has also deepened the sense of precarity: Aaron's stepmother whom they were living with had asked the couple to move out within three months as she wanted to make space in her apartment for her own biological son and his family. Without the cushioning effects of extended family support, securing the LTVP+ by committing to raising a child has moved the couple from one realm of precarity (tenuous residency status) to another (insecurity of finding affordable housing).

Prior to 2015, gaining PR was a crucial precondition for accessing other substantive rights, such as the right to work. For many migrant wives, the right to paid work was of paramount importance for generating an independent income to support both their natal and marital families, but achieving this goal was ultimately dependent on their husbands' financial standing and capacity to sponsor their PR applications. Ironically, those who needed to work to supplement family income were more likely to be among those with no easy pathway to access paid work. Binh (38-year-old Vietnamese, six-month SVP, pre-2011 interviewee), for example, had come to Singapore to 'find a husband' in order to support her three daughters from a previous marriage. Upon marriage, she found that her husband, a fishmonger, earned a small monthly income (S$1,700) with which he had to support, beside themselves, his elderly mother and his youngest teenaged son from a previous marriage. Binh herself made a small sum of money through offering tailoring services, but her home-based business was limited as she neither had a regular clientele nor a proper workspace. She considered renting a small retail space, but could not pursue this as she had no capital, and more crucially, was wary of the illegalities of conducting businesses on short-term SVPs. Marriage migrants like Binh thus found themselves in a difficult bind: they needed to work as their husbands were struggling to support the family, but their husbands' financial inadequacy in turn stood in the way of their right to long-term residency and paid work.

In another case, Nhan (32-year-old Vietnamese, LTVP, pre-2011 interviewee) had married Michael (32-year-old salesman) on the understanding that he earned a good monthly income (S$3,000), owned an apartment, and was able to provide her with 'a better life'. Upon marriage, Nhan found that her husband was in financial difficulties: his income, based on commissions, had dropped by a third due to the recession, and he also had to pay child support after his recent divorce. Michael's apartment now belonged to his ex-wife and the newlyweds had to share a rental flat with another Singaporean-Vietnamese couple. Under these circumstances, Nhan had little hope in progressing to PR, even though she yearned to be able to resume work (she owned and managed a hair salon in Vietnam) as 'staying at home and doing nothing was a torture'. She could work if an employer was willing to sponsor her work permit, but the lack of social networks and linguistic capital meant that she had little access to the local job market. Nhan had also considered working illegally but Michael refused to allow her to do so for fear of jeopardizing her PR application.

While the introduction of work rights for LTVP/LTVP+ holders in 2015 has lowered the barriers to paid work, it did not completely liberate marriage migrants from the nettle of reproductive citizenship. The arrival of children often confirmed the marriage migrant's primary role as a mother and homemaker while undermining her productive worker identity. The patriarchal bargain at the heart of the 'fecundity for citizenship' exchange takes on new complexities as the terms of bargaining morph into another family tradeoff, this time requiring migrant wives to forego paid work for full-time caregiving and homemaking. Having fought for and succeeded in securing Betty's residency status, Aaron – despite being in dire financial straits – asserted his patriarchal rights to keeping Betty at home to provide caregiving:

> No matter what, we as husbands, we don't want our wives to come out [to work] ... *I'm working*. I come out to work. You, best help me [by] looking after my child well ... while I slowly earn [money].

In turn, Betty had little choice but to acquiesce to the terms of the bargain, and suspend, at least in the short-run, her own desire to work:

> I've to look for opportunities to work when my child goes to school. Whenever I can work, I will. But now my child is [too young].

Like Betty, most marriage migrants, including those who had secured the right to work, did not engage in paid work when their children were young. In some cases, husbands (like Aaron) were explicit in 'preferring' their migrant wives to stay home and devote themselves to the children. Deliana (41-year-old Indonesian, PR, post-2018 interviewee), who worked as an accountant before marriage, explained that while she wished to continue working, she complied with her husband's wishes for her to stay home until their son reached school-going age. In other cases, the patriarchal bargain was an unstated assumption: migrant wives who climbed the citizenship ladder by producing children should fulfil their end of the bargain by demonstrating exemplary motherhood in providing full-time care for their children. In Kristy's (39-year-old Vietnamese, PR, post-2018 interviewee) case, despite a ten-year career as an accountant and then a tour guide in Vietnam, paid work was impossible in the early years of the marriage: she was already pregnant on register-ing her marriage in Singapore, and found herself overwhelmed by care duties and housework when her daughter turned a month old:

> I'd to do all the household chores, such as washing clothes, cleaning the house, sweeping the house ... holding my child with one hand, and cooking with another hand ... [One day], as I was lulling her [baby daughter] to sleep, my mother-in-law entered the room, kicked me and told me to wash the clothes. 'Your kid's already sleeping, why are you still lying here instead of waking up and washing clothes?' So I felt very, very sad, felt very ... hurt [voice cracking].

Despite having a supportive husband, Kristy knuckled down to her mother-in-law's view of women's roles vis-à-vis men's:

> My husband did help me with the housework. However, [when my mother-in-law found out], she shouted at him and didn't allow him to help. She said that my husband worked outside the whole day and was very tired. And as [I] just stayed home and looked after the kid ... So [I] have to do all the housework.

Stepping stones along the pathway of reproductive citizenship are not only dependent on powerful others (such as husbands and mothers-in-law) within the context of family-making, they also reflect a paradoxical process of moving up and down a slippery slope. While producing a child propels the marriage migrant closer to securing citizenship, it may also become an obstacle to accessing the substantive rights of her citizenship – in particular access to employment and a worker-identity in her own right. For marriage migrants, partial citizenship is hence a result of the state's hierarchical control of citizenship rights on the one hand, and family processes that confirm migrant women's primary subjectivity as wives, mothers and homemakers on the other.

In sum, the narratives illustrated how women marriage migrants are reduced to partial citizens through the layered and interactive effects of restrictions imposed by state policies, and family processes and circumstances. State policies expect women marriage migrants to be dependent on their husbands for their residency applications, which exacerbates their vulnerability when spousal relations sour. However, even when spousal relations are unobstructive, state policies restricting employment for marriage migrants have the effect of constraining pathways towards seeking independent identities or generating family income. Marriage migrants are thus confined to partial citizenship with low status in the family and diminished citizenship rights pertaining to residency and employment.

Leveraging on the family for substantive claims-making

While the intimate sphere of the family is paramount in framing the conditions under which marriage migrants negotiate pathways to citizenship, women who have committed to travelling this road also actively leverage on familial processes to widen the degree of latitude they have in claims-making beyond the bounds of reproductive, partial citizenship. Substantive claims-making in acquiring a worker identity by accessing external employment proved to be crucial in paving a way toward contributing to increasing household income, greater decision-making power, and a higher status in the family. In order to grasp the complexities of negotiations in the interstices of family processes, we focus on one woman's experience in navigating the pathway towards citizenship before giving attention to other intersecting accounts.

When Nhi (29-year-old Vietnamese, PR currently applying for SC, post-2018 interviewee) was twenty years old, she married a Singaporean man 31 years her senior, with two school-age children from a previous marriage, through a commercial agency. It was a decision that hung on a knife's edge as she vacillated amidst many tears and anxieties, but ultimately committed herself to marrying the 'fat and old' man. Her father had insisted that she need not force herself into being 'sold like fish' but her mother told her to be pragmatic. Having already spent a hefty sum (S$5000 to cover airfares and agency fees) on two trips to Singapore to find a match, she would be the 'laughing stock' of the village if she returned empty-handed. The agency also made it clear that she would be missing the boat if she did not take up her prospective husband's offer of marriage, as he was a factory-owner in comfortable circumstances and quite a 'catch'.

For Nhi, her marriage began inauspiciously: she was fearful of living in a 'super messy' house with altars in every room,[11] she could not communicate as she had little Mandarin, and worst of all, she felt extremely isolated as she was unable to step out of the house unaccompanied for the first three months of married life. However, within a few months, Nhi found ways of altering the patriarchal bargain to create more degrees of autonomy while continuing to prove herself a responsible member of the family.

Despite her husband's concerns that not having a child from the marriage might jeopardize her PR application, Nhi insisted on delaying childbearing and giving priority to finding work to gain independence and generate remittances for her natal family:

> [My husband] wanted a child but I didn't want one. I said I was still young, why give birth first? Let me work first to earn money to support my parents. Then after that, I can give birth. So that's what I did.

While her husband was willing to back down from insisting that Nhi produced a child (he already had two children from his previous marriage), he tried to maintain patriarchal control by 'paying' Nhi *not* to work. But Nhi resisted her husband's offer and was adamant that she took on a job to earn her 'own money':

> He didn't want me to work initially but I insisted ... he did give me $200 a month actually, but I insisted. He said, *don't work* and he would give me $500 a month. I didn't want that and still fought with him, that I wanted to work, so in the end he had no choice, he signed the papers to allow me to work.[12]

In order to recalibrate the patriarchal bargain in her favour, Nhi continually built up her social and linguistic capital. Six months after marriage, she found work at a food centre through her Vietnamese network of friends. Starting as an assistant serving behind the counter of a food stall, a role that required minimal language facility, she persevered through constant scolding from her supervisor and graduated to a more active role interacting with customers and collecting money:

> I first started at the 'economy rice' stall, it was easier since you don't need to talk right? [Customers] just point at the dishes they want right? You don't need to talk ... I was always scolded by my [Malaysian] supervisor, every day, I was scolded: 'Why do you work here when you can't speak Mandarin? You don't know Mandarin!' I just smiled. I understood what was being said but I couldn't reply. So, I started to learn Mandarin very quickly as I was really angry. I sold economy rice for 10 days and then [moved] to the duck rice stall where I worked for three years. I was [serving at tables] and collecting money. Soon, I was [able to retaliate]. I said: 'Look, my Mandarin is good now, I can even scold you!'

While she had begun learning Mandarin from a phrasebook upon marriage, it was her work at the food stalls that strengthened her facility in communication, and this in turn gave her ammunition to argue her case with her husband. When asked how she managed to have her own way, Nhi laughed and summed it up: 'I'm not afraid of him ... I learnt Mandarin in six months!' For marriage migrants, linguistic capital is not only a marker of social integration but an important condition that shapes claims-making both within and outside the family sphere.

When Nhi finally had a daughter six years into the marriage, she had already progressed to becoming an informal partner in a small business selling Singaporean snacks at food centres. Despite strong reservations at the start, her husband realized how entrepreneurial Nhi was and even came round to support her business venture by contributing some capital. However, establishing her right to work still meant that she had to resolve care deficits within the home. As her entrepreneurial role was not entirely compatible with the expectations thrust upon reproductive citizens, Nhi had to marshal replacement domestic labour to hold up her end of the patriarchal bargain. To do so, she brought her parents over from Vietnam through consecutive SVPs (eventually followed by a one-year LTVP under her husband's sponsorship for her mother) to help with the childcare, and also convinced her husband to hire a foreign domestic worker to take over household chores. By reworking the tradeoff between carework in the family and paid work in the public sphere, marriage migrants – with either tacit or active support of their husbands – who have moved from 'wife' to 'worker' are able to emulate the way Singaporean working women escape entrapment in the patriarchal bargain: by roping in unpaid grandparental labour or paying (other) migrant women as cheaper sources of substitute care labour.

In turn, proving herself a successful entrepreneur who also contributed to household expenses strengthened her position in family decision-making. When her husband felt that enrolling their young daughter in a private childcare facility was too expensive, Nhi, who wanted nothing but the best for her daughter's education, was able to fork out her own money:

> Every time I bring up the topic of pre-school, we would quarrel … I've told him, 'If you don't want to pay, I will do it'. Since she's my daughter, I want to give her the best.

While Nhi faced considerable delay in negotiating the pathway to legal citizenship (her PR application was successful only when she became pregnant after six years in Singapore), she was able to assemble support from family (both natal and marital) and co-ethnic networks (her business partners were also Vietnamese migrant wives) to gain what she considered the most important substantive right to secure – the right to work. Eschewing the set order seemingly prescribed for marriage migrants (marry, have a child, gain long-term residency, then work) due to her unwavering focus on independence and earning money, Nhi was able to leverage family processes to place work before children. While she eventually fulfilled her part of the patriarchal bargain and produced a child, her early access to work allowed her to expand her social circle, accumulate economic, social and linguistic capital, and eventually attain PR. In other words, while Nhi was cognizant of the advantages of having PR ('you can work anywhere [for any employer], the salary is higher and you can start your own business'), she was not willing to trade her rights to paid work for a PR status that seemed umbilically tied to having a child, as the latter would confirm her status as *only* a reproductive citizen. By the time we interviewed Nhi, she had gained a sufficient sense of economic and emotional security in Singapore to have the confidence to apply for SC.

For others, resisting being straightjacketed as a reproductive citizen was not possible in the beginning, and the patriarchal bargain only began tilting in their favour over time. Kristy, for example, expressed some bitterness that her own career plans were never discussed prior to her marriage and migration to Singapore. While her citizenship journey progressed relatively smoothly (she was accorded LTVP+ status upon marriage and PR three years later), she faced considerable struggles on the home front (as earlier accounted). Although she accepted staying home to take care of her young daughter as her maternal responsibility, she also yearned for work outside the home. The turning point came when her husband's company went bankrupt and he had to take on a low-paying job. To supplement household income, Kristy found work at a factory (which paid more than her husband's earnings) and placed her three-year-old daughter in a government-run kindergarten. She traced a significant change in her mother-in-law's attitude towards her to the day when, feeling the stresses of home and work, she had a relapse of a longstanding medical condition and had to be sent to the hospital in an ambulance. Afraid of losing her, her mother-in-law began from that point onwards to take on a share of the childcare and housework:

> Ah ... suddenly she was very scared, suddenly she changed. When I get back home (from work), everything is in order ... she'll sweep and clean the house ... previously I always needed to cook, but now, when I come back home, she's already cooked!

In her newfound role as a significant breadwinner cum caregiver, Kristy's status in the family improved, so much so that she now deserved to be cared for by the older non-working woman in the family.

In other cases, the rebalancing of the patriarchal bargain occurred even more gradually. Ai Khue (35-year-old Vietnamese, PR, post-2018 interviewee) began married life as a homemaker on an LTVP, receiving 'pocket money' from her husband who ran a food stall for daily expenses. She soon realized that her husband gambled heavily and ran up debts. He was also careless in watching over his workers. She felt that she had no choice but to step up, initially as his assistant, to help manage the business:

> I was pregnant, with a big tummy, about to give birth ... yet, I came out to help my husband. I took the chopper and chopped (the meat) ... I didn't know Mandarin, I didn't know anything ... [but] within one month, I learnt to take orders, I learnt *everything*. I caught two workers stealing money and chased them away. So everyone was very impressed by me ... Very strong woman, everyone says so, very strong.

Ai Khue picked up Mandarin, Hokkien and English, and eventually became adept in handling customers' orders. Ten years later, the mother of three is now also the 'boss' in charge of the business and family finances. A telling sign of how the patriarchal bargain had been recalibrated lay in the fact that it was Ai Khue who now provided her husband with 'pocket money', having found it necessary not only to control his expenditure, but to also buy cigarettes on his behalf to moderate his smoking habit.

The acquisition of PR was important in facilitating job searches for migrant wives such as Kristy, but less so for those who 'assisted' their husbands such as Ai Khue. More crucially, their capacity to exercise the right to work was inextricable from the dynamic power relations within the family.

Conclusion

In this paper, we have highlighted the importance of conceptualizing citizenship as both legal status and social practice, and given attention to the way the legal and the social are mutually constituted. On the one hand, states can effect hierarchical control by imposing differentiated legal categories of membership with graduated rights in different combinations and permutations. On the other hand, migrants can exercise agency in everyday practices of claims-making so as to 'transcend status categories and reconstitute the substantive meaning of citizenship' (Bloemraad and Sheares 2017, 852). For marriage migrants, this dynamic is located in the family sphere as the principal arena of control and struggle.

Inducted into the nation-state as 'reproductive citizens' (Turner 2008), marriage migrants' position within the host nation-state is premised on their gendered roles and identities within the marital family, as wives, mothers, daughters-in-law and home-makers. In Singapore, this mode of partial citizenship has two interrelated aspects. First, as a form of reproductive citizenship, fecundity pathways to citizenship valorise migrant women's bodies as fertility machines, while reinscribing reproductive relations as central to family norms and forms. In return for gaining a foothold on the citizenship ladder, marriage migrants are expected to demonstrate their value to the nation-state through reproduction, child-rearing and family-making. Second, marriage migrants become subjects of gendered power hierarchies within the family, where their mobility towards securing residency and citizenship depends on the sponsorship of their citizen-husbands and the support of their in-laws.

At the same time, while progress along pathways of reproductive citizenship is both slippery and dependent on more powerful familial others, marriage migrants are not necessarily entrapped reproductive subjects of gender and generational oppression. Women can navigate familial processes in order to find leverage for claims-making. In some cases, asserting their right to exceed reproductive citizenship by putting paid work before childbirth allowed them to assume worker identities synonymous with independence and economic productivity. This in turn strengthened their positioning within both natal and marital families, and advanced their residency claims (to a level allowing them the rights to work and stay for longer periods). In other cases, while the asymmetries of the patriarchal bargain that lies at the heart of conditional reproductive citizenship (alongside an unequal possession of human and social capital) had to be endured at the start, marriage migrants, over time, found ways to recalibrate the trade-off to move the bargaining in their favour through incremental steps.

As a primary site that mediates marriage migrants' claims-making, the family sphere is critical in determining how and when they can effectively exercise the graduated rights of partial citizenship. Within this sphere of intimate relations, migrant women find varying degrees of freedom to negotiate the paradox of being responsible affinal subjects of the family on the one hand, while being partial citizens of the nation-state on the other.

By tracing the complex negotiations and struggles that marriage migrants undertake in order to achieve citizenship and residency rights, and centring the family in the analytical frame, we have highlighted the disjuncture between the lived realities of family relationships on the one hand, and the boundary-making work of reproducing the nation-state on the other. While the interaction between state control of citizenship rights and family processes in shaping familial relations has created the marriage migrant as a category of partial citizenship, marriage migrants are nonetheless able to exercise agency to varying extents in navigating their way through gendered familial hierarchies to further their citizenship claims and reach beyond the confines of being partial citizens of the nation-state.

Notes

1. 'Responsibilisation' is a concept developed in the governmentality literature to refer to individuals who are active subjects responsible for managing their own welfare, security and the risks to these (Rose 1996; Wakefield and Fleming 2009). In this context, responsibilised marriage migrants are individually responsible for negotiating and securing their own citizenship pathways.
2. See https://www.ica.gov.sg/pass/LTVP/pass_LTVP_apply_ssc.
3. See https://www.guidemesingapore.com/in-the-news/2014/2014 https://www.guidemesinga pore.com/in-the-news/2014/2014—relaxed-rules-for-singaporean-foreign-spouses-brings-smiles-to-families-and-businesses-owners – relaxed-rules-for-singaporean-foreign-spouses-brings-smiles-to-families-and-businesses-owners.
4. See https://va.ecitizen.gov.sg/CSS/uploads/PMLA.pdf.
5. Companies employing LTVP/LTVP+ holders are not subject to foreign worker quotas or required to pay foreign worker levies, thereby reducing costs while augmenting the supply of labour (https://www.singaporecompanyincorporation.sg/blog/relaxed-work-visa-rules-for-foreign-spouses-of-residents-in-singapore-companies-set-to-benefit/).
6. See https://aware.org.sg/wp-content/uploads/Home-truly-respect-the-rights-of-foreign-wives.pdf.
7. See https://aware.org.sg/wp-content/uploads/Home-truly-respect-the-rights-of-foreign-wives.pdf.
8. This reflects the gradual decline of the need for commercial matchmaking services and the increasing importance of personal networks and social media over the decade as a result of increasing regional mobility (Yeoh, Chee, and Baey 2017).
9. Similarly, reasons for this change are likely interlinked and possibly attributed to factors such as policy changes, foreign wives' length of stay in Singapore as well as the recruitment of respondents from public spaces (often their workplaces). Being able to work is also a reflection of their longer-term visa status.
10. While the criteria for success remains a black box, most respondents thought that qualifying factors included the husband's education, employment status and history, income level, Central Provident Fund balance, and tax records.
11. Appeasing the deities was important to her husband's business.
12. Nhi was holding an LTVP then and needed her husband, as guarantor, to give formal permission for her to work.

Acknowledgments

We would like to thank Chiu Tuen Yi (Jenny), reviewers, research collaborators and respondents as well as organisers and participants of the Workshop on "Marriage Migration, Family and Citizenship in Asia" where an earlier version of this paper was presented.

Disclosure statement

No potential conflict of interest was reported by the author(s).

Funding

This work was supported by the Ministry of Education, Singapore, under its Academic Research Fund Tier 2 [T208A4103]' Wellcome Trust [General Purpose Fund].

ORCID

Brenda S.A. Yeoh ⓘ http://orcid.org/0000-0002-0240-3175
Heng Leng Chee ⓘ http://orcid.org/0000-0001-6731-8724
Rohini Anant ⓘ http://orcid.org/0000-0001-5166-9220
Theodora Lam ⓘ http://orcid.org/0000-0003-0342-5808

References

Asis, M. M. B., and G. Battisella. 2012. "Multicultural Realities and Membership: States, Migrations and Citizenship in Asia." In *Migration and Diversity in Asian Contexts*, edited by A. E. Lai, F. L. Collins, and B. S. A. Yeoh, 69–74. Singapore: Institute of Southeast Asian Studies.

De Hart, B. 2015. "Regulating Mixed Marriages through Acquisition and Loss of Citizenship." *The Annals of the American Academy of Political and Social Science* 662 (1): 170–187. doi:10.1177/0002716215595390.

Bloemraad, I., and A. Sheares. 2017. "Understanding Membership in a World of Global Migration: (How) Does Citizenship Matter?" *International Migration Review* 51 (4): 823–867. doi:10.1111/imre.12354.

Charsley, K., M. Bolognani, and S. Spencer. 2017. "Marriage Migration and Integration: Interrogating Assumptions in Academic and Policy Debates." *Ethnicities* 17 (4): 469–490. doi:10.1177/1468796816677329.

Cheng, C. M. C., and H. Y. Choo. 2015. "Women's Migration for Domestic Work and Cross-Border Marriage in East and Southeast Asia: Reproducing Domesticity, Contesting Citizenship." *Sociology Compass* 9 (8): 654–667. doi:10.1111/soc4.12289.

Cheng, I. 2013. "Making Foreign Women the Mother of Our Nation: The Exclusion and Assimilation of Immigrant Women in Taiwan." *Asian Ethnicity* 14 (2): 157–179. doi:10.1080/14631369.2012.759749.

Cheng, Y. 2012. "Transnational Masculinities in Situ: Singaporean Husbands and Their International Marriage Experiences." *Area* 44 (1): 76–82. doi:10.1111/j.1475-4762.2011.01045.x.

Chung, E. A. 2020. "Creating Hierarchies of Noncitizens: Race, Gender, and Visa Categories in South Korea." *Journal of Ethnic and Migration Studies* 46 (12): 2497–2514. doi:10.1080/1369183X.2018.1561061.

Constable, N. 2005. *Cross-Border Marriages: Gender and Mobility in Transnational Asia.* Philadelphia: University of Pennsylvania Press.

Douglass, M. 2006. "Global Householding in Pacific Asia." *International Development Planning Review* 28 (4): 421–446. doi:10.3828/idpr.28.4.1.

Erel, U. 2013. "Kurdish Migrant Mothers in London Enacting Citizenship." *Citizenship Studies* 17 (8): 970–984. doi:10.1080/13621025.2013.851146.

Friedman, S. 2010. "Marital Immigration and Graduated Citizenship: Post-Naturalisation Restrictions on Mainland Chinese Spouses in Taiwan." *Pacific Affairs* 83 (1): 73–93. doi:10.5509/201083173.

Hsia, H.-C. 2012. "The Tug of War over Multiculturalism: Contestation between Governing and Empowering Immigrants in Taiwan." In *Migration and Diversity in Asian Contexts*, edited by A. E. Lai, F. L. Collins, and B. S. A. Yeoh, 130–160. Singapore: Institute of Southeast Asian Studies.

Jongwilaiwan, R., and E. C. Thompson. 2013. "Thai Wives in Singapore and Transnational Patriarchy." *Gender, Place and Culture* 20 (3): 363–381. doi:10.1080/0966369X.2011.624588.

Kim, M. 2013. "Citizenship Projects for Marriage Migrants in South Korea: Intersecting Motherhood with Ethnicity and Class." *Social Politics: International Studies in Gender, State and Society* 20 (4): 455–81.

Kim, G., and M. Kilkey. 2018. "Marriage Migration Policy in South Korea: Social Investment beyond the Nation State." *International Migration* 56 (1): 23–38. doi:10.1111/imig.12350.

Kim, I., and Z. M. Vang. 2020. "Contending with Neo-Classical Patriarchal Bargain: Filipina Marriage Migrants' Negotiations for Naturalization in South Korea." *Citizenship Studies* 24 (2): 209–227. doi:10.1080/13621025.2019.1700915.

Kim, M. 2010. "Gender and International Marriage Migration." *Sociology Compass* 4 (9): 718–731. doi:10.1111/j.1751-9020.2010.00314.x.

Kim, M. 2013. "Citizenship Projects for Marriage Migrants in South Korea: Intersecting Motherhood with Ethnicity and Class." *Social Politics: International Studies in Gender, State and Society* 20 (4): 455–481. doi:10.1093/sp/jxt015.

Kim-Bossard, M. 2017. "Mothering as Laboring: Navigating Cultural Discourses of Mothering as Marriage-Labor Immigrants in Korea." *Anthropology of Work Review* 38 (2): 92–103. doi:10.1111/awr.12121.

Lee, H.-K. 2008. "International Marriage and the State in South Korea: Focusing on Governmental Policy." *Citizenship Studies* 12 (1): 107–123. doi:10.1080/13621020701794240.

Longman, C., K. De Graeve, and T. Brouckaert. 2013. "Mothering as a Citizenship Practice: An Intersectional Analysis of 'Carework' and 'Culturework' in Non-Normative Mother–Child Identities." *Citizenship Studies* 17 (3–4): 385–399. doi:10.1080/13621025.2013.791540.

López, J. L. 2015. "Impossible Families': Mixed-Citizenship Status Couples and the Law." *Law & Policy* 37 (1–2): 93–118. doi:10.1111/lapo.12032.

National Population and Talent Division, Strategy Group, Prime Minister's Office, Singapore Department of Statistics, Ministry of Home Affairs, Immigration & Checkpoints Authority, and Ministry of Manpower. 2020. *Population in Brief 2020*. Singapore: National Population and Talent Division, Strategy Group, Prime Minister's Office, Singapore Department of Statistics, Ministry of Home Affairs, Immigration & Checkpoints Authority, Ministry of Manpower.

Rose, N. 1996. "The Death of the Social? Re-Figuring the Territory of Government." *International Journal of Human Resource Management* 25 (3): 327–356.

Sheu, Y.-H. 2007. "Full Responsibility with Partial Citizenship: Immigrant Wives in Taiwan." *Social Policy Administration* 41 (2): 179–196. doi:10.1111/j.1467-9515.2007.00546.x.

Singapore Department of Statistics. 2020. "Number and Proportion of Inter-Ethnic and Transnational Marriages among Citizen Marriages, Annual." Singapore Department of Statistics, Accessed 19 October. https://www.tablebuilder.singstat.gov.sg/publicfacing/viewMultiTable.action

Song, J. 2015. "Five Phases of Brokered International Marriages in South Korea: A Complexity Perspective." *Asian Studies* 1 (1): 147–176.

Tan, T. 2011. "Bride and Gloom." In *The Straits Times*. Singapore: SPH.

Tham, B. 2019. "Help Available for Foreign Spouses of Singaporeans." In *The Straits Times*. Singapore: SPH.

Tsai, M.-C. 2011. "Foreign Brides' Meet Ethnic Politics in Taiwan." *International Migration Review* 45 (2): 243–268. doi:10.1111/j.1747-7379.2011.00847.x.

Turner, B. 2008. "Citizenship, Reproduction and the State: International Marriage and Human Rights." *Citizenship Studies* 12 (1): 45–54. doi:10.1080/13621020701794166.

Wakefield, A., and J. Fleming. 2009. "Responsibilization." In *The Sage Dictionary of Policing*, edited by A. Wakefield and J. Fleming, 277–278. London: SAGE Publications .

Wang, H.-Z., and D. Belanger. 2008. "Taiwanizing Female Immigrant Spouses and Materializing Differential Citizenship." *Citizenship Studies* 12 (1): 91–106. doi:10.1080/13621020701794224.

Yeoh, B. S. A., H. L. Chee, and G. Baey. 2017. "Managing Risk, Making a Match: Brokers and Sthe Management of Mobility in International Marriage." *Mobilities* 12 (2): 227–242. doi:10.1080/17450101.2017.1292779.

Yeoh, B. S. A., H. L. Chee, and T. K. D. Vu. 2013. "Commercially Arranged Marriage and the Negotiation of Citizenship Rights among Vietnamese Marriage Migrants in Multiracial Singapore." *Asian Ethnicity* 14 (2): 139–156. doi:10.1080/14631369.2012.759746.

Yeoh, B. S. A., H. L. Chee, and T. K. D. Vu. 2014. ""Global Householding and the Negotiation of Intimate Labour in Commercially-matched International Marriages between Vietnamese Women and Singaporean Men." *Geoforum* 51: 284–293. doi:10.1016/j.geoforum.2013.09.012.

Zhang, J., M. C.-W. Lu, and B. S. A. Yeoh. 2015. "Cross-Border Marriage, Transgovernmental Friction, and Waiting". *Environment and Planning D: Society and Space* 33 (2): 229–246. doi:10.1068/d24111.

Penalizing 'runaway' migrant wives: commercial cross-border marriages and home space as confinement

Sohoon Yi🆔

ABSTRACT

This study examines the use of the term *'gachul* (absconding from home)' in courts and immigration policies to punish the behavior of marriage migrant women who enter South Korea after marriage and then leave their husbands. The study focuses on penalized mobility outside migrants' marital homes, which is interpreted as deviance from the expected family role. By conceptualizing home as a *confinable* space, the paper discusses migrant women's exclusion from citizenship based on their contribution to the family. The paper draws from cases heard in criminal courts and laws and policies, paying attention to the conflation of criminal, immigration, and family laws and the effect on marriage and family. Notably, it highlights cases of uxoricide, marital rape, and international child abduction. The cases reveal that judicial and executive bodies penalize marriage migrants' departure from home, regardless of the justification for their actions.

Introduction

On 25 June 2007, Huynh Mai, a 19-year-old Vietnamese marriage migrant, wrote a sorrowful goodbye letter to her South Korean husband whom she met through a commercial marriage broker in Vietnam half a year earlier. Her husband, named Jang, had sought international marriage brokers because he was ashamed of being alone in his old age (he was 25 years older than Huynh) and not successful in finding a wife among Korean women (whom he blamed for being 'too realistic'). The next day, Jang came home drunk after work and found Huynh ready to leave with her suitcase and passport. Jang was 'consumed with rage;' he felt that the marriage was a 'swindle' and that he had been 'abandoned' by Huynh.[1] He had paid the marriage brokers 10 million won (approximately 10,000 USD), almost all his savings, to arrange a wedding with Huynh. He beat her to death and was charged with murder.

Huynh's death – one of many published deaths of marriage migrants at the hands of their intimate partners – exposes the extreme violence to which many of these women are subjected. Three months before Huynh's murder, Le Thi Kim Dong (also a marriage migrant from Vietnam) died from a fall while trying to escape her husband using a makeshift rope of curtains from the balcony of their apartment on the ninth floor (Viet Nam News 2007). The house she left was empty, indicating that she was likely locked in. More recently, in December 2018, a South Korean man murdered his Filipina wife. It was said that her husband sought to prevent her from going out or even putting on makeup. When the woman started working for pay out of necessity (the husband's poor health prevented him from working), the couple argued a lot about her employment until it led to her murder (Yun 2018).

This paper focuses on marriage migrants' freedom of mobility by examining their contested relationship to 'home'. The deaths of or domestic violence against migrant women (especially marriage migrants) are often the consequences of their inability to leave their partners or a struggle over women's autonomy of action and mobility. However, despite their vulnerability, official discourse on the protection of migrant women's freedom of mobility – and by extension, their safety and security – has seen mixed responses.

After Huynh Mai's death, the judges of her case produced a verdict that was sharply critical of the wider phenomenon of commercially-arranged marriage migration. They commented that this case exposed broader social problems of 'treating women from less affluent countries like imported goods as an answer for marrying old bachelors'.[2] Studies on violence against marriage migrant women and its implications have been conducted since Huynh's death (Kim, Kim, and Kim 2008; Hwang 2015). Scholars have noted the relationship between their legal precarity, dependence on their husbands for visas, and the extreme power inequality such immigration mechanisms engender (Choo 2016; Kim 2012, 2013; Kim 2016). Such circumstances may make it difficult for marriage migrants to leave their marriage even if it is abusive.

However, the South Korean government, especially the immigration authorities, have refused to recognize marriage migrants' freedom of mobility as a human right in a legal and moral sense. The South Korean government takes a socially conservative approach to marriage. It has mandated a law to encourage heteronormative marriages and prevent marital breakdowns, and marriage migrants are accepted under the government initiative to promote marriage and childbirth for their citizens. When marriage migrants arrive in South Korea, they are granted *temporary* (but renewable) marriage migration visas but are *not guaranteed* to receive permanent residency or citizenship.[3] Instead of legal stability, immigration restrictions function as a safety test for the government to ensure the 'genuineness' of cross-border marriages (see also, Yi 2021).

Scholarship on marriage migration in Asia analyzes social anxiety about foreigners that penetrate deep into society by marrying citizens and forming families in countries where the notions of multiculturalism are relatively new (Hsia 2007; Kim 2012; Friedman and Mahdavi 2015; Lan 2008). It would, however, be incorrect to say such anxiety is unique to Asia, as it is deeply rooted in social angst about citizenship of marriage migrants and migrant families, which is also evident elsewhere (see, for example, Bonjour and de Hart 2021; Griffiths 2021; Block 2021). Nonetheless, this paper focuses on women's physical location and social belonging in home space and family as a *condition to membership* specifically in the context of South Korea's legal and moral norms. In doing so, I pay attention to an aspect of citizenship which Bosniak (2009) called an 'exclusive national status' (128) that describes both the kind of relationship that members of a community maintain and rules associated with the maintenance of membership. I focus on home space and family as a site where politics of exclusion occur and bring to light the relational and normative nature of citizenship.

While marriage with a citizen grants a possibility of legal citizenship for marriage migrants, such possibility demands women to conform to certain rules about the family. What this paper shows is the other scenarios where women did not (or could not) conform to such rules, showing what Bosniak (2009) called 'the interplay of citizenships at stake' (128).

I place legal discourse on 'runaway' wives at the disjuncture between instrumentalizing migrants to address South Korea's perceived 'demographic crisis' (Lee 2012) and recognizing their agency and capability to make decisions to maximize personal interests.[4] I analyze the term *gachul* (家出), which can be translated to 'absconding' or 'running away' from home and is frequently used to describe runaway youths.[5] In addition, I criticize the assumed immorality of runaways embedded in South Korea's legal system to describe the actions of adult women. In addition to questioning and challenging the implied meaning in using such legal terms, I find the discourse on *gachul* as justifying migrants' *confinability* in home space. Using home space as a possible space of confinement (that is, *confinable* space), as it was the case for Huynh, Le and the Filipina woman, the home symbolically represents exclusion from the protections and rights that are available to citizens.

While the logic of immigration control provides important enforcement mechanisms through which women's mobility is confined, I argue that immigration is only part of a complex web of power. After all, Huynh wished to leave her husband *and* South Korea; immigration restrictions (the difficulty of further stay in South Korea after leaving marriage) thus mattered little to her. I pay attention to the intersection of jurisdictions of criminal, family, and immigration laws and the production of a disciplining force that penalizes women's mobility. In this intersectional space, one can find a mechanism that counters a constitutional right of personal autonomy and furthermore punishes a woman for leaving her husband and thus the family. Grounded in the patriarchal imaginations of women's needs as equal to the perceived 'needs of the family', women's mobility deemed 'contrary' to the benefit of the family are penalized and considered immoral. When women's 'natural' place is in the family, it becomes difficult to separate women's individual needs and desires from those of the family.

The use of the term 'home' is problematic because public institutions understand home space synonymously with patrilocality. When women migrate to join their husbands, their husbands' residence generally becomes the family residence (Palriwala and Uberoi 2008). Thus, when they leave their husbands, they are also said to leave the 'home'. I should note the paradox and politics of naming 'home' when it can function as a space of confinement, of which departure can result in death.

By focusing on confinability of home space, this paper contributes to the existing research on anxiety and suspicion about migrant women's citizenship based on their contested family roles. In particular, I note the literature on marriage migrants and debate over the 'authenticity' of their marriage (Bonjour and De Hart 2013; Eggebø 2013; Friedman and Mahdavi 2015; Wray 2006) and the literature on mother-work of migrant women as citizenship practice (Longman, De Graeve, and Brouckaert 2013; Erel 2011; ito 2005; Yi 2021). Whereas the mentioned literature focuses on the performance of migrant women's family roles as a condition of their acceptability as (potential) citizens, my study examines *penalization* of deviance of one's role as a wife and a mother upon departing (or attempting to depart) from home.

The rest of this paper is organized as follows. I first explain the theoretical entry points and background of this paper before explaining the data and methods. Namely, I explore research on criminalization of immigration and the meaning of state power in cross-border marriages. Then I draw on case laws on international marriages, focusing on marital rape and international child abduction. Lastly, I draw on policy documents from the Ministry of Justice (MOJ) (and its subsidiary Korea Immigration Service) and the media reports to further examine the mentioned cases of marital rape and international child abduction.

Coercing intimate labor by penalizing runaway marriage migrants

Spatial politics of criminalization and home space as confinement

Migration scholars have examined criminalization of immigration through the conflation of criminal law and immigration law. Stumpf (2006) defines 'crimmigration' on three fronts: (1) the overlapping substance of immigration law and criminal law; (2) resemblance between immigration and criminal enforcements; and (3) the effects of criminal procedure on the prosecution of immigration violations. Since Stumpf's work, immigration scholars in socio-legal studies have paid attention to the conflation of criminality and unauthorized migration (Coutin 2005; Kubal 2014; Reiter and Coutin 2017; Sarabia 2018). Such conflation is manifested in various techniques of penalizing immigration offenses, including incarceration, the increased technological sophistication of immigration enforcement (Menjívar 2014; Coutin 2005), the symbolic functions of criminal laws, and stigmatized identities (Kubal 2014; Reiter and Coutin 2017; Sarabia 2018).

However, this paper looks beyond the strict *criminalization* of immigration to examine the broad institutional consequences of the conflation of two jurisdictions on the lives of migrants. By focusing on confinability of migrants' marital homes, I examine the intersection of criminal law and immigration law more widely to look at their overlaps and indirect consequences of such overlaps. I focus on the impact of one's immigration status and experience in criminal cases. In particular, I pay attention to three aspects: 1) the creation of an experience of confinement in everyday life; 2) the criminal court's (arbitrary) interpretation of migrants' immigration status; and 3) the penalization of *gachul* at the intersection of immigration law and criminal law. I do not mean to imply that migrant 'runaways' are prosecutable subjects. Leaving one's home, family, or husband is not against the law. A man can report his spouse's disappearance at the local police (*gachulsin-go*), after which her profile is entered into a system. Nonetheless, unlike missing minors, the adult missing person's whereabouts are not revealed to her spouse against her wish.

However, reporting marriage migrants' disappearance from home has grave *immigration* consequences before they acquire citizenship or permanent residency because their visas depend on their marriage. The South Korean case study is noteworthy because of the high rate of precarious legal status holders among marriage migrants. Marriage migrants can acquire citizenship after two years of residence. Although not required by law, husbands' consent is usually asked by the immigration authorities when they apply for citizenship (Yi 2021). Although marriage migrants can extend their visas even after divorce if they can successfully prove their innocence and the inevitability of divorce (i.e.

domestic violence), these visas are nonetheless temporary and insecure. According to a study by the National Human Rights Commission of Korea, citizenship-holders were a minority among marriage migrants in 2016. There were 121,332 temporary (F-6) visa holders as opposed to 114,910 marriage migrants-turned citizens as of 2016 (Eunjeong et al. 2017). Before acquiring more stable legal status, the citizen-spouse who guarantees the marriage migration visa of the migrant spouse can withdraw his guarantorship at the local immigration office, making the migrant spouse's visa precarious and subject to cancelation. Her legal status is precarious anyway, because marriage migrants enter South Korea on temporary visas that must be renewed/extended every 1–3 years.

Cross-border marriages and state power

On 3 February 2004, the Constitutional Court of Korea ordered the abolition of the Head of Household System (*hojuje*), an outdated, hierarchal, and highly unjust arrangement of organizing family under the male head of a household. Nevertheless, just six days after the Constitutional Court decision, the Framework Act on Healthy Family (hereafter the Framework Act) was legislated, disappointing many who campaigned for the abolition of the Head of Household System in hopes of the official recognition of more diverse forms of family. The Framework Act labels families dichotomously as 'healthy' and 'unhealthy', with corrective measures to 'fix' the unhealthy. For instance, Article 8 of the Framework Act urges all citizens to recognize the importance of marriage and childbirth, and Article 9 encourages all family members to prevent the dissolution of the family.

The Korea Institute for Healthy Family (KIHF) was founded by the Framework Act under the Ministry of Gender Equality and Family and is responsible for providing support services for cross-border families. The KIHF operates the Multicultural Families Support Center, locally-based organization responsible for supporting families of marriage migrants. The goal is to create a 'healthy and wholesome culture of international marriages' (*geonjeonhan gukjegyeolhon munhwa*) with no thought of the relevance, validity, or benefits of such a model on the highly varied forms of cross-border marriages.

Marriage migration in Asia is unique in its prevalent use of commercial marriage brokerages and heavy state involvement in the creation of regulatory and protection mandates (Friedman and Mahdavi 2015, Piper and Lee 2016). Commercial matchmakers play a crucial role in recruiting potential brides (from 'developing' countries) and grooms (from 'developed' countries) and facilitating an overwhelmingly bureaucratic and technical process to arrange transnational marriages and migration. While the presence of matchmakers appears 'normal', if not 'traditional', in many Asian countries, it has been criticized as a 'commercial activity disguised as a traditional practice' (Lu 2005, 293). Wang (2007) argues that global economic inequality, which motivates commercially-arranged cross-border marriage, disembeds this form of marriage from 'traditional' practices in Taiwan.

Nonetheless, scholars are divided in their assessment of the state as the regulator of cross-border marriages in Asia. Some scholars focus on the government's disciplining mechanisms that compel migrants to perform roles that they would not otherwise do. For instance, Hyunok Lee (2012) holds the state accountable for using marriage migration as a response to a 'crisis' of social reproduction and devising discourse on 'multicultural families' as a disguise for the South Korean state's efforts to recruit reproductive labor. She also presents convincing evidence to prove that the state recruits foreign women for unpaid reproductive labor at the expense of their desire for paid employment.

Others point to the ambiguous role of the state, focusing on its inconsistent, changing, and conflicting mandates in multiple government bodies. For instance, Danièle Bélanger (2016) points to the Vietnamese state's ambivalent stance on seeing marriage migration as the trafficking of women. The 'state-produced ambiguity' (Bélanger 2016, 93) is embedded in the actions of local actors who may have positions of power in the local community. Despite the ban on commercially-arranged marriage migration, local endorsement is backed by the remittances emigrants send home to Vietnam (See also, Bélanger, Tran, and Le 2011, Bélanger et al. 2014).

Ambiguous *and* coercive forces enforce migrant women's commitment to marriage and unpaid reproductive labor at the intersection of multiple jurisdictions. It is grounded in a belief that justifies women's control by men in the name of the family, 'traditions', and the ideals of womanly virtue through which women's interests are neglected in the name of making 'sacrifice for family' (Song 2009). While different state authorities may produce divergent interpretations of such values, they collectively produce the conditions of captivity. As this paper shows, immigration measures strictly enforce an ambiguous idea of a 'normal' and 'authentic' family. South Korea's obsession with the normative models of family and corrective (if not forceful) measures to realize them is worthy of scholarly investigation.

Methods

This study draws from an analysis of case laws, other court documents, laws, policy documents, and policy reports related to international marriages (*gukjegyeolhon*). To investigate the representation of cross-border marriages in criminal trials, I utilized the case law database provided by the Supreme Court of Korea.[6] I searched for information using distinct keywords including a combination of 'international' (*gukje*) or 'foreigner' (*oegukin*) and 'marriage' (*gyeolhon* or *hon-in*) for cases related to cross-border marriages. Additionally, I re-searched for criminal cases and manually selected cases where the case laws mention cross-border marriages between 2000 and 2019. The search resulted in 17 criminal cases grouped in five thematic areas as outlined in Table 1, involving marriage migrants as defendants, victims, and involved parties.

This study focuses on the thematic areas of the kidnapping of a minor and marital rape in addition to the murder (the case of Huynh explained at the beginning of this paper).[7] I selected these thematic areas because of several distinguishing factors. First, the courts demonstrate varied interpretations of marriage migrants' *gachul* and its impact on the case where marriage migrants play opposite roles as a plaintiff (perpetrator, in the kidnapping case) and victim (the marital rape case). Moreover, the cases received society-wide attention and were widely published on media outlets. They also received ample attention from the South Korean legal scholarship because of their significance of being the first trial of kidnapping by a parent, and the first successful conviction of marital rape (see, for example, Oh 2013, Park 2009). As Zelizer (2005) and Reyes (2019) did in their methods, I analyze these cases like a sociologist not a legal scholar, using the case law to reconstruct how the intersection of criminal and immigration laws are enacted in migrants' daily lives.

In addition to case laws, I also drew on laws, policy documents, and policy reports from the MOJ. Data from the MOJ concern marriage immigration policies (F-6 visa) under the Immigration Act, with an emphasis on victim support. In addition, I reviewed official documents relating to the ratification of the Hague Convention on the Civil Aspects of International Child Abduction and the domestic legislation of the Act on the Implementation of the Hague Convention on the Civil Aspects of International Child Abduction.

Interpretation of women's mobility and family in criminal courts

Marital rape

The first criminal conviction of marital rape was against a South Korean man who raped his Filipina wife. The victim lived with the defendant for four months after their marriage on 30 August 2006. The marriage had been arranged by a commercial cross-border marriage brokerage service. The victim ran away from her husband because of his physical and economic violence (the defendant deprived the victim of material means by not giving her any money). She worked in a plastic manufacturing factory in Gimhae, a nearby city. She was captured by the immigration officer for her 'illegal' immigration status and brought to court on 15 July 2008. On 26 July 2008, the husband forced himself on his wife using a gas rifle and a small kitchen knife when she refused sexual intercourse due to menstruation.

This case was significant that it reversed previous case laws.[8] The Court writes,

> This case recognized the wife as the object of a rape crime because it saw that the benefit and protection of the law was not women's 'chastity' [jeongjo], meaning sexual integrity [seong-jeok seongsil], but 'sexual autonomy' [seongjeok jagigyeoljeong-gwon], which are personal rights [ingyeokgwon].[9]

Prior to this case, the husbands were not justiciable for raping their wives in the past, because sexual intercourse was understood to be a duty between a married couple. The title of Criminal Act Section 2 Chapter 32 (to which Article 297 on rape is included) used to be called 'Crimes against Chastity', which made punishing husbands as perpetrators impossible, before its revision on 29 December 1995. Moreover, the Civil Act stipulates that 'husband and wife shall live together and shall support and aid each other' (Article 826 clause 1). Cohabitation and care are the statutory duties of married couples, and case laws elaborate that these include the 'duty to share a sexual life' (seongsenghualeul hamkkye hal uimu).[10]

Although the judges made a precedent-setting ruling that recognized the need for the protection of woman's sexual autonomy, they still utilized a protectionist view of women's role in the family and endorsed a male-centered view of the family. The judges reasoned as follows:

> The victim suffered hardships and loneliness after leaving her motherland and family and arriving in a foreign country because she did not speak the language and had no extended family. *The victim married and migrated only for the trust of the defendant, and the defendant was naturally obliged to love and care warmly.* However, the defendant caused various difficulties for the victim and *made it even inevitable* for her to leave the defendant and their home. The defendant also *neglected her, causing her to work as a factory worker* in a vulnerable situation [*emphasis added*].[11]

By using the language of 'trust', 'love', 'care', and 'warmth', the judges rebuked the defendant for abandoning the idealized image of a husband in a heteronormative patriarchal family and faulted him for creating a circumstance wherein the wife had no choice but to leave the house. In doing so, the judges naturalized the husband's house as the couple's natural residence while describing her factory work and residence in Gimhae as showing she was 'vulnerable' and as a proof of his 'neglect'.

The judges did not comment on the immigration enforcement that not only captured the wife erroneously for her 'illegal status' but also brought her to her abusive husband. The immigration raid is fairly common in many industrial complexes where migrant workers work, as some migrant workers are undocumented (see Choo 2016). However, the wife was *made illegal* by the immigration authorities despite her 'valid' marriage relationship (see De Genova 2002). Marriage migrants in abusive situations can have their identity documents confiscated by their husbands or had fled from their home without the documents. Moreover, her husband could have withdrawn his immigration guarantorship, which would endanger her immigration status (for further discussion on guarantorship, see Yi 2021).

Instead of rebuking the immigration authorities, the court described her capture as a 'reunion' enabled by 'the cooperation of state (*dang-gukui hyeobryeok*)' and the opportunity for the husband to do right by her. The court even made a sweeping assessment that the couple had 'no problems' for five days after the wife's return and had 'consensual sex' before the rape. Such a simplistic generalization is alarming given the history of physical and economic violence, the wife's forced return, and the extreme violence at the time of a legally-recognized rape, where the defendant threatened to kill her with weapons.

Despite his crime, the defendant received a suspended sentence and was not jailed.[12] Among the reasons for suspension, the wife's desertion of home was mentioned, phrased as the fault of the victim.[13] The court commented, 'The victim ran away from home and came back only a while after, and the victim was lazy in her effort to converse and communicate about the circumstances in the meantime', contradicting its earlier statement that her departure was 'inevitable' because of her husband's abuse. The court applied a gendered role when it found the husband at fault for not 'protecting' the wife while apportioning some blame to the wife for her 'lethargy' in not reconciling the differences between her and her husband.

International abduction

On 21 March 2013, the Supreme Court of Korea broadcast a court hearing on live television for the first time in its history. A Vietnamese marriage migrant was charged with kidnapping a minor and trafficking in persons. Prosecutors appealed two previous rulings on the same incident, which found the woman not guilty. The court justified its decision to broadcast its hearing by stressing the need for a wider South Korean society to deliberate on the issue. While the justices ultimately agreed with the previous two courts and found the woman, named 'A', not guilty, the trial was closely debated. Five of 13 justices opposed the decision, and five of eight on the majority side produced a rebuttal to the opposition.

According to the court documents, a Vietnamese woman identified as 'A' came to South Korea in April 2006 after marrying a South Korean man in Vietnam in February of the same year through a commercial marriage brokerage.[14] In August 2007, she gave birth to a child. As A's husband worked full-time, she stayed home to care for the toddler. In August 2008, 'A' went to her friend's house 60–70 km away, but her social gathering went late. 'A' missed the last bus home and had to return the following day. Her husband was enraged and demanded that she leave his house, which 'A' interpreted as a sign that he did not need her any longer. Her lawyers testified that she was unhappy with his derogatory treatment of her and his previous comments that he 'paid for' her. She left him with her child to return to Vietnam three days later and withdrew just over 11 million won (about USD 11,000) from her husband's bank account without his consent. Their son was roughly 13 months old at the time she left with him for Vietnam. In September 2008, two weeks after leaving for Vietnam, she returned to South Korea so that she could work to pay for childcare costs, while the toddler was cared for by her mother in Vietnam.

The televised hearing was especially timely because the Act Concerning Implementation of the Hague Convention on International Child Abduction had come into force just 20 days before. South Korea had accepted the Hague Convention on the Civil Aspects of International Child Abduction four months before its domestic law came to force. A's case was an important trigger in the Ministry's decision to ratify the Hague Convention. The MOJ described the actions of 'A' pejoratively as 'absconding without authorization (*mudan gachul*)', conflating the woman's action as child abduction.

'A''s case is worth investigating for three main reasons. First, she faced a criminal trial under the charges of kidnapping of a minor (*miseongnyeonja yakchui*) and trafficking in persons (*piyakchuija guk-oeisong*), serious offenses with a minimum prison sentence of three years (Criminal Act Articles 287, 288, 289). The Hague Convention on Civil Aspects of International Child Abduction concerns the *civil* aspects of disputed or violated child custody between parents when the child leaves the country of ordinary residence. For this reason, the judges expressed concerns that criminal prosecution was inappropriate, and the actions of the defendant did not amount to the original intention of the legislation of Articles 287, 288, and 289:

> Justice: You are of the opinion that [the crime] is constituted when a child is taken overseas in international marriage such as this. But, if a divorce process is in place between a couple who are both South Korean citizens, are you of the opinion that it amounts to abduction if one parent leaves home with children without the other parent's consent? (KTV 2013, 59:10)

The prosecutor answered by mentioning equality before the law, which worried the Justice as she thought that such an application would render too many South Korean citizens in divorce processes criminally justiciable. The lawyer stressed that the application of criminal laws was excessive and disproportionate. After all, he argued that this was a case of a wife going to her natal home after a marital argument and taking her baby with her. Her natal home just happened to be in Vietnam. In doing so, they sought to justify the defendant's mobility by stressing the legitimacy of her alternative home in Vietnam in times of emergency. She moved 'back' to her natal home, and the woman's mobility between her natal and marital homes is something that many South Koreans can understand. Rather than stressing the woman's autonomy and independence, the lawyers stressed that the migrant dutifully returned to her parents after being 'expelled' from her husband, and she only left her parents to fulfill her duty as a mother.

Second, it is unclear whether the South Korean ex-husband of the defendant ever wanted custody of the son or wished his return. When her ex-husband found the defendant working in South Korea, he reported her to the police, and she was detained on 16 April 2010 for theft for withdrawing money from her husband's bank account without his consent when she had left him. Their divorce was settled on 13 May 2010, while the defendant was still in jail, with custody given to her by mutual agreement (Oh 2013). She was released on bail on 27 May 2010, and their son remained in Vietnam until the end of the trial, almost three years after he left South Korea. The husband made no appeals to the court for his son's return during the trials, and the justices (as well as the judges in the previous trials) agreed that the husband and his family were not in a circumstance to provide the intensive care necessary for the toddler. In addition, the money the defendant withdrew from her ex-husband's bank account was settled as the child support fund. The government's contention that fathers in such cases grieve for their lost children is contradicted by the silence of the husband in this case.

Third, what repeatedly appears in the court hearings is the idea that a nation-state, rather than a father, has lost a South Korean citizen-child, and this requires criminal prosecution. A substantial minority of five opposed the ruling of innocence on the grounds of two contentious issues: whether 'A' used force and whether the best interests of the child were violated. While the child was born to a Vietnamese mother and a South Korean father and his maternal relatives live in Vietnam, his South Korean identity was assumed and never questioned in any of the trials. The opposition statement rules the defendant's conduct as 'an illegal act that brought *our national* to a *foreign* country (*uri gukmineul oegukeuro derigo gan*) not in accordance with the process and method justified by the law' (*emphasis added*)[15]. However, the child can hold multiple citizenships by lineage under South Korea's Nationality Act; in other words, the defendant's child is entitled to South Korean and Vietnamese citizenships.[16] Therefore, the court's assumption of a singular citizenship is technically incorrect. Taking a broader view of substantive citizenship, such an assumption is especially misguided given the cultural plurality of a transnational household. During the hearing, one justice asked the defendant's expert witness, a university professor in criminal law, the following question:

> Justice: Given that the baby was born a South Korean citizen, would it not be better for his/her welfare to be raised in an environment where *our language* [*woorimal*] is spoken as a mother tongue? I am of the opinion that an environment where our language cannot be used at all is detrimental to the child's well-being [*emphasis mine*] (KTV 2013, 64:05).

Having noticed the intention of the question, the expert witness replied:

> Expert witness: Being born and raised in South Korea, I do not think that my well-being is worse compared with being born and raised in the United States. We must separate the issue of the child's well-being from whether the child grows up in South Korea or Vietnam. Given the inevitable dissolution of the marriage, either mother or father had to be chosen as a custodial parent anyway. For a 13-month old baby, it was clear that the child was in irreplaceable need of maternal care (KTV 2013, 64:27).

Nonetheless, the opposing opinion suggests that 'the child is to grow up suffering from a mental and psychological shock in a *foreign* country where the language, customs, culture, and living environment are drastically different from those of [his/her] own' (*emphasis added*).[17]

As reiterated by other justices, however, there are no objective grounds that the 'mental and psychological shock' to which the child is subjected in a 'foreign country' would have been prevented had he been raised by the father in South Korea and prevented from the cultural influence of and continued mental and psychological ties with his Vietnamese mother. Not only does such a statement reflect an essentialist understanding of a South Korean identity inherent in the baby of a transnational couple, but it also connotes the superiority of such identity, that the child *should* have a South Korean identity because it is better for his well-being.

In this particular case, the woman's departure from her marital home was criminalized by her decision to take her 13-month-old son with her, under the assumption that her son's citizenship was singularly South Korean and that it was against his interests to be raised in a 'foreign' country. Notwithstanding, the majority opinion, which found the defendant not guilty, interpreted her action as a continuation of care and protection of her son, a job that she had been responsible for since his birth; she did not move her son through the illegal use of force. While the court did not agree with the previous court that her son's best interests were not definitively violated, it found that it did not amount to the level of criminal prosecution appropriate for the kidnapping of a minor or trafficking in persons. The defendant's lawyer had argued that *if* she had left home *without her baby*, fully acknowledging that she was the primary caregiver and that her husband had limited capacity to provide care, then she would have risked the charges of child neglect. Here, the court recognized her decision and action justified for a mother. The defendant's decision to place her son in the care of her parents and her decision to return to South Korea to work to pay for his childcare costs were reasonable, given her specific circumstances.

Penalizing women's mobility in immigration

Controlling 'abnormal' marriage through immigration enforcement

The MOJ, in which the Korea Immigration Service (KIS) is housed, has put substantial effort into identifying 'inauthentic' marriages and enforcing immigration compliance on marriage migrants. Women's geographic location functions as significant evidence of the authenticity of marriage (Yi 2021). The KIS investigates whether a couple maintains a shared residence through documents and site visits and interprets it unfavorably when marriage migrants have a history of leaving their husbands, even if it is due to domestic violence.

In September 2013, four years after the conviction of marital rape in the case mentioned above, the media reported that the Busan Office of Immigration canceled the Filipina migrant's visa because she did not have a 'normal marriage'. The media also reported her tragic story after her husband's conviction. Contrary to the court's opinion that the husband had repented his crime (which the court cited as a reason for issuing a suspended sentence), he was outraged by the outcome of the trial, allegedly calling media outlets to plead his innocence (Law Issue 2013). Five days after the verdict, he committed suicide. Although the woman is said to have extended her visa a couple of times after his death, the immigration office conducted a site investigation when she applied to extend her visa in 2013. At that point, the immigration office concluded that she 'did not have a normal marriage because she absconded from home frequently'. The media reported that the site investigation consisted of immigration officials talking to the family of her late husband (Jiyeon 2013). The migrant organization that assisted her visa application said that they had an audio recording of the immigration official commenting that the woman was in fact a 'perpetrator' and should have gotten a divorce rather than reporting her husband for rape, as this led to her husband's death (Mingyu 2013). Ultimately, the case was resolved because the controversy generated after the publication of the media reports led the immigration office to reassess her case, resulting in her visa renewal.

The KIS takes seriously its responsibility to investigate and detect sham marriage. Nonetheless, cross-border marriages are measured against an ambiguous idea of 'normal' marriage, notwithstanding the unique conditions that challenge the conventional ideas of marriage in South Korean society. The commercial nature of the marriage, the involvement of brokers who specialize in cross-border bureaucracy and transactions, the severe economic inequality between men and women, and the unilateral nature of the payment from the groom to the broker and the bride are just some of the factors that complicate the economic exchange that happens within the institution of marriage (see Wang 2007). To say the least, this ignores the unique and uncommon demographic factors identified by the government survey on families of cross-border marriages. Marriage migrants are more likely to have their marriages commercially arranged, to reside in rural areas, to have a lower median income, to have a partner with a disability, and to have a wider age gap between partners than average South Korean couples (Yunjeong et al. 2019). These demographic characteristics mean that women are pressured to move to urban areas to seek employment to support their marital and natal families. The age and disability factors may lead to early widowhood. Given this demographic backdrop, imposing rigid rules on maintaining a 'normal' marriage is all the more unreasonable.

Given the inapplicability of 'conventional' marriage standards, the KIS turns to one familiar feature of 'traditional' marriage retained in cross-border marriages: gender power imbalance and control over women. An extreme power imbalance is a starting point for many commercially-arranged cross-border couples because of the economic inequality and citizenship difference. Given such a backdrop, a negative evaluation of women's departure from marriage by the authorities has far-reaching consequences. Court and immigration authorities de facto penalize women's 'uncontrolled' mobility by blaming them for acting against their marriage even if the marriage is strained with abuse.

International abduction and appearance of criminality

The MOJ has put substantial effort into identifying and returning the children of international marriages to their homeland of South Korea. The MOJ says that from January to May 2010, there were 63 cases where Vietnamese women left South Korea with their children and returned to South Korea alone. In most of these cases, the Ministry speculates that the departure of the children and mothers occurred after marital problems with husbands or in-laws, and mothers return to work after leaving the children with their families in Vietnam.[18] MOJ has continuously campaigned for 'our children lost overseas' (*haeoero ppaeatgin nae ai*), garnering widespread support from the government, the judiciary, and organizations of divorced husbands of international marriages.

While the Vietnamese woman, 'A', was waiting for her final trial, the MOJ prepared ratification of the Hague Convention on International Abduction of Children. Return of children is only possible between two signatory countries of the Hague Convention. However, from the beginning, the MOJ made it explicit that the ratification of the convention was intended to resolve the cases of international abduction by marriage migrants while recognizing that the migrants came from non-signatory countries. In other words, the Hague Convention, as it stands now, is legally irrelevant to solving what the MOJ sees as the problem of international abduction. Despite this reality, the MOJ continues to use countries such as China, Vietnam, and Cambodia, the main origin countries of marriage migrants, to showcase their ratification of the Hague Convention.[19] Such discourse produces a dangerous generalization of cases where women leave their husbands with their children. This is especially problematic given the high incidence of domestic violence in cross-border marriages (Eunjeong et al. 2017) and the ambiguous effect of the Hague Convention on women who flee their abusive partners with their children (Yamaguchi and Lindhorst 2016).

Furthermore, the MOJ's portrayal is far away from the criminal case that initiated the discussion about international child abduction. 'A' did not, in a technical sense, 'run away' from her husband but left him when he told her so during an argument. Moreover, the husband did not desire his son's custody, agreeing to the wife's custody while she was in jail. Nonetheless, highly moralizing discourse was built to couple runaway wives with child kidnapping and to prioritize the grief of husbands and paternal grandparents over that of wives and maternal families. The discourse was used to justify the extraordinary intervention by the prosecutor's office that sought criminal intervention as a means of settling a transnational family dispute. The government effort is buttressed by the symbolism of upholding 'international standards' of the Hague Convention without considering its weaknesses and the limits in applicability.

Conclusion

This study has examined the treatment of migrant women's mobility outside their 'homes' against the will of their citizen-husbands or the destination state. Notable attempts have been made by the government agencies to support marriage migrants settle in South Korea and protect them from domestic violence in the last decade. However, this paper shows that the protection and support have been conditional upon a particular understanding of women's roles in marriage and the family. That marriage and home space function as conditions for legal citizenship for some migrants and legal penalization for the others may represent what Bosniak (2009) called 'the interplay of citizenships at stake' (128), demonstrating exclusive citizenship and the multiple and simultaneous manifestation of inclusion in and exclusion from membership.

By exploring the marriage migrants' freedom of mobility as a contested site, I challenged the perceived dichotomy between the tropes of personal autonomy and commitment to marriage, 'authentic' marriage and runaway wives, the duty of sexual care and 'abnormal' family, and being a good mother and a child kidnapper. Particularly, this study examined the case studies of murder, marital rape, and international child abduction from cross-border marriages, analyzing the judges' interpretation of *gachul*, its impact on the family/marriage, and the culpability of women who 'absconded from homes'. I found that the judges normatively rebuked the women's action of deserting their husbands even if the husband has been abusive.

My argument that sees confinability in home space is supported by the complex process of penalization where the spheres of family, immigration and criminal enforcement and process merge. It is in this space that the husband abused his Filipina wife and restricted her personal freedom. The judge ruled the husband guilty of rape but nonetheless faulted the wife for committing *gachul*. The women in this paper were penalized for their mobility at the intersection of criminal and immigration laws. The immigration authorities apprehended the Filipina woman for doing nothing other than leaving her 'home', forcing her to return to her abusive husband, and even canceled her visa even after his conviction. In the kidnapping case, the MOJ indicted the Vietnamese woman by mobilizing the discourse of immoral wife who committed *gachul* and stole a child. The defense team, however, successfully refuted the discourse by presenting her mobility as morally justified, arguing that her husband treated her badly and compelled her to move, she went back to her maiden home, and she acted responsibly for her child. What remains to be seen is the immigration consequences of her case, as she carries on with her precarious legal status that may not be renewed at any year (as it happened with the Filipina woman).

This intersection of criminal and immigration laws is contested, contradictory, and ambiguous. However, it is precisely this chaos that enables the transformation of a trite space such as one's home turns into a disciplining space of confinability. The cases that I present in this paper present useful addition to the literature that critically examines the increasing merger of criminal and immigration enforcement and the use of criminal penalty as a way of controlling immigration. Not only are criminal and immigration offenses conflated, the gendered notion of women's roles in the family also further complicates the construction of women's culpability because marriage migrants are penalized for deviance of one's role as a wife and a wife upon departing (or attempting to depart) from home. Thus, the merger of immigration and criminal enforcements yields a result that could endanger an extreme form of vulnerability.

End notes

1. These are Jang's expressions, as told by the Court. Daejeon High Court, 2007*no*425 (Jan 23, 2008).
2. Daejeon High Court, 2007*no*425 (January 23, 2008). All translations of case laws are mine.
3. See Lee (2008) for discussion about marriage migration policies in South Korea.
4. 'Demographic crisis' such as low birth rate and gender imbalance in rural areas are the reasons the government welcomed marriage migrants (Lee 2012).
5. For stylistic and technical purposes (after all, '*gachul*' is a legal term), I omit the use of quotation marks in the rest of this paper and use more charged terms (such as 'runaway' or 'deserting one's home') together with more neutral expressions (such as 'leaving her husband').

6. The database is available on this website: https://glaw.scourt.go.kr/wsjo/intesrch/sjo022.do (last visited on January 15, 2021)
7. Among the remining, 'illegal marriage brokerage' and 'fabrication of public documents and obstruction of justice' are criminal charges applied to irregular migration practices such as identity document fabrication, marriage of convenience and unlawful actions during commercial cross-border matchmaking. While they may be of interest to those investigating criminalization of immigration violation, they are beyond the scope of this paper.
8. For example, Daegu High Court, 70*no*138 (June 24, 1970) and Supreme Court 70*do*29 (March 10, 1970)
9. *Pangyeolyoji* [Case Summary], Busan District Court, 2008*gohab*808, January 16, 2009 https://glaw.scourt.go.kr/wsjo/panre/sjo100.do?contId=1980678&q=2008%EA%B3%A0% ED%95%A9808&nq=&w=panre&section=panre_tot&subw=&subsection=&subId=1&csq= &groups=6,7,5,9&category=&outmax=1&msort=&onlycount=&sp=&d1=&d2=&d3=&d4= &d5=&pg=1&p1=&p2=&p3=&p4=&p5=&p6=&p7=&p8=&p9=&p10=&p11=&p12= &sysCd=WSJO&tabGbnCd=&saNo=&joNo=&lawNm=&hanjaYn=N&userSrchHistNo= &poption=&srch=&range=&daewbyn=N&smpryn=N&idgJyul=01&newsimyn=Y&tabId= &save=Y&bubNm=#Body (accessed on July 28, 2020)
10. Supreme Court 2012*do*14788,2012*jeondo*252 (16 May 2013)
11. Busan District Court, 2008*gohab*808 (January 16, 2009)
12. The defendant was sentenced to two years and six months of imprisonment, suspended for three years.
13. Aside from the wife's *gachul*, other grounds for the suspension was the defendant's repentance, the lack of criminal history, and the wife's petition for clemancy.
14. Details about the case come from Supreme Court, 2010*do*14328 (June 20, 2013) and the transcription of the televised hearing (KTV 2013).
15. 2010*do*14328
16. The revised Nationality Act (revised June 14, 1998) allows a child to inherit nationality of both the mother and the father and those born with dual citizenship can legally hold dual citizenship until the age of 22 (Article 12). While dual citizenship holders previously had to choose one citizenship only, under the revised law, those born with multiple citizenships do not have to renounce other citizenships if they make an oath not to practice the foreign citizenship while in South Korea (Article 12 revised on May 4, 2010).
17. 2010*do*14328
18. This was reported in JoongAng Ilbo, '"21st Century Lai Dai Han" abandoned in Vietnam' (pet'ŭname pangch'itoenŭn '21seki laittaihan') 21 October 2010 (http://article.joins.com/news/article/article.asp?total_id=4551254&ctg= Last accessed on 30 March, 2015) The article quotes materials by the Ministry of Justice submitted to a Member of the National Assembly.
19. See, for example, the MOJ blog (in Korean, http://blog.daum.net/mojjustice/8705314, last accessed on July 31, 2020)

Acknowledgement

This research was supported by Kyungpook National University Research Fund, 2019.

Disclosure statement

No potential conflict of interest was reported by the author(s).

ORCID

Sohoon Yi (iD) http://orcid.org/0000-0003-0452-9246

References

Bélanger, D., G.L. Tran, and B.D. Le. 2011. Marriage migrants as emigrants: Remittances of marriage migrant women from Vietnam to their natal families. *Asian Population Studies*7(2): 89–105.

Bélanger, D. 2016. "Beyond the Brokers: Local Marriage Migration Industries of Rural Vietnam." *Positions* 24 (1): 71–96. doi:10.1215/10679847-3320053.

Bélanger, D., Giang Linh Tran, Bach Duong Le, and Thu Hong Khuat. 2014. „From Farmers' Daughters to Foreign Wives: Marriage, Migration and Gender in the Sending Communities of Vietnam.„ In *Asian Women and Intimate Work, edited by E. Ochiai and K. Aoyama*, 191–216. Leiden and Boston: Brill.

Block, L. 2021. "'I'm Not Entitled to Be Married in Germany? Am I German or Am I Not?' Narratives and Discursive Strategies of Citizen Sponsors in the German Spousal Migration Context." *Identities* 28 (1): 56–73. doi:10.1080/1070289X.2020.1723327.

Bonjour, S., and B. De Hart. 2013. ""A Proper Wife, a Proper Marriage: Constructions of 'Us' and 'Them' in Dutch Family Migration Policy". *European Journal of Women's Studies* 20 (1): 61–76. doi:10.1177/1350506812456459.

2021. "Intimate Citizenship: Introduction to the Special Issue on Citizenship, Membership and Belonging in Mixed-status Families." *Identities*. 28 (1):1–17. 10.1080/1070289X.2020.1737404.

Bosniak, L. 2009. "Citizenship, Noncitizenship, and the Transnationalization of Domestic Work." In *Migrations and Mobilities: Citizenship, Borders, and Gender, edited by S. Benhabib and J. Resnik*, 127–156. New York and London: New York University Press.

Choo, H. Y. 2016. *Decentering Citizenship: Gender, Labor and Migrant Rights in South Korea*. Stanford, CA: Stanford University Press.

Coutin, S. B. 2005. "Contesting Criminality: Illegal Immigration and the Spatialization of Legality." *Theoretical Criminology* 9 (1): 5–33. doi:10.1177/1362480605046658.

De Genova, N. P. 2002. "Migrant 'Illegality' and Deportability in Everyday Life." *Annual Review of Anthropology* 31 (1): 419–447. doi:10.1146/annurev.anthro.31.040402.085432.

Eggebø, H. 2013. "A Real Marriage? Applying for Marriage Migration to Norway." *Journal of Ethnic and Migration Studies* 39 (5): 773–789. doi:10.1080/1369183X.2013.756678.

Erel, U. 2011. "Reframing Migrant Mothers as Citizens." *Citizenship Studies* 15 (6–7): 695–709. doi:10.1080/13621025.2011.600076.

Eunjeong, G., J. Myeongseon, J. S. Jeong Sundul, and H. Yeongsuk. 2017. *Gyeolhonijuminui Anjeongjeok Cheryubojangeul Wihan Siltaejosa*. National Human Rights Commission of Korea.

Friedman, S. L., and P. Mahdavi. 2015. "Introduction: Migrant Encounters." In *Migrant Encounters: Intimate Labour, the State, and Mobility across Asia,*1-22. edited by Sara L. Friedman and Pardis Mahdavi. Philadelphia: University of Pennsylvania Press.

Griffiths, M. 2021. "'My Passport Is Just My Way Out of Here'. Mixed Immigration Status Families, Immigration Enforcement and the Citizenship Implications." *Identities* 28 (1): 18–36. doi:10.1080/1070289X.2019.1625568.

"Hangukin Nkmpyeone Sklhaedanghan Pilripin Ijuyeoseong ... 'Tto Dareun Jukeum Makaya'."
2018. OhMyNews. 19 December 2018. http://www.ohmynews.com/NWS_Web/Mobile/at_pg.
aspx?CNTN_CD=A0002497179#cb

Hsia, H.-C. 2007. "Imaged and Imagined Threat to the Nation: The Media Construction of the
'Foreign Brides' Phenomenon' as Social Problems in Taiwan." *Inter-Asia Cultural Studies* 8 (1):
55–85. doi:10.1080/14649370601119006.

Hwang, J-M. 2015. "Gyeorhonijuyeoseongui gajeongpokryeoke pihae-e daehan jaegochal:
'chuiyakseong'peureimeseo in-gananbo(human security) gwanjeomeuro [Reconsidering
Domestic Violence Against Marriage-Migrant Women in Korea: from Vulnerability to
Human Security]." *Journal of Korean Women's Studies 31(4): 1-39.*

Issue, L. 2013. "Bubuganggan Cheot Pihae Ijuyeoseong Bijayeonjang Bulheohaetda Jaeyeonhang
Wae?" Law Issue. 5 September 2013. http://lawissue.co.kr/print.php?ud=
201309051019120015444_12

Ito, R. 2005. „Crafting Migrant Women's Citizenship in Japan: Taking "Family" as a Vantage
Point.„ *International Journal of Japanese Sociology 14*: 52–66.

Jiyeon, S. 2013. "'Bubuganggan' Pihae Gyeolhonijuyeoseong Bija Jaeyeonhang Bulheo Pamun".
Busan Ilbo. 5 September 2013. http://www.busan.com/view/busan/view.php?code=
20130905000163

Kim, H. M., M-J. Kim and J. S. Kim. 2008. „'Anjeonhan gyeorhon iju'?: Mong-gol yeoseongderui
hangukeuroui iju gwajeong-gwa gyeongheom. [Safe Marriage Migration'?: Migration Process
and Experiences of Mongolian Marriage Migrants in South Korea].„ *Journal of Korean Women's
Studies. 24* (1): 121–154.

Kim, M. 2013. „Citizenship Projects for Marriage Migrants in South Korea: Intersecting
Motherhood with Ethnicity and Class.„ *Social Politics 20*(4): 455–481.

Kim, N. H.-J. 2012. "Multiculturalism and the Politics of Belonging: The Puzzle of
Multiculturalism in South Korea." *Citizenship Studies* 16 (1): 103–117. doi:10.1080/
13621025.2012.651406.

Kim, N. H-J. 2016. „The Janus-Faced Court of Naturalisation: Marriage and Kinship in
Naturalisation Litigation in South Korea.„ *Journal of Ethnic and Migration Studies 42*(9):
1536–57.

KTV. 2013. Daebeopwon 2010do14328 Gukoeisongyakchuisageon Gong-Gaejaepan Jung-
Gyebangsong [Broadcast Open Hearing of Supreme Court 2010do14328]. http://www.ktv.go.
kr/content/view?content_id=458590

Kubal, A. 2014. "Struggles against Subjection: Implications of Criminalization of Migration for
Migrants' Everyday Lives in Europe." *Crime, Law, and Social Change* 62 (2): 91–111.
doi:10.1007/s10611-014-9527-5.

Lan, P.-C. 2008. "Migrant Women's Bodies as Boundary Makers: Reproductive Crisis and Sexual
Control in the Ethnic Frontiers of Taiwan." *Signs* 33 (4): 833–861. doi:10.1086/528876.

Lee, H. 2012. "Political Economy of Cross-Border Marriage: Economic Development and Social
Reproduction in Korea." *Feminist Economics* 18 (2): 177–200. doi:10.1080/
13545701.2012.688139.

Longman, C., K. De Graeve, and T. Brouckaert. 2013. "Mothering as a Citizenship Practice: An
Intersectional Analysis of 'Carework' and 'Culturework' in Non-normative Mother-child
Identities." *Citizenship Studies* 17 (3–4): 385–399. doi:10.1080/13621025.2013.791540.

Lu, M. C. W. 2005. „Commercially Arranged Marriage Migration: Case Studies of Cross-Border
Marriages in Taiwan.„ *Indian Journal of Gender Studies12*(2-3): 275–303

Menjívar, C. 2014. "Immigration Law beyond Borders: Externalizing and Internalizing Border
Controls in an Era of Securitization." *Annual Review of Law and Social Science* 10 (1): 353–369.
doi:10.1146/annurev-lawsocsci-110413-030842.

Mingyu, J. 2013. "Bubuganggan Pihaeyeoseongi Oegukinimyeon Gahaeja?" OhMyNews. 3
September 2013. http://www.ohmynews.com/NWS_Web/View/at_pg.aspx?CNTN_CD=
A0001902850

News, V. N. 2007. "Bride Deaths Raise Awareness about Mixed Marriages." Viet Nam News. 31 August 2007. https://vietnamnews.vn/society/168248/bride-deaths-raise-awareness-about-mixed-marriages.html#cSgOBjM3xCU0bhf4.97

Oh, Y.-K. 2013. „Damunhwa gajeongeseo miseongnyeonja yakchui mit gukoeisongjoeui munje [The Problem of the Child Kidnapping and Deportation in the Multi-Culture Family].„ *Hangukhyeongsabeobhakhoe.* 25(3): 365–90.

Palriwala, R. and P. Uberoi. 2008. Marriage Migration and Gender. New Delhi: Sage

Park, G. 2009. „Bubugang-ganjoiui panremit Ipbobane daehan gochal [A Study on Cases and Legislation of Marital Rape].„ *Han Yang Law Review* 27: 253–72.

Piper, N., and S. Lee. 2016. „Marriage Migration, Migrant Precarity, and Social Reproduction in Asia: an Overview.„ *Critical Asian Studies* 48(4): 473–493.

Reiter, K., and S. B. Coutin. 2017. "Crossing Borders and Criminalizing Identity: The Disintegrated Subjects of Administrative Sanctions." *Law & Society Review* 51 (3): 567–601. doi:10.1111/lasr.12281.

Reyes, V. 2019. *Global Borderlands: Fantasy, Violence, and Empire in Subic Bay, Philippines.* Stanford: Stanford University Press.

Sarabia, H. 2018. "'Felons, Not Families': Criminalized Illegality, Stigma, and Membership of Deported 'Criminal Aliens'." *Migration Letters* 15 (2): 284–300. doi:10.33182/ml.v15i2.374.

Song, J. 2009. *South Koreans in the Debt Crisis: The Creation of a Neoliberal Welfare Society.* Durham, NC: Duke University Press.

Stumpf, J. 2006. „The Crimmigration Crisis: Immigrants, Crime, and Sovereign Power.„ *American University Law Review* 56(2): 3.

Wang, H.-Z. 2007. "Hidden Spaces of Resistance of the Subordinated: Case Studies from Vietnamese Female Migrant Partners in Taiwan." *International Migration Review* 41 (3): 706–727. doi:10.1111/j.1747-7379.2007.00091.x.

Wray, H. 2006. "An Ideal Husband? Marriages of Convenience, Moral Gate-keeping and Immigration to the UK." *European Journal of Migration and Law* 8 (3–4): 303–320. doi:10.1163/157181606778882582.

Yamaguchi, S., and T. Lindhorst. 2016. "Domestic Violence and the Implementation of the Hague Convention on the Civil Aspects of International Child Abduction: Japan and U.S. Policy." *Journal of International Women's Studies* 17 (4): 16–30.

Yi, S. 2021. "Suspicious Mothering: Maternal Labor and Marriage Migration in South Korea." *Social Politics* 28 (1): 71–93. doi:10.1093/sp/jxz018.

Yun, S. 2018. „Hangukin nampyeone sarhaedanghan pilipin yijuyeoseong. . .„ddo dareun jugeum makaya„ [Filipina Migrant Woman Murdered by Korean Husband. . .„Another Death Should Be Prevented„].„ *OhMyNews.* 19 December 2018.

Yunjeong, C., G. Iseon, D. J. Seon Boyeong, Y. G. Jeong Haesuk, and H. J. I. Euna. 2019. *2018nyeon Jeongukdamunhwagajoksiltaejosa Yeonau.* Korea Women's Development Institute.

Zelizer, V. 2005. *The Purchase of Intimacy.* Princeton and Oxford: Princeton University Press.

Discretionary maternal citizenship: state hegemony and resistance of single marriage migrant mothers from mainland China to Hong Kong

Tuen Yi Chiu (iD)

ABSTRACT

This article contributes to the scholarship on marriage migration and citizenship by drawing attention to an under-studied group of single marriage migrant mothers who are widowed, divorced, or separated from their citizen-husbands. It examines the ways in which nation-states regulate the dissolution of cross-border marriages and allocation of citizenship rights to single marriage migrant mothers. Drawing on the experiences of 25 mainland Chinese single marriage migrant mothers, this article unravels the dynamic process of citizenship negotiation between top-down state hegemony and single marriage migrant mothers' bottom-up resistance to the exclusionary immigration system in Hong Kong by claiming maternal citizenship through state discretion. As the article illuminates how discretion has been used as a strategic mechanism by both the state and single marriage migrant mothers to negotiate the boundaries and substance of citizenship, it offers insights into how the family becomes a critical site where citizenship is experienced, negotiated, and contested.

Introduction

The proliferation of cross-border marriages around the globe has attracted much public and scholarly attention. Despite the burgeoning scholarship on cross-border marriages, most extant studies have examined spousal power dynamics and the vulnerability of female marriage migrants *within* the marriage. Much less attention has been paid to situations where cross-border marriages dissolve (see also Fresnoza-Flot 2018; Quah 2020). As a result, the experiences of marriage migrants with non-normative marital statuses, namely those who are widowed, divorced, or separated from their citizen-husbands, remain under-studied. In particular, the ways in which nation-states regulate the dissolution of cross-border marriages and allocation of citizenship rights to marriage migrants who are no longer in a marital relationship with a local citizen have not been sufficiently understood. To address these issues, this article focuses on non-citizen female marriage migrant mothers with non-normative marital status (single marriage migrant mothers hereafter) to examine their post-marital experiences of making citizenship claims.

While a substantial amount of research has suggested that female marriage migrants generally experience legal precarity and gender inequalities due to their coerced dependence on their husbands to petition for their legal right to remain in the host country (e.g. Chiu 2017; Friedman 2015; Yeoh, Chee, and Vu 2013; Coté, Kérisit, and Coté 2001), non-citizen single marriage migrants are further disadvantaged as their rights to reside in or immigrate into the host country are forfeited when their marriage with a citizen is dissolved. Previous studies have suggested that when the migrant mother lacks residency and social citizenship rights, the precariousness she experiences may spill over to her children, citizens and non-citizens alike (Chiu 2020; Enriquez 2015; Fix and Zimmermann 2001). Questions of how single marriage migrant mothers respond to the deprivation of their right to remain and how they make citizenship claims to care for their citizen-children in the host society, therefore, carry important research and social significance. Against this background, this article examines how single marriage migrant mothers attempt to claim *maternal citizenship* from the host state based on their biological and caregiving role as mothers of their citizen-children (Kim 2013). As their citizenship claim shifts from marital citizenship to maternal citizenship, their maternal role in the family is substituted for their marital role in becoming the vital resource for citizenship negotiation and contestation. The existence and experiences of cross-border families led by non-citizen single marriage migrants (i.e. non-normative cross-border families) have transformative potential to challenge the substance, meanings, and boundaries of the state framework of citizenship.

Building on the concept of citizenship as 'a terrain of struggle' (Stasiulis and Bakan 1997), this article examines the dynamics between top-down state hegemony and bottom-up resistance of single marriage migrant mothers in the context of non-normative cross-border families between mainland China and Hong Kong. The mainland China-Hong Kong case is particularly relevant and theoretically interesting because some single marriage migrant mothers – despite being institutionally marginalized and excluded – have managed to use mothering as a critical resource to strive for maternal citizenship through appealing to the state to exercise its *discretion* over their cases. This pathway to citizenship through discretion is largely unexplored in the scholarship on marriage migration and citizenship. This article contributes to the scholarship by revealing how discretion has been used as a strategic mechanism by both the state and single marriage migrant mothers to negotiate the boundaries and substance of citizenship, and how the family, as a nurturing ground for biological and social reproduction, mediates such negotiation.

In the following, I first draw upon the literature on cross-border marriage to elucidate why and how many marriage migrant-receiving states in East Asia (including Hong Kong) operate a hegemonic and exclusionary immigration system, which I conceptualize as one based on so-called 'marrytocracy'. I then introduce the research site as well as the methods and data used in this research. The analysis section examines the politics of state de-legitimization and single marriage migrants' strategies in re-legitimizing themselves for Hong Kong residency. As I illustrate how these mothers appeal for maternal citizenship through the discretion of the state, i.e. *discretionary maternal citizenship*, I elucidate how a hidden yet hierarchical framework of legitimacy exists to serve as an institutional leeway for the state to manage 'irregular' marriage migration from mainland China, which simultaneously provides an *uncertain* pathway for non-citizen marriage migrant mothers to claim residency and citizenship. The last section discusses the implications of discretionary maternal citizenship at the individual, family, and state levels.

'Marrytocracy-based' immigration system and its implications on single marriage migrants

In the public discourse of many host countries, female marriage migrants are depicted as materialistic 'gold diggers' who take advantage of local men for money, employment opportunities, and citizenship (Chiu 2017; Hsia 2007; Yamaura 2020). The involvement of commercial matchmaking agencies and the prevalent stories of 'runaway brides' has further brought about suspicion from the public and host states (Faier 2008). Given this atmosphere, the nation-states of popular marriage migrant receiving countries have been active in implementing various measures, such as setting up sponsorship schemes and 'authenticity paradigms' (Friedman 2015) to combat bogus cross-border marriages. Marriage migrants are often put on a probationary period (usually two to four years), during which they may lose their right to stay in the country and be deported as an illegal alien if the marriage dissolves before they are granted full rights of residency (Chiu and Choi 2020; Friedman 2015). Marriage migrants are legally dependent on their citizen-husbands as their right to residency is inextricably tied to their marriage (Liversage 2012; Wang and Bélanger 2008). This unequal power relation may put marriage migrants at a heightened risk of spousal violence victimization (Chiu 2017).

As host states recognize marriage migrants *exclusively* by their marital relationship with a citizen, a hegemonic immigration system has been conceptualized by this study, as one based on 'marrytocracy'. The neological term of 'marrytocracy' is conceptually derived from the concept of meritocracy – a social system in which individuals are rewarded or given power based on their abilities and talents. What is distinctive about a 'marrytocracy-based' system is that it legitimizes or gives power to marriage migrants solely based on their *marriage* with a citizen, irrespective of their personal characteristics and other social identities, responsibilities, or needs, such as maternal identity and caregiving duties. Notably, once their marriage is dissolved, as in cases of divorce, widowhood, and separation, marriage migrants are no longer considered as deserving subjects of rights and entitlements. In this regard, marriage migrants' commitment to their legal marriage appears to be a type of 'merit' in the eyes of some host states. Just as individuals must work hard to climb the socioeconomic ladder through the meritocracy system, marriage migrants in the 'marrytocracy-based' immigration system must devote continuous time and effort to fulfil the spousal role to maintain their marriage for a more secure legal status. Those who 'fail' to maintain their marriage will be penalized by losing their right of abode.

While existing studies have documented that married marriage migrants are often treated as second-class or partial citizens (Friedman 2016; Yeoh, Chee, and Vu 2013; Wang and Bélanger 2008) with unequal access to rights and entitlements under the graduated citizenship regime in the host countries (Ong 2006), single marriage migrants are further marginalized as they are *legally non-existent* in the immigration system. Some scholars conceptualize the institutional and legal exclusion of single marriage migrants as a form of administrative violence (Quah 2020) or legal violence that has not only restricted non-citizen marriage migrants' ability to care for their children, but also brought suffering to these mothers when trying to fulfil their caregiving responsibilities (Abrego and Menjívar 2011). These measures also separate families led by single marriage migrants, as their ties with the citizen family, including their biological children, are immediately disposed of upon marital dissolution (Quah 2020). The loss of access to substantive and social rights (e.g. paid work, healthcare, and social welfare), and the possible deportation due to loss of eligibility for citizenship, severely harm single marriage migrants' post-marital lives (Quah 2020; Kim, Park, and Shukhertei 2017). These disadvantages, brought about by the legal precarity of non-citizen mothers, in turn affect the wellbeing of their dependent children, even if the children are indeed citizens themselves (Chiu 2020; Enriquez 2015; Fix and Zimmermann 2001). This form of *intergenerational precarity* makes it even more pressing for single marriage migrant mothers to secure long-term residency and citizenship rights.

In Taiwan, mainland Chinese marriage migrants who are widowed, and have received legal custody of a dependent citizen-child following a divorce, can still maintain their legal residency and pathway to citizenship (Friedman 2016). In South Korea, a divorced marriage migrant is granted a 'marriage migration visa' so that she can continue to see and care for her citizen-child, but legitimate evidence of proximate mothering is needed when making such a claim (Yi 2019). These examples of granting residency/citizenship rights to non-citizen single marriage migrant mothers of a dependent citizen-child allude to a kind of *maternal citizenship*. More than merely emphasizing reproduction and the right to reproduce[1] (as in the case of reproductive citizenship), maternal citizenship here is conceptualized based upon mobilizations around the 'politics of care' (To 2019a; Van Walsum 2016). In family-related migration contexts, scholars have argued that the connection between migrants and society should be understood through the lens of care (Huang 2016) and that care should be conceptualized as a set of relational practices and social relations (Duffy 2011). Thus, to ensure that citizen-children can effectively enjoy their citizenship rights, their primary caregiving parent, which is usually the mother, should be given corresponding rights to carry out their caregiving duties. In the European Union (EU), residency is granted to a non-citizen migrant mother of citizen-children so that the children can effectively enjoy their right to reside as well as be brought up and educated in the region (Van Walsum 2016). This article builds on these insights to examine how mothering and intergenerational care becomes an important resource of legitimacy for single marriage migrants to make citizenship claims. It further examines whether such claims are deemed sufficient by the host state; if yes, how does the state handle such claims? If not, on what grounds does the state reject such claims?

The current study

The dearth of studies on transnational marital dissolution suggests that the scholarship on the dissolution of cross-border marriages is still at an embryonic stage; questions as to whether, why, and how marriage migrants with non-normative marital status could achieve citizenship has not been sufficiently understood. This article contributes to this body of scholarship by unpacking how non-citizen single marriage migrant mothers proactively mobilize their maternal role and family rights to claim citizenship, how nation-states respond to their claims, and what implications these have on the notion of maternal citizenship. It extends the discussion on maternal citizenship by presenting how single marriage migrant mothers make maternal citizenship claims through *state discretion* – a pathway that is largely unexplored in the scholarship on marriage migration and citizenship. Existing migration research on state discretion has focused on street-level discretion made by frontline public workers such as teachers, social workers, and visa officers (Lipsky 2010; Satzewich 2014), as well as the prosecutorial discretionary power that police and immigration officers have to defer law enforcements to arrest, detain, or deport undocumented immigrants (Chand and Schreckhise 2015; Coutin et al. 2017). While these studies shed important light on the arbitrary and tenuous nature of state discretion, they mostly see discretion as a useful device to 'humanise decision-making and to acknowledge that the circumstances of individuals do not always fit into predefined rules and procedures' (Satzewich 2014, 1452). By examining the state politics of delegitimization and single marriage migrant mothers' strategies of claiming maternal citizenship through state discretion, this article extends the literature on marriage migration, citizenship, and discretion. It does so by showing that, rather than merely being a mechanism to provide *flexibility* for bureaucrats and law enforcement officers to respond to special circumstances of individual migrants (to the interest of the individuals), discretion should also be understood as a way for states to maintain the *rigidity* of their immigration system and citizenship laws (to the interest of the state). It underscores how discretion becomes an important mechanism for citizenship contestation and how intergenerational care relation becomes a critical resource for such contestation to occur. To contextualize the experiences of single marriage migrant mothers, the next section provides an overview of the marriage migration system between mainland China and Hong Kong.

Marriage migration between mainland China and Hong Kong

With increasing social and economic integration between mainland China and Hong Kong over the past decades, cross-border marriages between the two places have proliferated as a result. Since 2003, over 30% of the total registered marriages in Hong Kong have involved a Hong Kong spouse and mainland Chinese spouse (Census and Statistics Department 2019). In 2018, the number of such marriages was 32%, (or 15,959 marriages). Among them, most involved Hong Kong men and mainland Chinese women. While official statistics on the dissolution of cross-border marriages are unavailable, one local study suggests that cross-border marriages may account for one third of all divorce cases in Hong Kong, with a greater likelihood of divorce in cross-border marriages (Law et al. 2019).

Hong Kong was once a British colony, and its sovereignty returned to the People's Republic of China in 1997. However, the immigration of Mainland spouses is still governed by the 'One-way Permit' (OWP) scheme established in 1950, which sets a daily limit of 150[2] on the number of Mainland residents who wish to settle in Hong Kong for family reunification. Under the quota system, Mainland spouses must wait for at least four years to obtain the OWP, with which they can settle in Hong Kong as an ordinary resident. Before that, they can apply for a temporary visitor visa called the 'Two-way Permit' (TWP), which enables them to visit Hong Kong for up to 90 days each time. Once the Mainland spouse has continuously resided in Hong Kong for seven years, he/she is eligible for obtaining permanent residency (analogous to citizenship in other countries), which entitles them to right of abode, rights to vote and to stand for election, and social benefits such as public housing.

As with other East Asian countries, the marriage migration system between mainland China and Hong Kong is operated on a 'marrytocracy' basis. First, while the OWP scheme provides marriage migrants with the most direct route to long-term residency, it only recognizes marriage migrants based on their marriage with a citizen spouse. As such, marriage migrants' legal marriage becomes the *necessary* condition for obtaining residency. Yet, legal marriage *per se* may not be sufficient for claiming residency; marriage migrants' 'marrytocracy' is also predicated on their *continuous and ongoing* marital relationship with a citizen. Commitment to their marriage therefore constitutes another critical criterion of the 'marrytocracy-based' immigration system. In 1997, a points-based system was introduced in mainland China, stipulating that Mainland spouses must accumulate 'eligibility points' based the number of days they have queued for OWP (Legislative Council Secretariat 2014). In this system, Mainland authorities announce the points required for OWP issuance and applicants can check their application status online. Notably, this system exemplifies the reliability and predictability of the 'marrytocracy-based' immigration system between mainland China and Hong Kong. As long as marriage migrants remain in legal marriage, sooner or later they will be granted long-term residency and the rights enjoyed by ordinary residents. However, marriage migrants who are divorced, widowed, or separated from their Hong Kong husband are excluded from this 'marrytocracy-based' immigration system.

As of 2011, an estimated 5,000–10,000 cross-border single mothers have been unwillingly staying on TWP due to changes in their marital status, and about 70% of TWP holders are single mothers (Huang 2016). Despite this substantial number, there is no institutionalized pathway for Mainland single marriage migrant mothers to obtain Hong Kong residency. Some local residents and public workers have urged single marriage migrant mothers to bring their children back to mainland China for care. However, children who are Hong Kong permanent residents (PRs) are considered foreigners in mainland China, and therefore face difficulties enrolling in public schools there. Although these children may turn to private or international schools, many single marriage migrant mothers cannot afford the exorbitant tuition fees. Therefore, they can only raise their children in Hong Kong, where children can enjoy 12 years of free education. The only opportunity for single marriage migrant mothers to obtain Hong Kong residency is to appeal to the Hong Kong state to exercise its *discretion* over their case.

As of mid-2016, the Immigration Department of Hong Kong received around 150 requests for assistance from Mainland single marriage migrant mothers, involving a total of around 180 minor children in Hong Kong. However, only around half (80) of the single marriage migrant mothers have been granted OWPs with Hong Kong residency on a discretionary basis. Among the remaining 70 unsuccessful cases, over half were issued a 'one-year multiple exit endorsement' as an expedient measure for them to look after their children in Hong Kong (The Government of HKSAR 2016). This low success rate means that single marriage migrant mothers must endure long periods of legal precarity. Moreover, they can only wait until they reach the age of 60 and their children reach the age of 18 in order to apply for OWP. The mainland China-Hong Kong case therefore provides fertile ground for investigating the case of *discretionary maternal citizenship*.

Data and methods

To examine the experience of single marriage migrants, 25 Mainland single marriage migrant mothers (aged 29–54) were interviewed between 2012 and 2017. Among them, 10 obtained Hong Kong ordinary residency through the OWP scheme before they became widowed, divorced, or separated from their Hong Kong husbands. Among the remaining interviewees, four widowed mothers obtained OWP with the aid of NGOs through state discretion within one to four years, and they were Hong Kong ordinary residents at the time of the interview. The remaining 11 were still fighting for OWP (three were widowed, six divorced/separated, and two abandoned by their Hong Kong husbands). Since this article aims to examine the process in which single marriage migrant mothers claim discretionary maternal citizenship, it has focused on the experiences of the 15 respondents who had not obtained OWP at the time of becoming single. Among this group, most were in their 30s (range: 29–51) and started an intimate relationship with their husbands in the mid-2000s (range: 2000–2012). They had been single mothers for an average of seven years (range: 1–11 years). When they became single, all of their children were studying at kindergartens or primary schools, except four interviewees, whose children were at or under the age of three. All the children are Hong Kong PRs.

Since 2009, Mainland marriage migrants waiting for OWP and with children under the age of 18 can apply for the 'one-year multiple exit endorsement for visiting relatives', which allows them to make multiple visits to Hong Kong with maximum 90 days each time within the one-year validity period (Security Bureau 2014). However, those who are widowed, divorced, or separated from their Hong Kong husbands are not eligible for such endorsement as they are no longer in the OWP system. Therefore, most respondents of this study were holding TWPs that required renewals on the Mainland every 90 days. Only five of them managed to receive the endorsement via state discretion.

The respondents were recruited through two NGOs providing services to mainland China-Hong Kong cross-border families using purposive and snowball sampling methods. The only recruitment criterion was being former spouses of Hong Kong PRs. The interviews were based on a semi-structured interview protocol that asked about union formation, immigration experience, everyday family life, and future plans of the respondents. Furthermore, five social workers and staff working in three related NGOs were interviewed to better understand their experiences in helping Mainland migrants to obtain Hong Kong residency. All interviews were transcribed verbatim and coded line-by-line for thematic analysis (Braun and Clarke 2006). Pseudonyms were used to protect the identity of the respondents. To supplement the interview data, participant observations were conducted intermittently in two NGOs. Secondary data including reports, legal documents, and newsletters from the government and the NGOs were collected for data triangulation. The three sets of data were synthesized for a more comprehensive and in-depth understanding of single marriage migrants' experiences of citizenship claims-making.

State politics of de-legitimization

Under the 'marrytocracy-based' immigration system, marriage migrants can only immigrate into Hong Kong as 'wives of citizens' but not 'mothers of citizens'. Even with their Hong Kong resident children to look after, it is not considered a sufficient reason for obtaining residency, signifying that the family has not been considered as part of marriage migration. In other words, marriage migrants only comprise a marriage and not a family from the state's perspective. When explaining why single marriage migrant mothers are denied residency, the Hong Kong state cites the difficulties in verifying the matrimonial relationship between a Mainland single marriage migrant mother and her former Hong Kong husband as a major obstacle and claims that 'allow[ing] Mainland single mothers to apply under the OWP Scheme may [...] give rise to the problem of bogus marriage' (Legislative Council Secretariat 2016, 6). Under this narrative, all Mainland single mothers are imagined as potential lawbreakers and opportunists who take advantage of Hong Kong men and public resources. By highlighting the suspicious intent of Mainland single marriage migrants, the state justifies the exclusionary nature of the 'marrytocracy-based' immigration system in the name of safeguarding Hong Kong's resources. It can thus effectively reinforce the rigid boundaries of citizenship by de-legitimizing single marriage migrant mothers, even though they were once legitimate 'wives of citizens'.

Some legislative councillors have proposed that a channel should be set up for Mainland single mothers to apply for Hong Kong residency so that they can reunite with their children in Hong Kong. Citing cases in which the custody of a Hong Kong resident child is awarded to his Mainland single mother by the court, it is put forth that 'a court order should be treated as a qualifying condition for approving the OWP applications from Mainland single mothers, as it is not reasonable for a mother without the right to abode in Hong Kong to assume the responsibility of taking care of her Hong Kong resident children' (Legislative Council Secretariat 2016, 5). Nevertheless, no major changes to the immigration system have been made, even though the daily quota of 150 applications has not been reached over the years (see Table 1).

Official documents show that the average daily numbers of Mainland residents coming to Hong Kong on OWPs were 129 and 116 in 2017 and 2018, respectively (The Government of HKSAR 2019). The unused quotas signify that the Hong Kong state has deliberately excluded Mainland single mothers from the OWP scheme, despite the capacity to receive them for family reunification.[3]

Single marriage migrant mothers' strategies of re-legitimization

Facing state de-legitimization, the Mainland single marriage migrant mothers we interviewed generally think the immigration system is 'very discriminatory', 'unreasonable' and 'unfair'. Confronted by the prevalent public discourse that Mainland women would run away after obtaining residency, some respondents contended that the seemingly high marital dissolution rate of cross-border marriages might have to do with the state-stipulated separation between the spouses:

> Many cross-border marriages failed because the couple did not understand each other well. They did not have time to get along with each other [before settling in Hong Kong] and were not able to see the drawbacks of each other's personality and habits. Even though they have spent time together on the Mainland, it was more like a honeymoon period, conflicts between the spouses have not emerged. So, when they co-reside in Hong Kong, they have conflicts and call for a divorce. (Yue-ming, a divorced mother of a 11-year-old son.)

Table 1. Number of OWP holders and unused quotas 2009–2018.

	2009	2010	2011	2012	2013	2014	2015	2016	2017	2018
(a) Holders of Certificate of Entitlement	5,025	4,662	3,758	3,750	4,329	4,938	3,655	3,508	2,795	2,407
(b) Spouses separated for 10 years or more and their accompanying children	829	651	619	733	742	791	753	870	690	573
(c) Spouses separated for less than 10 years and their accompanying children	38,592	33,446	31,461	25,746	23,193	23,528	25,142	45,261	36,847	31,513
(d) Joining parents in Hong Kong [1]	3,336	2,942	6,702	23,401	15,832	10,282	7,909	6,800	5,535	6,681
(e) Joining children in Hong Kong [2]	566	646	550	714	713	803	780	898	1,079	1,143
(f) Others [3]	239	277	289	302	222	154	99	50	25	14
Total	48,587	42,624	43,379	54,646	45,031	40,496	38,338	57,387	46,971	42,331
Quotas unused [4]	6,163	12,126	11,371	104	9,719	14,254	16,412	−2,637	7,779	12,419
	(11%)	(22%)	(21%)	(0.2%)	(18%)	(26%)	(30%)	(−4.8%)	(14%)	(23%)

Source: The Government of HKSAR (2019)

Notes:

1. Excluding accompanying children whose parents joined their spouses in Hong Kong in items (b) and (c) of the above table.
2. Including unsupported elderly people coming to Hong Kong to join their children settled in Hong Kong.
3. Exceptional cases such as unsupported elderly people coming to join their relatives, etc.
4. Calculated by using the maximum quotas each year (150*365 days) to deduct the quotas actually used.

Yue-ming's account aptly points out the negative consequences of the OWP scheme. As the granting of residency to Mainland spouses is delayed, cross-border couples have to put up with geographical separation for at least four years. This may bring instability to their marriage. Most of the respondents' husbands are blue-collar workers and some are unemployed, hence they cannot afford their own housing in Hong Kong and are living with other family members. To avoid over-crowdedness and conflicts with the in-laws, Mainland wives often stay in mainland China until their children need to attend school in Hong Kong. Although Mainland wives can visit their husbands in Hong Kong using TWPs, the short validity of the TWP and/or the short period of their visits do not allow them to have sufficient time to get along with their husbands. Some Hong Kong husbands may take advantage of the geographical separation to conceal their problems, such as excessive gambling, debts, extra-marital affairs, and aggressive behaviours, from their Mainland wives. Our respondents who encountered marital problems disclosed that they had been clueless about their husbands' problems prior to their eventual immigration. Some were abandoned before or upon arrival in Hong Kong. While previous local studies have found that cross-border marriages are more prone to marital conflict and spousal violence than local marriages, due to the socioeconomic disadvantages (Choi and Cheung 2016) and unequal characteristics of the spouses in terms of education and age (Pong et al. 2014), the findings of this research suggest that institutionalized separation between cross-border spouses is also a risk factor leading to the dissolution of cross-border marriages.

Our respondents also refuted that the verification of Mainland single mothers' identity is not as difficult as the state claimed:

> Our children are living in Hong Kong, the government can check that. If I am divorced, that means I was once married. For those who are divorced, we have the divorce certificate, the child custody verdict from the court, and the birth certificate of my daughter (which states the name of her Hong Kong father). I also have the phone number of my ex-husband; the government can investigate whether I have been taking care of my daughter. My marriage was a fact. My care for my daughter is also a fact that can be traced. It is unfair to exclude us altogether. (Yi-lin, a divorced mother of a 15-year-old daughter.)

For Mainland single marriage migrant mothers, even though they are no longer wives of Hong Kong residents, they are still mothers of their Hong Kong resident children. During the interviews, they reiterated that they were fighting for Hong Kong residency 'for their children'. They lamented that the children are innocent and should not bear the suffering of not having their mothers around them.

Apart from stressing the rights of their children to grow up in Hong Kong with the care of their mothers, the single mothers also re-legitimized themselves as deserving recipients of Hong Kong residency by emphasizing their contribution to Hong Kong society through nurturing their children:

> We want to reunite with our children because they need our care and company so that they will not go astray and will not become a burden to Hong Kong society in the future. We have to be here to nurture them. (Tian-yu, an abandoned single mother of a 15-year-old daughter.)

Shi-Ying, another abandoned single mother of a seven-year-old daughter, also asserted that allowing them to reside in Hong Kong could benefit Hong Kong society:

There are around 100 Mainland single mothers waiting for Hong Kong residency. Offering residency to all these women would not influence the quota system much, but it makes a big difference to these families. If the single mothers are given residency, more than 100 children will have a stable family and can enjoy warmth and care from their mothers. These children will become members of society and make contributions when they are grown up. Whether they are well taken care of determines the future stability of Hong Kong. If some of them become rebellious or criminals, the public order of Hong Kong will be destroyed.

In their narratives, the family is an important avenue for nurturing the future pillars of society. Intergenerational care becomes a critical resource for making citizenship claims and countering state governmentality. It is within this 'rhetoric of the family' (Chee, Lu, and Yeoh 2014, 835) that single marriage migrants find sources of legitimacy and empowerment for making citizenship claims, thereby resisting the negative stereotypes imposed on them. Apart from daily caregiving, some single marriage migrant mothers also volunteer at the NGOs to help other marriage migrants. They stressed that, even though they are not legally regarded as Hong Kong residents, they have nevertheless been residing in Hong Kong, albeit intermittently, and have undeniable family links with Hong Kong citizens. Advocating for their rights to family is advocating for the wellbeing of their citizen-children. These provide strong motivations for them to contribute to Hong Kong society through voluntary work and continue their citizenship struggles. The NGOs provide a platform for single marriage migrant mothers to transform themselves from being passive recipients of assistance to active agents who contribute to Hong Kong society, which further legitimizes their claims as deserving subjects of residency. Nevertheless, their contributions have been undervalued and they are not rewarded with access to legal and substantive rights when they carry out care and voluntary work in Hong Kong (To 2019a).

Discretionary maternal citizenship: the hidden and unequal pathway to family reunification

Being disqualified from OWP applications, Mainland single marriage migrant mothers can only appeal to the Director of the Immigration Department, hoping that he/she will exercise *discretion* over their case. According to the NGO staff that were interviewed, there are several ways to do so, most important of which is to submit a petition letter to the authorities. The letter can be submitted directly to the Immigration Department, which seldom yields positive results, or to the Legislative Council Redress System,[4] which receives and handles complaints from the public about government actions, legislation, or policies, through the Public Complaints Office (PCO) of the Legislative Council Secretariat. The letter will then be examined, and each case evaluated. NGOs and petitioners may also request to meet legislative council members through the PCO. If the complaint is justified, legislative council members may ask the government to take remedial action and/or refer the issue to the relevant Legislative Council committee or raise the issue at a Legislative Council meeting, if a change in policy or law is deemed necessary. Although these mechanisms are not established specifically for single marriage migrants, they provide a pathway for single marriage migrants to make collective claims in the public realm towards changing immigration policies (such as adding a legal category in the quota system for single marriage migrant mothers to obtain OWP), as well as to submit individual requests to the Immigration Department.

Eule, Loher, and Wyss (2018) cautioned that 'discretionary practices cannot only be observed in the context of state authorities', the role of NGOs in the governance of citizenship is non-negligible. Indeed, NGOs play a critical role in single marriage migrant mothers' citizenship struggles. Mainland marriage migrants usually come from lower educational backgrounds and are not well-equipped to argue their case and articulate their needs and difficulties in relation to the limitations of the immigration system and policies. Thus, NGOs provide them with training to help them navigate the complex immigration and welfare systems as well as the discretionary pathway described above. As officials make discretionary judgements based on the petition letters and supporting documents, it is paramount for single marriage migrant mothers to present their case in an organized and convincing way. During training, the NGO staff interviewed explained that they would help single marriage migrants organize their stories by helping them to tease out the main points that they should emphasize in their letters or during meetings with officials. In their petitions, single marriage migrant mothers typically mobilize their family link to and genuine needs of caring for their children. Based on the petition letters gathered and interview data with an NGO staff member, widowed marriage migrants also stress the 'unexpected and uncontrollable' nature of their widowhood (i.e. not their fault that their marriage ended) to further legitimize their claims, whereas divorced or separated marriage migrants emphasize the 'social and interpersonal factors' (e.g. financial crisis, unemployment and/or the difficult personality of the husband) that led to their marital dissolution. The training by the NGOs partly shapes these narratives.

Proactively, the NGOs would also invite officials from relevant departments to communicate face-to-face with single marriage migrant mothers. However, opportunities like this only occur once a year. For urgent cases, the NGOs would organize press conferences to draw public attention and depend on reporters to question relevant departments, hoping that said departments would urge frontline workers to follow up with the concerned cases. The NGO staff explained that they need to make phone calls to follow up with each case, which may take another month or so to get concrete responses. Ultimately, they considered these procedures 'too bureaucratic', 'mechanistic', and 'lacking humanistic considerations'. While successful results are not guaranteed, their actions at least increase awareness among officials of the needs of single marriage migrant mothers, so that officials then look into these cases. In doing so, an unofficial channel is shaped through continuous grassroots advocacy and bottom-up activism.

Nevertheless, this pathway to discretionary citizenship is largely hidden, as it is not institutionalized or publicized. Only those who have access to the NGOs have knowledge of such a channel. Those who do not have access to these important parties, such as those residing in mainland China, may be indefinitely trapped in 'legal limbo' (Menjívar 2006). Further, the discretionary pathway is operated using a black-box approach – the vetting process is 'shadowy, never fully articulated and often inconsistent' (Maynard-Moody and Musheno 2000, 333). According to the two NGO staff we interviewed, there is no guideline on the procedures for discretionary appeals, and approval can be given to one case but not the other in the same situation. Even so, the handful of successful cases appears to be a source of hope for single marriage migrant mothers.

Given the precedent that some Mainland single marriage migrant mothers are given residency on a discretionary basis, one might question why the Hong Kong state has not institutionalized a pathway for Mainland single marriage migrant mothers to acquire Hong Kong residency. First, it justified the discretionary approach by trivializing the issue, quoting that the number of cases is 'limited' (Legislative Council Secretariat 2016, 5). This way, the Hong Kong state has conveniently shed its responsibility over the mothers of its citizens, disregarding the fact that these mothers are victims under the restrictive and exclusionary immigration system. Second, it refused to change the OWP scheme by saying that 'once it becomes a policy to include Mainland single mothers with minor children in Hong Kong in the OWP Scheme, Mainland parents may be encour-aged to seek to obtain OWPs through this special channel, which may in turn induce more Mainland pregnant women to give birth in Hong Kong' (Security Bureau February 2014, 5). From the state perspective, it has to consider the broader biopolitical context where citizenship control is exercised on other migrant categories, such as Mainland women who come to Hong Kong to give birth (i.e. birth tourists) and foreign domestic workers who give birth in Hong Kong during their employment (Constable 2014). Given the contested debates over the citizenship rights of children whose parents are not Hong Kong PRs, the Hong Kong state is reluctant to establish a formal pathway for Mainland single marriage migrant mothers to claim maternal citizenship, as this may open legal grounds for birth tourists and foreign domestic workers to claim citizenship. As such, reinforcing an exclusionary immigration system helps the Hong Kong state to achieve easier governance over migrant populations as well as political legitimacy amidst the rising tide of xenophobia. Third, under the current immigration system, the applica-tion, approval, and issuance of the permits falls within the remit of Mainland authorities. The Hong Kong state facilitates at the case level to issue the CoE as well as verify the supporting documents and claimed relationship of the applicants with their husbands in Hong Kong (The Government of HKSAR 2014). By not initiating the establishment of a formal pathway for Mainland single mothers, the Hong Kong state can avoid any law amendments that may bring uncertainty or complications to its relationship with Mainland authorities. Making the discretionary pathway ad hoc and hidden helps the Hong Kong state maintain its political interests and stability. Hence, in the replies to the NGOs and Mainland single mothers' petitions, officials simply reiterated that they would convey to Mainland authorities the exceptional cases that deserved discretionary consideration.

Endless process, hidden hierarchy of legitimacy, and intergenerational precarity

For Mainland single marriage migrant mothers, the state's account appears to be counter-logical because the state has literally turned what they originally deserve (i.e. Hong Kong residency) into an exceptional privilege that it offers out of mercy. Not to mention that many cases might have gone unnoticed, given the invisible nature of the discretionary pathway, those who managed to make appeals have suffered from immense stress and frustration throughout the process. Very often, multiple appeals have to be made before one is given discretionary residency. Although five respon-dents, with NGO assistance, managed to obtain the 'one-year multiple exit endorsement', it was granted on a one-time basis. Lan, a divorced mother of an eight-year-old child, lamented, 'I have to do this every year and I never know if I can get the endorsement next time. This is endless. I feel so lost and anxious, as I have no clue about when I will be granted an OWP'. In other words, the single marriage migrant mothers felt that they could only petition again and again until they finally obtained residency.

More importantly, previously approved discretionary cases are not set as precedents for future appeals. The only certainty that NGOs and Mainland single mothers have is that those with a Hong Kong resident child and those who are widowed have a higher chance of obtaining residency. This is based on the observations of the NGO staff and Mainland single mothers that discretionary approval towards divorced and separated Mainland mothers is far less forthcoming than for widows. According to the NGO staff and single mothers we interviewed, very few divorced marriage migrant mothers are granted discretionary residency if their children have severe health issues and need intensive care. Divorced mothers with healthy children have a slim chance. Those who are separated but have not legally registered their marriage with their ex-Hong Kong spouses stand no chance at all. Online documents submitted by other NGOs to the Legislative Council, as well as responses from the government,[5] corroborate the observation that widowed marriage migrant mothers have a higher chance of getting state discretion. One NGO staff member explained that 'Those who are divorced or whose husband has disappeared [face more difficulties] because it is difficult for them to present evidence to eradicate the authority's suspicion of them being involved in a bogus marriage'. Such a hierarchy of legitimacy underscores the patriarchal logic of state ideology – only those who are loyal to their marriage (by submitting and being committed to their husbands) and compliant with the law (by adhering to the formal marriage system) are recognized and rewarded. This signifies that, even when single marriage migrants as a category exists outside the state citizenship framework, widowed, divorced, and separated marriage migrants are still subject to a hidden graduated structure that prescribes them with variegated degree of legitimacy. This may further intensify the inequalities between citizens and non-citizens, as well as between non-citizens with different degrees of 'marrytocracy'.

Notably, marriage migrant mothers holding a TWP are temporary visitors and not entitled to the rights of paid employment and other social welfare in Hong Kong. The temporary visitor visa issued to them represents the state's intention to mobilize the unpaid reproductive labour of Mainland single mothers without taking responsibility for them (see also Chiu and Choi 2020). As such, even though many divorced marriage migrants have obtained full custody of their children, they lack the economic resources to provide for their children. Rather, they depend on the welfare given to their children, which is barely enough to offset the rental expenses. Respondents who have depleted their savings explained that they depend on charities for subsistence. Furthermore, as single marriage migrant mothers have to bring their children along when they renew their TWPs on the Mainland (usually every 90 days, and each renewal takes a few weeks to complete), the children's learning progress is unavoidably obstructed. Under these circumstances, even though state regulations do not target citizen-children, the children nevertheless share their mothers' legal precarity and experience its consequences in their own lives (see Chiu 2020 for a detailed discussion). This lived reality of intergenerational precarity is a result of the restrictive 'marrytocracy-based' immigration system, and underscores how citizenship is experienced at the family level.

Conclusion

Despite the burgeoning scholarship on cross-border marriages, family-level experiences and outcomes of cross-border marriages have been under-examined. In particular, the experiences of non-normative cross-border families have rarely been put in the spotlight. This article contributes to the literature by drawing attention to the under-studied group of marriage migrants who are widowed, divorced, or separated from their citizen-husbands. Drawing on the post-marital experiences of Mainland single marriage migrant mothers, this article illustrates how the state idealizes and institutionalizes certain types of cross-border intimacy (those that are intact and normative) while ostracizing those who do not fit the hegemonic definitions of marriage and family through the exclusionary 'marrytocracy-based' immigration system. Although restrictive control is thought to be necessary to combat bogus cross-border marriages, it tends to operate at the expense of the wellbeing of non-normative cross-border families, constricting not only the autonomy of single marriage migrants but also their dependent citizen-children. Diverging from the primary analytic focus of previous studies on marriage, this article uses the family as the unit of analysis to examine single marriage migrants' citizenship struggles and their legal precarity. By examining single marriage migrant mothers' resistance and strategies of re-legitimizing themselves for discretionary maternal citizenship, vis-à-vis the state's hegemonic politics of de-legitimization, this article extends Stasiulis and Bakan's (1997, 118) concept of 'citizenship as a terrain of struggle' by drawing attention to the ways single marriage migrant mothers mobilize the rhetoric of 'politics of care' during their citizenship struggles. The findings reveal that, although the exclusionary immigration regime disregards their caregiving needs, single marriage migrant mothers strategically mobilized their intergenerational care relationships with their citizen-children as a critical resource for making legitimate citizenship claims. While previous studies have criticized nation-states' patriarchal mode of incorporation (which essentializes marriage migrants as domestic caregivers) for intensifying female marriage migrants' subordination and vulnerability within the family and the nation-state (Kim 2013; Yeoh, Chee, and Vu 2013; Wang and Bélanger 2008), this article adds to the literature by illuminating the resilient agency of single marriage migrant mothers in re-appropriating their maternal and caregiving role as a feminized weapon to confront the state and re-legitimize themselves for maternal citizenship. This strategic mobilization of maternal caregiving reflects the paradoxical effects of the gendered mode of maternal citizenship.

Despite the agency of the single marriage migrant mothers in capitalizing on their maternal role as a source of legitimacy, their maternal identity *per se* does not automatically qualify them as legitimate residency/citizenship recipients. State refusal to institutionalize the discretionary pathway for single marriage migrant mothers signifies its determination to sustain the hegemonic 'marrytocracy-based' immigration system. At the state level, the discretionary pathway is used as institutional leeway for the Hong Kong state to manage 'irregular' marriage migration from mainland China without opening legal grounds for birth tourists and foreign domestic workers to claim citizenship or risking any complications that law amendments may bring to its relationship with

Mainland authorities. This form of governance is therefore conducive to maintaining the state's political legitimacy. However, because a hidden hierarchy of legitimacy underpins the pathway to discretionary maternal citizenship, the inequalities between cross-border families led by widowed, divorced, and separated marriage migrant mothers are likely to be further widened, leading to an even more rigorous intergenerational disadvantage at the family level. Nevertheless, this institutional leeway, albeit unequal, provides room for some non-citizen migrant mothers to make patriarchal bargains and permeate the rigid boundaries of citizenship at the individual level. These findings shed light on how a graduated citizenship structure exists in the context of cross-border marriage migration, and indicate how the state's citizenship regime is further graduated and differentiated based on patriarchal principles of 'marrytocracy'. Furthermore, the findings point to the fact that discretion is not only used by the state to continue its governance over migrant populations but also utilized by marginalized single marriage migrant mothers to open up possibilities for claiming citizenship and maneuver their disadvantaged position within the graduated citizenship regime.

Overall, this article contributes to the scholarship of marriage migration and citizenship by revealing how discretion has been used as a strategic mechanism by both the state and single marriage migrant mothers to negotiate the boundaries and substance of citizenship, and how citizenship is experienced, negotiated, and contested within the family realm. As the effects of legal precarity is likely to spill over from single marriage migrant mothers to their dependent citizen children, researchers should pay attention to the intergenerationality of citizenship (Chiu and Yeoh 2021, this issue), particularly the ways in which the family may reproduce intergenerational precarity when one or more members are being legally marginalized, and re-consider how citizenship should be conceptualized as a family-level concept. Moreover, by presenting a special case of the granting of maternal citizenship through discretion, this article opens up new inquiry into the opportunities and limitations brought by the distinct form of *discretionary citizenship*. Further comparative studies would help to unpack how discretionary citizenship opens up or limits space for migrants and nation-states to negotiate the substance and boundaries of citizenship.

Notes

1. Including the right to choose with whom and under what conditions one may reproduce (Richardson and Turner 2001).
2. Among the quotas, 60 places are allocated to children holding Certificates of Entitlement (CoE; signifying their right of abode); 30 to spouses separated for 10 years or above and their accompanying children; and the remaining 60 to other categories of applicants, including spouses separated for less than 10 years and their accompanying children, unsupported children and elderly people who need to join their relatives in Hong Kong, and persons coming to Hong Kong to take care of their unsupported aged parents (Legislative Council Secretariat 2016).
3. The unused quotas mainly come from the categories of CoE holders and spouses separated for 10 years or above, but they are not re-allocated to spouses separated for less than 10 years and single mothers (To 2019a).
4. Details of the system can be found at https://www.legco.gov.hk/general/english/sec/corg_ser/redress.htm

5. Sources: https://www.legco.gov.hk/yr14-15/english/hc/sub_com/hs51/minutes/
   hs5120151123.pdf (p.5) https://www.legco.gov.hk/yr14-15/chinese/hc/sub_com/hs51/
   papers/hs5120151223cb2-517-4-c.pdf (p.7 in Chinese) https://www.legco.gov.hk/yr14-15/
   chinese/hc/sub_com/hs51/papers/hs5120151223cb2-517-1-c.pdf (p.2 in Chinese)

Acknowledgments

The author would like to thank Brenda Yeoh, Sohoon Yi, and the reviewers for their thoughtful comments on the earlier drafts of this article, as well as the respondents in this project for sharing their valuable insights and experiences. This project is supported by the Asia Research Institute at the National University of Singapore and the Hong Kong Research Grant Council (grant number GRF2120461).

Disclosure statement

No potential conflict of interest was reported by the author(s).

ORCID

Tuen Yi Chiu (iD) http://orcid.org/0000-0002-5901-236X

References

Abrego, L. J., and C. Menjívar. 2011. "Immigrant Latina Mothers as Targets of Legal Violence." *International Journal of Sociology of the Family* 37 (1): 9–26.
Braun, V., and V. Clarke. 2006. "Using Thematic Analysis in Psychology." *Qualitative Research in Psychology* 3 (2): 77–101. doi:10.1191/1478088706qp063oa.
Census and Statistics Department. 2019. *Women and Men in Hong Kong Key Statistics.* Hong Kong: Hong Kong SAR.
Chand, D. E., and W. D. Schreckhise. 2015. "Secure Communities and Community Values: Local Context and Discretionary Immigration Law Enforcement." *Journal of Ethnic and Migration Studies* 41 (10): 1621–1643. doi:10.1080/1369183X.2014.986441.
Chee, H. L., M. C. Lu, and B. S. A. Yeoh. 2014. "Ethnicity, Citizenship and Reproduction: Taiwanese Wives Making Citizenship Claims in Malaysia." *Citizenship Studies* 18 (8): 823–838. doi:10.1080/13621025.2014.964545.
Chiu, T. Y. 2017. "Marriage Migration as a Multifaceted System: Intersectionality of Intimate Partner Violence in Cross-Border Marriages." *Violence Against Women* 23 (11): 1293–1313. doi:10.1177/1077801216659940.
Chiu, T. Y. 2020. "Everyday Mixed Status: Spillover Effects of State Power in Cross-Border Families." *Gender, Place and Culture* 27 (5): 643–659. doi:10.1080/0966369X.2019.1615411.

Chiu, T. Y., and B. S. A. Yeoh (2021, this issue). "Marriage Migration, Family and Citizenship in Asia." *Citizenship Studies*. Advance online publication. doi:10.1080/13621025.2021.1968680.

Chiu, T. Y., and S. Y. P. Choi. 2020. "The Decoupling of the Legal Migration and Spatial Migration of Female Marriage Migrants." *Journal of Ethnic and Migration Studies* 46 (14): 2997–3013. doi:10.1080/1369183X.2019.1585018.

Choi, S. Y. P., and A. K. L. Cheung. 2016. "Dissimilar and Disadvantaged: Age Discrepancy, Financial Stress, and Marital Conflict in Cross-Border Marriages." *Journal of Family Issues* 38 (18): 2521–2544. doi:10.1177/0192513X16653436.

Constable, N. 2014. *Born Out of Place: Migrant Mothers and the Politics of International Labor.* Berkely, Los Angeles and London: University of California Press.

Coté, A., M. Kérisit, and M. L. Coté. 2001. *Sponsorship–for Better or for Worse: The Impact of Sponsorship on the Equality Rights of Immigrant Women.* Ottawa: Status of Women Canada.

Coutin, S. B., S. M. Ashar, J. M. Chacón, and S. Lee. 2017. "Deferred Action and the Discretionary State: Migration, Precarity and Resistance." *Citizenship Studies* 21 (8): 951–968. doi:10.1080/13621025.2017.1377153.

Duffy, M. 2011. *Making Care Count: A Century of Gender, Race, and Paid Care Work.* New Brunswick, New Jersey and London: Rutgers University Press.

Enriquez, L. 2015. "Multigenerational Punishment: Shared Experiences of Undocumented Immigration Status within Mixed-Status Families." *Journal of Marriage and Family* 77 (4): 939–953. doi:10.1111/jomf.12196.

Eule, T. G., D. Loher, and A. Wyss. 2018. "Contested Control at the Margins of the State." *Journal of Ethnic and Migration Studies* 44 (16): 2717–2729. doi:10.1080/1369183X.2017.1401511.

Faier, L. 2008. "Runaway Stories: The Underground Micromovements of Filipina *Oyomesan* in Rural Japan." *Cultural Anthropology* 23 (4): 630–659. doi:10.1111/j.1548-1360.2008.00021.x.

Fix, M., and W. Zimmermann. 2001. "All under One Roof: Mixed-Status Families in an Era of Reform." *International Migration Review* 35 (2): 397–419. doi:10.1111/j.1747-7379.2001.tb00023.x.

Fresnoza-Flot, A. 2018. "Social Citizenship and Divorce: Filipino Migrant Women (Un)claiming Social Rights in the Netherlands and in Belgium" *Nijmegen Migration Law Working Papers Series* 2018/01.

Friedman, S. L. 2015. "Regulating Cross-Border Intimacy: Authenticity Paradigms and the Specter of Illegality among Chinese Marital Immigrants to Taiwan." In *Migrant Encounters: Intimate Labor, the State, and Mobility across Asia*, edited by S. Friedman and P. Mahdavi, 206–230. Philadelphia: University of Pennsylvania Press.

Friedman, S. L. 2016. "The Right to Family: Chinese Marriage Immigrants, Chinese Children, and Graduated Citizenship in Taiwan." In *Gender and Citizenship in Historical and Transnational Perspective*, edited by A. R. Epstein and R. G. Fuchs, 211–231. London: Palgrave.

Hsia, H. C. 2007. "Imaged and Imagined Threat to the Nation: The Media Construction of the 'Foreign Brides' Phenomenon' as Social Problems in Taiwan." *Inter-Asia Cultural Studies* 8 (1): 55–85. doi:10.1080/14649370601119006.

Huang, S. M. 2016. "Can Travelling Mothers Ever Arrive? Articulating Internal and International Migration within a Transnational Perspective of Care." *Population, Space and Place* 22 (7): 705–717. doi:10.1002/psp.1953.

Kim, H. M., S. Park, and A. Shukhertei. 2017. "Returning Home: Marriage Migrants' Legal Precarity and the Experience of Divorce." *Critical Asian Studies* 49 (1): 38–53. doi:10.1080/14672715.2016.1266679.

Kim, M. 2013. "Citizenship Projects for Marriage Migrants in South Korea: Intersecting Motherhood with Ethnicity and Class." *Social Politics* 20 (4): 455–481. doi:10.1093/sp/jxt015.

Law, Y. W., M. Chan, H. Zhang, L. Tai, S. Tsang, P. Chu, and P. Yip. 2019. "Divorce in Hong Kong SAR, 1999–2011: A Review of 1,208 Family Court Cases." *Journal of Divorce & Remarriage* 60 (5): 389–403. doi:10.1080/10502556.2018.1558855.

Legislative Council Secretariat. 2014. *Press Release: LCQ2 One-way Permit Scheme.* Hong Kong: Hong Kong SAR government.

Legislative Council Secretariat. 2016. *Report of the Subcommittee to Study Issues Relating to Mainland-HKSAR Families.* Hong Kong: Hong Kong SAR government.

Lipsky, M. 2010. *Street-level Bureaucracy: Dilemmas of the Individual in Public Services.* Expanded ed. New York: Russell Sage.

Liversage, A. 2012. "Transnational Families Breaking Up: Divorce among Turkish Immigrants in Denmark." In *Transnational Marriage: New Perspectives from Europe and Beyond,* edited by K. Charsley, 145–160. New York: Routledge.

Maynard-Moody, S., and M. Musheno. 2000. "State Agent or Citizen Agent: Two Narratives of Discretion." *Journal of Public Administration Research and Theory* 10 (2): 329–358. doi:10.1093/oxfordjournals.jpart.a024272.

Menjívar, C. 2006. "Liminal Legality: Salvadoran and Guatemalan Immigrants' Lives in the United States." *American Journal of Sociology* 111 (4): 999–1037. doi:10.1086/499509.

Ong, A. 2006. "Mutations in Citizenship." *Theory, Culture & Society* 23 (2–3): 499–505. doi:10.1177/0263276406064831.

Pong, S. L., D. Post, D. Ou, and M. S. Fok. 2014. "Blurring Boundaries? Immigration and Exogamous Marriages in Hong Kong." *Population and Development Review* 40 (4): 629–652. doi:10.1111/j.1728-4457.2014.00004.x.

Quah, S. E. L. 2020. *Transnational Divorce: Understanding Intimacies and Inequalities from Singapore.* Abingdon, Oxon: Routledge.

Richardson, E. H., and B. S. Turner. 2001. "Sexual, Intimate or Reproductive Citizenship?" *Citizenship Studies* 5 (3): 329–338. doi:10.1080/13621020120085289.

Satzewich, V. 2014. "Visa Officers as Gatekeepers of a State's Borders: The Social Determinants of Discretion in Spousal Sponsorship Cases in Canada." *Journal of Ethnic and Migration Studies* 40 (9): 1450–1469. doi:10.1080/1369183X.2013.854162.

Security Bureau. 2014. *Panel on Security of the Legislative Council: Immigration Arrangements for Entry of Mainland Residents for Family Reunion.* Hong Kong: Author.

Stasiulis, D., and A. B. Bakan. 1997. "Negotiating Citizenship: The Case of Foreign Domestic Workers in Canada." *Feminist Review* 57 (1): 112–139. doi:10.1080/014177897339687.

The Government of HKSAR. 2014. *Press Release: LCQ2 One-way Permit Scheme.* Hong Kong: Author.

The Government of HKSAR. 2016. *Press Release: LCQ4: Single Mothers Issued with OWPs by Mainland Authorities on Discretionary Basis.* Hong Kong: Author.

The Government of HKSAR. 2019. *Press Releases: LCQ1: Operation of One-way Permits Scheme.* Hong Kong: Author.

To, C. W. C. 2019a. "Civic Stratification within Cross-Border Families: Mainland Chinese Children and Wives in Hong Kong." *Migration Letters* 16 (2): 301–316. doi:10.33182//ml.v16i2.743.

Van Walsum, S. 2016. "The Contested Meaning of Care in Migration Law." In *Family Life in an Age of Migration and Mobility: Global Perspectives through the Life Course,* edited by M. Kilkey and E. Palenga-Möllenbeck, 313–335. London: Palgrave Macmillan.

Wang, H. Z., and D. Bélanger. 2008. "Taiwanizing Female Immigrant Spouses and Materializing Differential Citizenship." *Citizenship Studies* 12 (1): 91–106. doi:10.1080/13621020701794224.

Yamaura, C. 2020. *Marriage and Marriageability: The Practices of Matchmaking between Men from Japan and Women from Northeast China.* Ithaca and London: Cornell University Press.

Yeoh, B. S. A., L. H. Chee, and T. K. D. Vu. 2013. "Commercially Arranged Marriage and the Negotiation of Citizenship Rights among Vietnamese Marriage Migrants in Multiracial Singapore." *Asian Ethnicity* 14 (2): 139–156. doi:10.1080/14631369.2012.759746.

Yi, S. 2019. "Suspicious Mothering: Maternal Labor and Marriage Migration in South Korea." *Social Politics: International Studies in Gender, State & Society* 28 (1): 71–93. doi:10.1093/sp/jxz018.

From 'social problems' to 'social assets': geopolitics, discursive shifts in children of Southeast Asian marriage migrants, and mother-child dyadic citizenship in Taiwan

Hsiao-Chuan Hsia

ABSTRACT

In recent years, the discourse surrounding children of Southeast Asian (SEA) marriage migrants in Taiwan has seen a dramatic shift from the discourse of 'social problems' to that of 'social assets'. By integrating perspectives of critical geopolitics and critical discourse analysis, this paper shows that this discursive shift has resulted from the dual impacts of the 'mother-child dyadic citizenship' and the geopolitics of the triad of Taiwan, SEA, and China. It is argued that the state formulates laws and policies concerning marriage migration based on the mother-child dyad rather than the individual-state nexus, while SEA is used merely as leverage against China. Moreover, confronted with an increasingly competitive global economy, especially the impending threat of a rising PRC, Taiwan's immigration laws have become more classist, discriminating against Southeast Asian marriage migrants in contradiction with the current positive discourse, which reveals that the state–citizen relationship has evolved into a corporate-consumer relationship.

My mother is from Indonesia. As I was growing up, I was scared whenever I saw TV news portraying immigrants and migrants in very negative ways . . . One of my classmates in junior high school was bullied after they learnt that his mother was from Vietnam. I felt that I would also be bullied if I revealed that my mom is an Indonesian, so I did not lend any help to this bullied classmate, which I have regret ever since. My mom never attended any activities in my schools. I didn't know why until I complained to her. She finally told me, 'I was afraid to make you ashamed.'. . . . Now I can proudly say I am the 'Second Generation Immigrant' and I am the mixed child of Indonesian and Taiwanese.

Introduction

The above quote comes from one of my undergraduate students enrolled in a 2019 Migration, Human Rights and Multiculturalism class. Though I never asked, several students revealed their family backgrounds; all recalled negative experiences growing up labelled as children of so-called 'foreign brides'.

These students' stories are indeed testimonials of the shifting gaze on the children of marriage migrants from Southeast Asia (SEA). In recent years, media and governmental discourses in Taiwan have begun promoting the presumption that second-generation immigrants (SGI) are advantaged for inheriting Southeast Asian cultures and languages. Their mothers, marriage migrants from SEA, are celebrated as markers of Taiwan's multicultural society[1] and encouraged to pass their native languages and culture down to their children so that these children can ultimately boost Taiwanese economic expansion to SEA, becoming the 'vanguards of Taiwan's deployment in Southeast Asia.'[2] Success stories such as *Using Mother Tongue as Springboard, Cheng Yao-Tieng Earns a Million Annually Before Age 30*[3] have been celebrated by the media, promoting children of SEA marriage migrants as the 'vanguards of the New Southbound Policy' for their multilingual capabilities, while SEA marriage migrants have been featured national anthem singers and ceremony hosts at National Day Celebrations, thereby representing Taiwan's 'tradition of inclusiveness'.[4]

Such positive discourse represents a drastic shift. As in Japan and South Korea, the other two receiving countries for marriage migrants in Asia, these migrants and their children have historically encountered derogatory public discourse (e.g. Nakamatsu 2005; Shin 2019).

More than a decade ago, these children were portrayed in both media and governmental discourses as having many problems, especially 'developmental delay', while their mothers were perceived as lacking child rearing capacity because of their so-called 'inferior population quality' (Hsia 2007), a term commonly used in governmental documents[5] and media reports.

The population quality of SEA mothers was questioned because of their socio-economic backgrounds. Since the phenomenon of marriage migration caught the public's attention in Taiwan in early 1990s, female marriage migrants from SEA and People's Republic of China (PRC), especially the former, were perceived as a threat to Taiwan's population quality because they frequently came from disadvantaged families in SEA and the PRC, which were then considered less developed than Taiwan. According to official statistics, one in every four new marriages in 2002 occurred between a citizen and a foreigner, although the percentage decreased after 2003, hovering between 12 and 20% of all marriages registered annually. The vast majority of foreign spouses remain women from the PRC and SEA, including Vietnam, Indonesia, the Philippines, Thailand and Cambodia.

While these children were born with Taiwanese nationality, and their mothers were spouses of Taiwanese citizens, both were considered in public discourse as 'undesirable', as reflected in discriminatory policies and laws (Hsia and Huang 2010). Marriage migrants from the PRC are governed differently and face far stricter laws and regulations due to the political tension between Taiwan and the PRC since 1949 when the KMT (Chinese Nationalist Party) government lost the civil war to the Communist Party and retreated to Taiwan. This antagonistic attitude toward PRC migrants has remained stable even through transitions of power between Taiwan's two dominant political parties, KMT and DPP (Democratic Progressive Party).

However, the discourse surrounding SEA marriage migrants and their children in Taiwan has turned positive in recent years as captured in media trends. In a study on media reports from 1994 to 2012, Fung and Wang (2014) showed that marriage migrants had been discussed in overwhelmingly negative terms such as 'foreign brides' from 1994 until 2002, when increasingly positive portrayals began to emerge. From 2010 on, media reports of marriage migrants have delivered relatively equal percentages of neutral and positive images. These trends in media portrayals parallel changing attitudes of the general public toward marriage migrants, as revealed in the series of National Image Surveys conducted by the Academia Sinica. Accordingly, the percentage of the inter-viewees perceiving SEA marriage migrants as negatively impacting Taiwanese society dropped significantly from 74.6% in 2004 to 54.3% in 2012, while the percentage of interviewees agreeing that the government should not restrict SEA marriage migrants from obtaining Taiwanese citizenship increased from 19% in 2004 to 28% in 2016.

The discourse on the children of SEA marriage migrants has followed a similar trend. These children were first labelled as 'New Taiwan's Children' (NTC hereafter) in 2003 with entirely negative images (ibid.) Lee and Chueh (2018) analyzed mainstream media reports between 2005 and 2016 and found that these children were portrayed with mostly negative terms, such as 'problems', 'developmental delay', and 'counselling', until media portrayals from 2014 to 2016 became positively associated with terms like 'talents' and 'advantages'.

While studies have clearly documented a discursive shift, the explanation of why this shift is occurring needs to be deepened. Fung and Wang (2014) and Lee and Chueh (2018) both attributed this discursive shift to social movements advocating for human and cultural rights of marriage migrants and their children. However, as the pioneering long-term activist referenced by Lee and Chueh in their discussion of these social movements, this attribution overly romanticizes our impact. The 2016 Amendments to the Nationality Act, rendering Southeast Asian marriage migrants vulnerable to state-lessness, was passed only months after the 'New Southbound Policy' (NSP hereafter) was launched to promote Taiwan's connection with SEA, which resulted in a positive dis-course surrounding children of SEA marriage migrants.

Additionally, Lee and Chueh (2018) argued that children of SEA marriage migrants have been valued in recent positive discourse because their human capital is imagined as a buttress for the NSP, reflecting the ideology inherited from the 'Go South Policy' (GSP hereafter) of the 1990s. While Lee and Chueh were correct to point out the impact of the NSP on the discursive shift, they failed to identify economic and political differences between the GSP and the NSP.

While both the NSP and GSP are governmental policies towards SEA, each was built on contrasting images of Southeast Asian countries and their citizens. One question that must be addressed is why the social construction of Southeast Asian marriage migrants was overwhelmingly negative in the context of the GSP and it turned positive in the context of the NSP? The answers lie in examining the relationship between immigration discourse and geopolitical context.

Immigration discourse and geopolitical context

Children of migrants have been given labels associated with different meanings. For example, the label 'multicultural children' refers to the children of an underprivileged Korean man and a female marriage migrant from a less industrialized neighboring country. In a study of news articles from 2009 to 2013, Shin (2019) identified three main discourses on so-called multicultural children: 'marginalized group', 'threat to the future of Korea', and 'global human resources'. Shin contended that the ideologies of democracy, nationalism, and neoliberalism penetrated the notion of multiculturalism in Korea. While correctly recognizing the importance of nationalism and neoliberalism, the analysis lacks a temporal dimension which is crucial to deepen our understanding of the phenomenon of marriage migration present in East Asian countries for more than two decades.

In the historical study of the changing discourse on mixed-race children in modern Japan, Horiguchi and Imoto (2016) traced different categories representing children born to Japanese and non-Japanese parents. From Meiji (1868–1992) to the pre-war period, these children were referred to as *konketsu* (mixed blood) and mostly associated with social problems, except for mixed-race children of Western mothers, who were symbols of desirable Japanese modernity. During the 1930s and 1940s, portrayals of mixed-race children focused on their healthy development since inter-marriage in colonized Korea and Taiwan were promoted in the imperialization policy. In the post-war period, there were almost no media reports on *konketsu* until 1952, when the General Headquarters ended its occupation in mainland Japan and the images of 'impure', 'polluted' mixed-raced children became widely reported, reflecting the prevailing anti-U.S. sentiment in Japan. As cross-border migration intensified, the number of children of Filipino mothers and Japanese fathers significantly increased beginning in the 1980s, and negative portrayals began to be challenged in the 1990s by civil society organizations advocating for the rights of the Japanese-Filipino children; thus, the term *kokusai-ji* (international children) was promoted.

While Horiguchi and Imoto (2016) contended that the labels of mixed-race children symbolize larger socio-political issues of the time, including race, Westernization, colonization, and globalization, their analysis did not further elaborate on the connection between discursive changes and broader socio-political contexts.

To articulate this connection, the lens of critical geography can shed some light. Dempsey and McDowell (2019) examined the connection between the EU's discourse on 'migration crisis' and geopolitical dynamics by analyzing media portrayals of migrants in 2015 and 2016. Migrants were initially described as 'humans' migrating to Europe, then likened to a 'natural disaster', and finally labelled as a geopolitical 'threat' to security. The intensification of negative representations reveals European geopolitical conceptualizations of belonging and sovereignty that are often at odds with the principles and values to which the EU subscribes. The labelling of migrants is a geopolitical narrative revealing EU member states' efforts to stabilize their system and protect the privileges that Europeans enjoy behind their once 'borderless' supra-national entity's increasingly militarized borders.

Many scholars in critical geopolitics have pointed out the close connection between immigration discourse and geopolitics. As Hyndman (2012) contended, migration has long been a barometer of geopolitics. Therefore, immigration discourse can be seen as geopolitical discourse (Mamadouh 2012), as illustrated in the discursive construction of Arab immigrants in the U.S. as terrorists in the aftermath of September 11, which led to a flurry of new immigration proposals to tighten border security (Nagel 2002).

The close connection between discursive shifts in immigration and geopolitical circumstances is clearly revealed in the study of immigration narratives in France and the Netherlands from the 1970s to 1990s, in which Mamadouh (2012) distinguished three storylines regarding the 'invasion' of immigrants at different scales: invaded neighborhoods, nations at risk, and Western Europe under siege. 'Invaded neighborhoods' represented a storyline in the 1970s when immigration was framed as a local problem, affecting issues such as lack of housing in the communities. This narrative of invasion was scaled up to 'nation at risk' in the 1980s after the oil crisis when a rise in unemployment led to the perception that immigrants were 'stealing jobs', and 'taking advantage of our welfare state'. The storyline of 'Western Europe under siege' emerged in the 1990s when asylum seekers became the predominant figures in anti-immigrant narratives, pointing to the notion of a common fate faced by a unified Western European society facing similar population flows. This immigration discourse is scaled up to the regional level emphasizing the need to construct a Fortress Europe to limit immigrant flows.

Similarly, to understand why the discourse on SEA marriage migrants' children in Taiwan has changed from the negative label of NTC to the positive label of SGI, this article also considers such discourse as a form of geopolitical discourse and will examine the geopolitical dynamics underlying the discursive shift with a temporal dimension.

However, unlike in the EU and the U.S., where tightening of immigration policies corresponds to negative immigration discourses, securitization of migration for SEA marriage migrants co-exists with the positive discursive shift in Taiwan. While discriminatory immigration laws and policies corresponded with negative images of SEA marriage migrants and their children in the past, the shift toward positive images of them has not been correspondently reflected in relevant laws. This article will further analyze this incongruence.

Research questions and methods

Informed by the perspectives of critical geography, this article aims to analyze how the discourse on children of SEA marriage migrants has shifted as the dynamics of geopolitics has changed over the past decades. To understand the reasons behind these discursive shifts, this paper adopts the lens of critical discourse analysis (CDA), whose purpose is '*to systematically explore often opaque relationships of causality and determination between (a) discursive practices, events and texts, and (b) wider social and cultural structures, relations and processes*' (Fairclough 1995, 132). The analysis will focus on the meso and macro levels of the three interrelated dimensions of the discourse developed by Fairclough (1995), since micro-level discursive practices surrounding children of SEA marriage migrants have already been established by previous studies (Fung and Wang 2014; Lee and Chueh 2018).

On the meso level, this paper investigates how the labels of NTC and SGI have been produced in the media and governmental narratives. On the macro level, the analysis focuses on geopolitical context within which the discursive shift arises. Specific research questions include: how have the labels of the children of Southeast Asian marriage migrants been constructed by the government and media? Why have these labels and their associated meanings shifted? What is the geopolitical context of this discursive shift? Why have legal changes contradicted this seemingly positive discursive shift?

Drawing on my long-term action-oriented research since 1994 as an organizer and advocate for the rights and welfare of marriage migrants and their children (for details of the processes and my roles, see Hsia 2019), the methods employed include participant observation in campaigns for policy and law changes since late 2003 (especially regarding the amendments to the Nationality Act from 2012 to 2016), analysis of media reports, and governmental statements of related policies and laws beginning in the early 2010s when the discourse began to change (particularly regarding the NSP and the 2016 Amendments to the Nationality Act).

The following sections will examine the connection between the discourse on the children of SEA marriage migrants, relevant policies and laws, and the geopolitical context, as summarized in Table 1.

Discursive shift from NTC as 'social problems' to SGI as 'social assets' in Taiwan

NTC had been the most popular term referring to children of marriage migrants until 2014, while SGI first appeared in the media in 2010 but remained rare until 2014 when its appearance significantly increased and surpassed NTC. SGI has become the most popular term since 2016. Moreover, the NTC discourse had been overwhelmingly negative while the SGI discourse has been very positive (Lee and Chueh 2018).

My previous study (Hsia 2007) showed that NTC was first coined in 2003 in a well-known magazine and subsequently widely circulated at the peak of national anxiety concerning negative impacts of foreign brides' children on Taiwan's 'population quality'. This anxiety led to a drastic shift in the government's position from neglecting issues of marriage migration to quickly formulating immigration policies to control the inflow of marriage migrants and initiating programs to presumably improve the 'quality' of their children, though these had no basis in solid research. This increasing concern over the 'quality' of foreign brides' children coexisted with proliferating media coverage concerning these children's higher risks of 'developmental delay'.

The NTC discourse centered around issues of 'population quality', which began to target foreign brides for the New Family Planning Programs in 1998, shortly after the 1997 Asian Financial Crisis followed by heated media discussion concerning Taiwan's global competitiveness. Rising anxiety that the PRC's emergence as a 'world's factory' would threaten Taiwan's economy was juxtaposed with concerns about how foreign brides, particularly those from SEA, would deteriorate Taiwan's population quality to compete globally (ibid). This fear of losing global competitiveness derives from Taiwan's conception of national pride as being rooted in prosperity, which led to the National Security Council pinpointing the 'incapable motherhood' of foreign brides as a national threat to the sustainability of Taiwan's economic development (Cheng 2013). This overwhelmingly negative NTC discourse was replaced by positive SGI discourse, which has become significantly popularized since the NSP was launched in 2016 (Lee and Chueh 2018).

The NSP's Promotion Plan was announced in September 2017, shortly after the inauguration of President Tsai Ing-wen (DPP).[6] The Office of the New Southbound Policy was established on 15 June 2016, directly under the Office of the President. One of the four main tasks of the promotion plan is to 'conduct talent exchange' and 'new immigrants', i.e. marriage migrants, compose one of the focus areas: '*Help first-*

Table 1. Geopolitics and the discourse on the children of Southeast Asian marriage migrants in Taiwan from 1990s to 2010s.

	Naming of Children of SEA Marriage Migrants	Dominant discourse	Immigration laws and policies	Economic policies	Regional and global political economy context
Early 1990s	None	'Foreign brides' as social problems (e.g. fake marriages)	None Ignored and hope it would disappear	1993 (to 2002) Go South Policy	rise of the PRC as a World's factory; capital flight from Taiwan to the PRC
Late 1990s	None	Deterioration of population quality			1997 Asian Financial Crisis
2003	New Taiwan's Children (NTC)	Developmental delay	Targeted SEA marriage migrants for New Family Planning Programs (birth control) 2003: National Immigration Agency established 2004: announced plan to establish the Foreign Spouse Care and Guidance Fund 2005: Fund established 2003–2007: increased barriers for marriage migrants to obtain citizenship	Go South Policy continued from 2002 to 2008	Rising power of the PRC
2010	Second-Generation Immigrants (SGI)	Respect multiculturalism	2012 Nationwide Torch Project for New Immigrants		
2014	SGI surpassed NTC; vanguards of Taiwan's deployment in Southeast Asia	SEA wave		Friendlier relationship with the PRC	Rising ASEAN
2016	SGI popularized; Seeds of New Southbound		Amendments to the Nationality Act (easier for professional foreigners to obtain citizenship but more barriers for marriage migrants)	Launching New Southbound Policy; more antagonistic toward the PRC	

generation immigrants use their linguistic and cultural advantages to obtain work certification and job opportunities (such as language teaching and tourism-related work). Help second-generation immigrants connect with their ancestral countries by encouraging universities to establish appropriate departments or curriculums, and give admission priority to students speaking Southeast Asian languages'.[7] The NSP promoted directly by the President has significantly contributed to the emerging 'Southeast Asian Wave' in Taiwan, and the children of SEA marriage migrants are expected to be the 'seeds of the New Southbound Policy'. As President Tsai stated at the Taiwan-ASEAN Dialogue in November 2016[8], *'We will also invest in second-generation immigrants in Taiwan, and encourage them to join our New Southbound Policy efforts'*, because SGI are believed by Tsai's Administration to be Taiwan's *'best connectors'* with SEA nations and their people.

During the presidency of Ma Ying-Jeou (KMT) prior to President Tsai's election, the National Immigration Agency (NIA) implemented the 'Nationwide Torch Project for New Immigrants' in 2012 with a budget for a Foreign Spouse Care and Guidance Fund (the Fund hereafter) under the Ministry of the Interior (MOI). The Fund was established in 2005 during President Chen Shui-bian's administration (DPP) to support programs that provided services such as Chinese language course, vocational training, counseling, and medical subsidies for marriage migrants, particularly those from SEA. With the Torch Project in 2012, most budget from the Fund was shifted to education programs for marriage migrants' children, especially those encouraging them to learn Southeast Asian cultures and languages. As the Torch project began to promote the multicultural advantages held by children of SEA marriage migrants, the term SGI became more popular while the previously dominant naming, NTC, began to fade away.

As part of the Torch Project, the NIA initiated an annual program called 'Talent Cultivation Camp for Second Generation Immigrant Youth' in 2014, whose aim was to *'make Southeast Asian language-speaking children of the new immigrants from SEA valuable assets for Taiwan; enhance their global competitiveness; and become trade vanguards in emerging markets'*. The official rationale behind such camp was that *'the global competitiveness of ASEAN has been rising, so that the SEA markets have unlimited potentials in the future and Taiwanese businesses have increased investment in SEA and doubled their need of talents'*. With the promotion of this camp, featuring Mr. Cheng Yao-Tieng, son of an Indonesian marriage migrant whose annual income reached a million NT in his late 20s, the term SGI became increasingly popular and, according to Lee and Chueh (2018), its number of appearances in the media exceeded that of NTC for the first time in 2014.

Mother–child dyadic citizenship in the wave of marriage migration

Discourses surrounding the children of SEA marriage migrants in Taiwan, both negative and positive, have been closely linked to that of their mothers. While NTC discourse was prevalent, the national anxiety began as apprehension about the impending threat of the PRC to Taiwan's global competitiveness, yet SEA marriage migrants quickly became the target because it was presumed that their 'inferior population quality' would lead to inferior quality children. The positive turn of SGI discourse also reveals this close connection as it assumes SGI's natural inheritance of Southeast Asian languages and cultures from their mothers. This connection is rooted in the position of marriage migrants in Taiwan's citizenship regime.

Taiwan's citizenship laws have been based on the principle of *jus sanguinis*, which reflects a traditional Chinese emphasis on lineage and ancestry that privileges patrilineal descent in the tracing of one's nationality, while nationality through maternal decent is conferred as an exception (Chen 2009). Prior to changes in the Nationality Act in 2000, no foreigners could be naturalized as citizens except for women married to Taiwanese men. Female marriage migrants are considered 'naturalizable' as they are included as members of the nation via motherhood (Cheng 2013; Lan 2008).

However, in NTC discourse, their 'incapable motherhood' (Cheng 2013) became a source of national anxiety rooted in fears of their deteriorative impacts on the Taiwan's population quality. (Hsia 2007). As the wives of Taiwanese citizens, the Taiwan government could not reject their access to Taiwanese citizenship and consequently adopted a 'dual exclusion-assimilation scheme' (Cheng 2013) that aimed at increasing barriers[9] for marriage migrants to acquire citizenship and initiated programs to assimilate them into Taiwanese culture and 'improve' their 'population qualities' (Hsia 2009).

These discriminatory immigration policies assume that since marriage migrants hail from developing countries, they must lack the qualities necessary to perform motherhood (Hsia 2013; Cheng 2013). In other words, their citizenship is intertwined with their children. Hence, the granting of citizenship to marriage migrants is premised upon motherhood on one hand, while on the other hand, they are discriminated against because of their children's presumably 'inferior quality'.

Conversely, their children's citizenship is premised upon that of their mothers. As Chen (2009) argued, Taiwan's regime of citizenship draws national borders along gender lines: women who marry across national borders, female immigrants, and interethnic or mixed-race children are constantly excluded from the national community. Though the children of marriage migrants were granted Taiwanese nationality by birth through their fathers' citizenship, they were still considered inadequate and assumed to be 'developmentally delayed' because of their mothers' origins. Therefore, despite formal citizenship, children of marriage migrants lacked substantive citizenship.

To improve their 'qualities', government-initiated programs discouraged marriage migrants from bearing more children and compelled them to put their children in after-school classes regardless of their academic performance (Hsia 2007). Consequently, most children of SEA marriage migrants were not acculturated in their mothers' native languages and cultures because the assimilation scheme constrained mother-child intimacy and impeded SEA marriage migrants from passing down their cultural inheritance (Cheng 2013). Ironically, this same group of children that was portrayed as being of inferior population quality when they entered primary school has suddenly been rebranded as 'talents' and 'seeds of the New Southbound' in their early twenties. Again, this recent discursive change regarding children of SEA marriage migrants assumes maternal cultural inheritance, which is also premised upon marriage migrants' motherhood, since women are perceived as 'cultural reproducers' (Yuval-Davis and Anthias 1989).

As illustrated, neither marriage migrants nor their children in Taiwan are situated in relation to the state as individuals. While many feminist scholars (ibid.) have criticized women's motherhood as the basis for their incorporation in the nation, this paper further contends that the ways in which their children are incorporated into the nation cannot be separated from those of their mothers; that is, the citizenship of marriage migrants and that of their children are mutually premised upon each other. In other words, the state formulates policies and laws regarding marriage migrants and their children based on the consideration of 'mother-child dyad' rather than the individual-state nexus. This concept of 'mother-child dyadic citizenship' is in contrast with conceptualizations of migrants' children's citizenship in North America and the EU, which perceive these children, even those of refugees and undocumented migrants, as vulnerable victims and give a superior moral status to children, whose individuality should be ensured by the state (Doná and Veale 2011; Kronick and Rousseau 2015; Hollekim, Anderssen, and Daniel 2016).

This 'mother-child dyadic citizenship' reveals the responses of Taiwan's state, whose citizenship regime has been based on *jus sangunis*, to the influx of marriage migrants. Therefore, to further understand the formation of citizenship in the wave of marriage migration in Taiwan and other emerging immigrants-receiving countries whose traditions of citizenship are based on blood, such as South Korea and Japan, it is crucial to investigate the '*mother-child dyadic citizenship*' instead of viewing the citizenship of marriage migrants and that of their children separately.

Geopolitics of the triad of Taiwan, SEA and the PRC

As previously indicated, the current SGI discourse has in part become prevalent because Taiwan's government wishes to deepen economic ties with SEA. However, SEA's primary value to the Taiwan government is as a leverage against the PRC, which will be illustrated in the following triadic relationship between Taiwan, SEA, and the PRC.

New Southbound Policy as strategy competing with the PRC in rising ASEAN

President Tsai's declaration of the NSP revealed the DPP government's urgency to gain an advantageous position in the ASEAN region within 5 years. As pointed out by Mr. James Chih-Fang Huang, the founding Director of the Office of the NSP: '*Taiwan may only have five years of advantage . . . . If we don't grasp this opportunity now, we will not have any advantage in ASEAN.*'[10]

The economic motivation behind the NSP is clearly stated in President Tsai's speech at the Taiwan-ASEAN Dialogue in November 2016: '*Taiwan's economic development cannot be separated from that of neighboring countries. Our economies are highly complementary . . . . Today, ASEAN is Taiwan's second biggest trade partner, and also our second biggest export market.*' However, the public rhetoric of the NSP emphasizes the so-called '*people-centered concept*' as Director Huang differentiated the NSP from the GSP: '*The New Southbound Policy is not a policy with the goal of certain numbers in trade. Rather, it is a new foreign economic strategy based on a people-centered concept . . . actively promoting mutual exchange and collaboration between Taiwan and ASEAN as well as South Asian countries in the fields of talents, industries, educational investment, cultures, tourism, agriculture, etc. We hope to build new partnerships with ASEAN and South Asian countries in the 21st century . . . . Not only do we go to ASEAN and South Asia, but we also hope that their people come to Taiwan as tourists and investors*'.

One of the reasons why the NSP is 'people-centered' is that many Taiwanese enterprises in SEA rely on employees from the PRC rather than from Taiwan. According to Director Huang, '*There are 6,400 Taiwanese enterprises in Vietnam, which create millions of job opportunities in Vietnam annually. However, these 6,400 Taiwanese enterprises employ 80,000 mainland Chinese staff ... Taiwanese businessmen also face problems identifying successors and lacking managerial staff*'. Moreover, since Taiwan's domestic market is limited, the NSP targets SEA as an extension of Taiwan's domestic market; solidifying this link would require significantly more personnel. As Director Huang pointed out, '*the cultivation of talents*' is the key to '*link to ASEAN and South Asian countries*', which will solve '*all the problems about the industries*'. This so-called people-centered concept highlights the need for 'personnel' and 'staff' for Taiwanese businesses in SEA, implying a utilitarian rather than humanist perception of people. Within the NSP framework, SGI are perceived as instrumental tools for Taiwanese business expansion rather than as citizens entitled to the state's good-faith efforts to reach their fullest potential, including nurturing cultural inheritance from their Southeast Asian mothers.

The NSP is also political. At her welcome remarks at the 2016 Taiwan-ASEAN Dialogue, whose guests of honor included former ASEAN Secretary General Ambassador Surin Pitsuwan and members of parliament from ASEAN nations, President Tsai elaborated on the two levels of the objective of expanding two-way exchanges:

> On the governmental level, we will push for closer interactions betweengovernment departments and mutual visits by senior officials .... On the societal level, we are already making progress. ... Right after we simplified visa applications for ASEAN citizens, more than 120,000 ASEAN visitors came to Taiwan this September .... So, we are making strides on our second objective and foresee that two-way exchanges will continue to expand at a brisk and steady pace.

While President Tsai mentioned twice that exchanges at the societal level have been significantly increasing, her emphasis was indeed on the governmental level, especially concerning mutual visits by *senior* officials. As a result of the tension between Taiwan and the PRC, Taiwan is not a member of the U.N., and it is almost impossible to arrange for visits of high-ranking officials from most countries. From the welcome speech at this 2016 Dialogue and the list of invited guests of honor, the political motivation behind the NSP to compete with the PRC was revealed.

Go South Policy as strategy against a rising PRC

The NSP was not the first policy adopted by the Taiwanese government to compete with the PRC. At the beginning of capital flight in the 1980s, most Taiwanese businesses turned to the PRC to take advantage of lower labor costs and linguistic and cultural affinity. To confront the PRC's rising power as a 'world's factory' that was siphoning off Taiwanese investors, President Lee Teng-hui (KMT), the first President born in Taiwan and nicknamed as 'Godfather of Taiwan's independence,' launched the GSP in 1993, providing incentives for Taiwanese businessmen to invest in SEA instead of the PRC (Huang and Chou 2014).

The original GSP was designed for only one three-year term, but due to the expansion of ASEAN, the policy was extended for two more terms to 2002. President Chen Shui-bian, the first non-KMT (DPP) President, was elected in 2000 and renewed the GSP in July 2002 to continue efforts to divert Taiwanese investment from the PRC during his presidency (2000–2008). During the presidency of KMT's Ma Ying-jeou (2008–2016), the policy content remained similar but was not named 'Go South' focusing instead on trade and investment to downplay political tones and maintain a friendlier relationship with the PRC (ibid.).

In addition to the GSP, President Lee's Administration initiated a 'labor-import policy' of recruiting blue-collar migrant workers from SEA to discourage Taiwan-to-PRC capital flight (Tseng 2004). As economic relations between Taiwan and SEA developed, the number of marriage migrants from SEA increased significantly in the 1990s (Hsia 2004).

In response to the increasing number of working-class people from SEA, including marriage migrants and migrant workers, the MOI drafted the Immigration Policy Guidelines in 2003 under the presidency of Chen Shui-bian, which clearly stated that to enhance Taiwan's competitiveness, the government should create incentives for a 'high quality population', meaning professional, managerial and skilled foreigners, and provide counseling and guidance to the presumably low-quality foreign brides already living in Taiwan. The Guidelines also stipulated that blue-collar migrant workers from SEA were not allowed to apply for permanent residency and naturalization. Additionally, as previously mentioned, the government established more barriers for marriage migrants to obtain citizenship and adopted programs aiming to improve the quality of their children.

Interestingly, these measures were adopted after President Chen's renewal of the GSP in July 2002, indicating that during this phase of the GSP, SEA was still perceived as the 'inferior other', and the GSP existed only to take advantage of cheaper labor and resources in SEA. The people of the Southeast Asian countries were not considered to have the 'quality' to become one of 'superior us' and thus must be excluded from full integration (like the blue-collared migrant workers), while the quality of those who could not be excluded (i.e. marriage migrants and NTC) had to be brought closer to our 'superior quality'.

However, though the government has attempted to attract foreign investors and professionals to become Taiwanese citizens through schemes such as allowing high-level professionals to apply for permanent residency in the 2002 Amendments to the Immigration Act, the number of these so-called 'high quality' foreigners obtaining Taiwanese citizenship has been extremely limited. According to the Assessment Report on Our Government's Immigration Policy and Institutions conducted by the Control Yuan[11] in the 2003–2004 period, one of the weaknesses needing correction was the '*lack of incentives to attract excellent professional talent*'.[12]

The main reason why high-level professionals or investors had little interest in obtaining Taiwanese citizenship is the requirement to renounce their original nationality as stipulated in the Nationality Act. As Tseng (1997) argued, in the global immigration market where nation-states are competing to attract potential business immigrants, the price of the rights of residency/citizenship depends on the position of the host country in the world system. Because Taiwan's position in the world system is not particularly high for its citizenship to be considered a privilege to highly skilled, educated, and wealthy people, the requirement to renounce their original nationality has made Taiwan much less competitive in the global immigration market; only marriage migrants from less developed countries would renounce their original nationalities to become naturalized Taiwanese citizens. This barrier for so-called 'high quality' foreigners to become Taiwanese citizens was removed in amendments to the Nationality Act at the end of 2016, soon after President Tsai launched the NSP.

Southeast Asia as Taiwan's leverage against the PRC

While both NSP and GSP appear as policies towards SEA, their ultimate objective is to respond to the impending threat of the PRC. Unlike studies on geopolitics and immigration discourses that reveal bilateral relations between the host country and specific sending country or area (e.g. between the U.S. and the Middle East), this paper shows that the PRC is the true driver behind Taiwan's immigration discourse on SEA. SEA has been utilized by Taiwan's government as leverage against the PRC. Therefore, to understand immigration discourses on SEA marriage migrants and their children, it is crucial that they be contextualized within the triad of Taiwan, SEA and the PRC.

SEA is perceived as an economic option for Taiwan to reduce its reliance on the PRC market. Significantly, the fact that ASEAN Plus Three (the PRC, South Korea and Japan) enhanced the relationship between ASEAN and the PRC also meant that if Taiwan failed to put a foot in the door, it would both end up reliant on the PRC market and also lose ASEAN markets. In addition to these economic incentives, there is a political reason behind the NSP and the GSP: to improve diplomatic relations with ASEAN countries to counter PRC's 'One China Policy'.

Consequently, in the context of implementing the NSP, a drastic discursive shift occurred: the 'social problems' (low quality 'foreign brides' and NTC) suddenly became 'social assets' (new immigrants and SGI with the advantage of Southeast Asian cultures and languages). The PRC and ASEAN countries have moved upward in the World System while Taiwan's economy has been stagnant and even regressed, so SEA citizens can no longer be considered the 'inferior other' that would cause deterioration of Taiwan's population quality. On the contrary, as President Tsai stated in her speech at the Taiwan-ASEAN Dialogue, 'ASEAN is Taiwan's second biggest trade partner and second biggest export market;' Southeast Asian citizens are now perceived as 'new partners' whom Taiwan should win over in order to help fight the 'evil other', the PRC. President Tsai emphasized this attempt in her speech: 'Taiwan is an important member of the Asia-Pacific region. We have a responsibility to contribute to regional peace, stability and prosperity. We fully embrace our role, and as ASEAN embarks on further integration, Taiwan will be a most reliable partner for ASEAN on this journey'.

Previously, under Chiang Kai-shek's regime in the Cold War structure, the PRC had been constructed as evil communists whose people suffered from poverty and oppression. With the rise of the PRC as one of the fastest growing economies in the world, Taiwan's prosperity-based national identity has been so shattered that the discourse has been thoroughly revised: although the PRC is becoming wealthy, it is portrayed as a vicious giant bullying its neighbors, while Taiwan is still 'morally' superior because of its proclaimed principles of freedom, democracy, and human rights. The aim of constructing Taiwan as a friendly partner and good neighbor in the region, in contrast to the

PRC, the unsaid yet most crucial subject, was revealed in President Tsai's speech where she proclaimed Taiwan as the '*most reliable partner for ASEAN*' and assumed responsibility to contribute to '*regional peace*'.

The emerging consumer citizenship underlying the incongruence between immigration discourse and laws

In light of the zeal evident in promoting the NSP, it is especially ironic that laws regulating SEA marriage migrants have tightened. This incongruence between immigration discourse and immigration law is particularly clear in the 2016 Amendments to the Nationality Act, signed soon after President Tsai launched the NSP.

One major amendment is that high-level professional foreigners can now obtain Taiwanese citizenship without renouncing their original nationality. Nevertheless, SEA marriage migrants remain required to renounce their original nationality for naturalization. More ironically, Article 19 of the 2016 Amendments even holds marriage migrants under the life-long threat of statelessness because after renouncing their original nationality, their hard-earned Taiwanese citizenship can be revoked anytime in their life if their marriage to a Taiwanese citizen is deemed fraudulent in court. Defective documents and malicious testimony from Taiwanese spouses and in-laws could be considered evidence of 'fraudulent marriage'.

As Tseng (2006) argued, Taiwan's immigration policy is in essence 'classist' but appears as 'racialized classism' in which blue-collar Southeast Asians are classified as a cultural race that are 'incompatible' with Taiwan. However, as neoliberal globalization intensifies, the Taiwanese government has revealed straightforward classism, as vividly illustrated in the 2016 Amendments that assign more rights to the upper-class, especially the right to retain original nationality while being naturalized as Taiwanese citizens. In the promotion of the 2016 Amendments,[13] the MOI explains that the rationale of exempting 'high-level professional' foreigners from renouncing original nationality is '*to enhance competitiveness of our nation in recruiting excellent foreign talents . . . who are beneficial to our nation*'.

Furthermore, in this current dominant discourse, upper-class foreigners are perceived as not only 'superior' in terms of their economic capital, but also in terms of their 'moral capital'. As part of the immigrants' rights movement campaigning for amendments to the Nationality Act since 2012, I personally witnessed government officials and legislators from various political parties rejecting our proposed amendment to accept dual citizenship to prevent marriage migrants from becoming stateless in the process of applying naturalization. Their primary reasoning was to ensure 'loyalty' of foreigners in times of war, and hence the principle of single citizenship was non-negotiable. The 2016 Amendments allowing dual citizenship only to 'high quality' foreigners indicates the assumption that the loyalty of 'high quality' foreigners is beyond doubt, thus making them 'morally superior' to the 'low quality' foreigners, mostly marriage migrants from SEA.

Moreover, this incongruence between positive discourse on SGI and stricter immigration laws for SEA marriage migrants indicates an evolving state-citizen relationship in Taiwan. The Taiwanese government has been in increasingly urgent need of 'high population quality' to enhance its global competitiveness because it has been confronted with greater economic pressure, especially from the PRC. Previously, based on the discourse surrounding the inferior quality of Southeast Asian marriage migrants and their children, the state legitimated its exclusion of marriage migrants and blue-collar migrant workers from SEA in the name of 'protecting the public interest' of Taiwanese citizens. In other words, the goal was to prevent deteriorative impacts of inferior foreigners on our superior population quality for the sake of Taiwan's competitive advantage in the global market. In this quasi-war discourse, what was at stake was the 'quality' of the population, perceived as the weapon needed to win the war in the competitive globalized market. However, ASEAN's subsequent rise since the 2010 has made negative framing of SEA marriage migrants and their children untenable. At the same time, the PRC began expanding its influence in SEA, so the Taiwanese government shifted to utilizing SGI in an attempt to link with SEA. Ironically, while the recent 'social assets' discourse apparently contradicts the previous 'social problems' discourse, the Taiwanese government has never publicly acknowledged its mistakes in previous policies regarding NTC.

Without reflecting on this contradiction, the state apparatus appears to be a *corporate-like* entity whose ultimate objective is to advance its competitiveness in the global economy rather than ensuring equality and justice for all citizens, including marriage migrants and their children. In turn, citizens have assumed a *consumer-like* status by merely demanding that the state (the corporation) ensure the 'quality' of the 'commodities' they purchase (Hsia 2015) (e.g. migrant women as reproducers of citizens and SGI as personnel working for Taiwanese companies in the ASEAN) rather than exercising their rights and responsibilities to hold the state accountable for providing welfare and advancing equality and justice.

For instance, in late 2020, a small group of SGI held a public protest when they learned of the NIA's plan to reduce the number of marriage migrants and SGI in the Committee governing the Fund. The Quarterly issued by an NGO active in marriage migrant and SGI issues published an article by an SGI leader in that protest. Since this Quarterly has been sponsored by the Fund, this NGO was required to make a mid-term report to the Committee. At the Committee meeting, the SGI editor of the Quarterly was scolded by an NIA senior staff, the key person administrating the Fund: 'The Fund has fed you large herd of new immigrants and SGI. We fund you, yet you published such an article agreeing with its criticism against us'.[14] The SGI editor was threatened that 'the final payment of this Quarterly will be retained if your mistakes are not corrected'.

The government's perception of citizens as consumers is justified by intensifying globalization. As a result of increasingly volatile economic development, the skills and human resources in highest demand today can soon become obsolete, leading individuals and countries to lose competitiveness in the global market. To attract global financial capital, the state must be able to quickly deploy the most competitive expertise and skills. In turn, the governors of the state apparatus have essentially become 'CEO' of the corporation (Hsia 2015). To maintain corporate advantage in the global market, the CEO must dispatch any personnel in need, such as SGI needed to help Taiwan's business expansion in the ASEAN. The government, as the CEO, can thus legitimate its endeavors to employ all means to recruit 'high quality' foreigners, including amending immigration laws, without apprehension of criticism by citizens. When the 2016 Amendments confronted a series of protests by NGOs regarding Article 19, the government did not respond. It was only until the passing of the amendments that the MOI issued a PowerPoint presentation promoting the 2016 Amendments on its Facebook Page that emphasized in one slide: '*Procedural Justice exists: difficult to revoke certification of naturalization*'. Instead of responding to NGOs' criticism of injustice, the MOI merely perfunctorily mentioned the difficulty in revoking nationality.

This emerging state–citizen relationship as one of corporation-consumer echoes the 'consumer citizenship' concept formulated by Turner (2017), who argued that the state has withdrawn from its commitment to full employment and the provision of social security, while civil society has been eroded under neoliberal globalization. With the emphasis on individualism and privatization, citizens have increasingly become consumers exercising individual choices in a society dominated by the market and commercial values.

Consumer citizenship has emerged strongly in Taiwan, as the state has not been held accountable for previous discriminatory policies and laws. Moreover, in Taiwan's case, the state's retreat from accountability and push toward prioritizing class-based immigration policies have been further justified by the long-term rivalry with the PRC. As the PRC continues to grow as the world's top economic power, Taiwan's prosperity-based sense of superiority relative to the PRC can no longer be sustained; consequently, Taiwan's government has attempted to construct Taiwan as the 'morally superior' alternative to the PRC in the region. In this new framing of Taiwan as the PRC's moral superior, SGI are utilized not only as cultural ambassadors to build bridges with SEA but also as showcases of Taiwan's adherence to multiculturalism and human rights as opposed to the PRC's ethno-nationalism and authoritarianism. Consequently, the state cannot afford to admit and apologize for previous discriminatory policies. In order to quickly mobilize an army of such 'cultural ambassadors', Taiwan's government employed and reinforced the frame of mother–child dyadic citizenship by constructing SGI as citizens already equipped with SEA cultures and languages. With such a utilitarian image of SGI in Taiwan's urgent competition against the PRC, the resources recently allotted to promote cultural inheritance from SEA marriage migrants to their children are perceived as a favor bestowed by the government rather than an entitlement the government is obligated to ensure.

Conclusion

Marriage migration has been significant in East Asia for more than two decades, and changing discourses on marriage migrants and their children need to be examined from a temporal perspective. By investigating discursive shifts regarding SEA marriage migrants and their children in Taiwan, this paper proposes a concept of '*mother-child dyadic citizenship*' and argues that the citizenship of marriage migrants and that of their children are mutually premised. As a state whose traditional citizenship laws have been based on blood, when confronted with a strong wave of marriage immigration, Taiwan's governments employ the 'mother-child dyad', not the individual-state nexus, to frame policies regulating SEA marriage migrants and their children (Figure 1).

As shown in the framework, the discursive shift in the children of SEA marriage migrants has resulted from the *dual* impacts of mother-child dyadic citizenship and the geopolitics of the Taiwan, SEA, and PRC triad. By expanding Taiwanese business presence and improving diplomatic relations with ASEAN countries to rival the PRC,

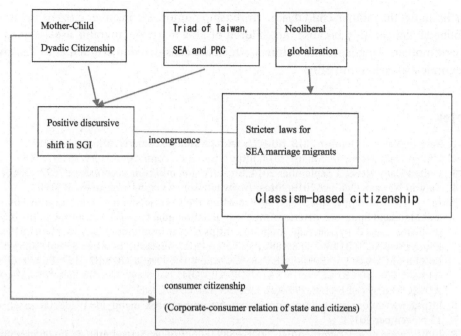

Figure 1. Analytical Framework of the Discursive Shift in the Children of SEA Marriage Migrants in Taiwan

the NSP attempts to mobilize children of SEA marriage migrants by leveraging their presumed cultural inheritance from their mothers; consequently, a positive discourse on SGI and their Southeast Asian mothers has emerged in contrast with the previous negative discourse on NTC, who had not been acculturated to their mothers' original language and culture because of severe discrimination. The current positive discourse is merely a tactic under the NSP that uses SEA as a leverage against the PRC in response to regional geopolitical dynamics.

This recent shift to positive discourse regarding SGI ironically coexists with the tightening of immigration laws regulating SEA marriage migrants. The ideology embedded in the 2016 Amendments to the Nationality Act is classism, which assigns more rights to upper-class foreigners than to SEA marriage migrants, who are mostly from the lower-class. While Taiwanese immigration policy has been loaded with 'racialized classism', recent changes in immigration laws reveal that the underlying ideology has become straightforward classism.

The contradiction between positive immigration discourse and discriminatory laws has not received much criticism from civil society. Without reflection on this contradiction, the state–citizen relationship has evolved into a corporate-consumer relationship within which the state is not held accountable for equality and justice, while resources provided to citizens, including SGI and their mothers, are perceived as favors bestowed by the state rather than entitlements. With this emerging framework of 'consumer citizenship', the positive discursive shift is taken for granted while the government evades the responsibility to publicly acknowledge mistakes when formulating discriminatory policies and laws regulating NTC and their Southeast Asian mothers. This evasion of governmental responsibilities has been justified by the long-term rivalry with the PRC.

Furthermore, the mother-child dyadic citizenship reinforces consumer citizenship under neoliberal globalization because the children of SEA marriage migrants are assumed to inherit mothers' languages and cultures, which are considered instrumental to Taiwan's economic expansion into SEA.

Notes

1. Taiwan News, 8 October 2018, https://www.taiwannews.com.tw/en/news/3547755
2. United Daily News, 18 August 2014, http://vision.udn.com/vision/story/7689/735688
3. United Daily News, 1 September 2014, https://vision.udn.com/vision/story/7697/735624
4. Taiwan News, 7 October 2019, https://www.taiwannews.com.tw/ch/news/3791900
5. In MOI's 2013 report titled 'Special Report on the Counselling and Education of Foreign and Mainland Spouses,' 'deteriorating the population quality' was listed as one of the major problems caused by marriage migrants. https://www.immigration.gov.tw/media/5194/% E5%A4%96%E7%B1%8D%E8%88%87%E5%A4%A7%E9%99%B8%E9%85%8D%E5%81% B6%E8%BC%94%E5%B0%8E%E8%88%87%E6%95%99%E8%82%B2%E5%B0%88%E6% A1%88%E5%A0%B1%E5%91%8A-92%E5%B9%B412%E6%9C%8823%E6%97%A5%E8% A1%8C%E6%94%BF%E9%99%A2%E9%99%A2%E6%9C%83.odt
6. https://www.moea.gov.tw/mns/otn_e/content/Content.aspx?menu_id=19288 (accessed on 13 November 2017)
7. https://www.ey.gov.tw/otnen/64C34DCA8893B06/9c560855-1ecd-4f58-9c3f-c065d9e58f89 (accessed on 18 January 2019)
8. https://english.president.gov.tw/NEWS/5022 (accessed on 10 January 2020)
9. Including language requirements, nationality test, financial requirements, etc.
10. Central News Agency, 17 May 2016. http://www.chinatimes.com/realtimenews/ 20160517003417-260407
11. An independent investigatory and auditory agency of the government.
12. http://www.cy.gov.tw/AP_HOME/op_Upload/eDoc/%E5%85%AC%E5%A0%B1/96/ 0960000192588_%E5%85%A7%E6%96%87(%E7%80%8F%E8%A6%BD%E7%94%A8). pdf□(accessed on 6 October 2017)
13. https://www.facebook.com/moi.gov.tw/posts/1477223388972726   (accessed   on 10 January 2021)
14. Notes of the SGI editor shared to the author.

Disclosure statement

No potential conflict of interest was reported by the author(s).

References

Chen, C.-J. 2009. "Gendered Borders: The Historical Formation of Women's Nationality under Law in Taiwan." *Positions* 17 (2): 289–314. doi:10.1215/10679847-2009-003.

Cheng, I. 2013. "Making Foreign Women the Mother of Our Nation: The Exclusion and Assimilation of Immigrant Women in Taiwan." *Asian Ethnicity* 14 (2): 157–179. doi:10.1080/14631369.2012.759749.

Dempsey, K., and S. McDowell. 2019. "Disaster Depictions and Geopolitical Representations in Europe's Migration 'Crisis'." *Geoforum* 98: 153–160. doi:10.1016/j.geoforum.2018.11.008.

Doná, G., and A. Veale. 2011. "Divergent Discourses, Children and Forced Migration." *Journal of Ethnic and Migration Studies* 37 (8): 1273–1289. doi:10.1080/1369183X.2011.590929.

Fairclough, N. 1995. *Critical Discourse Analysis.* London: Longman.

Fung, H., and T. P. Wang. 2014. "Vietnamese Marriage Migrants and the Changing Public Discourse in Taiwan." In *The Age of Asian Migration: Continuity, Diversity, and Susceptibility (Volume One),* edited by Y. W. Chan, D. Haines, and J. Lee, 211–242. Newcastle upon Tyne, UK: Cambridge Scholars Publishing.

Hollekim, R., N. Anderssen, and M. Daniel. 2016. "Contemporary Discourses on Children and Parenting in Norway: Norwegian Child Welfare Services Meets Immigrant Families." *Children and Youth Services Review* 60: 52–60. doi:10.1016/j.childyouth.2015.11.004.

Horiguchi, S., and Y. Imoto. 2016. "Historicizing Mixed-Race Representations in Japan: From Politicization to Identity Formation." In *Multiculturalism in East Asia: A Transnational Exploration of Japan, South Korea and Taiwan,* edited by K. Iwabuchi, H. M. Kim, and H.-C. Hsia, 163–182. London: Rowman & Littlefield International.

Hsia, H.-C. 2004. "Internationalization of Capital and the Trade in Asian Women—The Case of 'Foreign Brides' in Taiwan." In *Women and Globalization,* edited by D. Aguilar and A. Lacsamana, 181–229. Amherst: Humanity Press.

Hsia, H.-C. 2007. "Imaged and Imagined Threat to the Nation: The Media Construction of 'Foreign Brides' Phenomenon as Social Problems in Taiwan." *Inter-Asia Cultural Studies* 8 (1): 55–85. doi:10.1080/14649370601119006.

Hsia, H.-C. 2009. "Foreign Brides, Multiple Citizenship and Immigrant Movement in Taiwan." *Asia and the Pacific Migration Journal* 18 (1): 17–46. doi:10.1177/011719680901800102.

Hsia, H.-C., and H. L. Huang. 2010. "Taiwan." In *For Better or for Worse: Comparative Research on Equity and Access for Marriage Migrants,* edited by H.-C. Hsia, 27–73. Hong Kong: Asia Pacific Mission for Migrants.

Hsia, H.-C. 2013. "The Tug of War over Multiculturalism: Contestation between Governing and Empowering Immigrants in Taiwan." In *Migration and Diversity in Asian Contexts,* edited by L. A. Eng, F. L. Collins, and B. Yeoh, 130–149. Singapore: Institute of Southeast Asian Studies Publishing.

Hsia, H.-C. 2015. "Reproduction Crisis, Illegality, and Migrant Women under Capitalist Globalization: The Case of Taiwan." In *Migrant Encounters: Intimate Labor, the State and Mobility across Asia,* edited by S. Friedman and P. Mahdavi, 160–183. Philadelphia: University of Pennsylvania Press.

Hsia, H.-C. 2019. "Praxis-Oriented Research for the Building of Grounded Transnational Marriage Migrant Movements in Asia." In *Research, Peasant and Urban Poor Activisms in the Americas and Asia,* edited by D. Kappor and S. Jordan, 248–269. London: ZED Books.

Huang, K.-B., and R.-H. Chou. 2014. "The Retrospect and Influence of Taiwan's 'Southward Policy'." *Prospect & Exploration* 12 (8): 61–69. (in Chinese).

Hyndman, J. 2012. "The Geopolitics of Migration and Mobility." *Geopolitics* 17 (2): 243–255. doi:10.1080/14650045.2011.569321.

Kronick, R., and C. Rousseau. 2015. "Rights, Compassion and Invisible Children: A Critical Discourse Analysis of the Parliamentary Debates on the Mandatory Detention of Migrant Children in Canada." *Journal of Refugee Studies* 28(4), 1–26.

Lan, P.-C. 2008. "Migrant Women's Bodies as Boundary Markers: Reproductive Crisis and Sexual Control in the Ethnic Frontiers of Taiwan." *Signs* 33 (4): 833–861. doi:10.1086/528876.

Lee, M.-H., and H.-C. Chueh. 2018. "The Image of the 'New Second Generation' in Taiwan's Mainstream Newspapers." *Communication, Culture and Politics* 7: 133–174. (in Chinese).

Mamadouh, V. 2012. "The Scaling of the 'Invasion': A Geopolitics of Immigration Narratives in France and the Netherlands." *Geopolitics* 17 (2): 377–401. doi:10.1080/14650045.2011.578268.

Nagel, C. R. 2002. "Geopolitics by Another Name: Immigration and the Politics of Assimilation." *Political Geography* 21 (2002): 971–987. doi:10.1016/S0962-6298(02)00087-2.

Nakamatsu, T. 2005. "Faces of "Asian Brides": Gender, Race, and Class in the Representations of Immigrant Women in Japan." *Women's Studies International Forum* 28 (5): 405–417. doi:10.1016/j.wsif.2005.05.003.

Shin, J. 2019. "The Vortex of Multiculturalism in South Korea: A Critical Discourse Analysis of the Characterization of 'Multicultural Children' in Three Newspapers." *Communication and Critical/Cultural Studies* 16: 61–81. doi:10.1080/14791420.2019.1590612.

Tseng, Y.-F. 1997. "Commodification of Residency: An Analysis of Taiwan's Business Immigration." *Taiwan: A Radical Quarterly in Social Studies* 27: 37–67. (in Chinese).

Tseng, Y.-F. 2004. "Politics of Importing Foreigners: Taiwan's Foreign Labor Policy." In *Migration between States and Markets*, edited by H. B. Entzinger, M. Martiniello, and C. Wihtol de Wenden, 101–120. Burlington, VT: Ashgate.

Tseng, Y.-F. 2006. "Who Can Be Us? Class Selection in Immigration Policy." *Taiwan: A Radical Quarterly in Social Studies* 61: 73–107. (in Chinese).

Turner, B. S. 2017. "Contemporary Citizenship: Four Types." *Journal of Citizenship and Globalization Studies* 1 (1): 10–23. doi:10.1515/jcgs-2017-0002.

Yuval-Davis, N., and F. Anthias. 1989. *Woman-Nation-State*. London: Macmillan.

Motherhood, empowerment and contestation: the act of citizenship of Vietnamese immigrant activists in the realm of the new southbound policy

Isabelle Cheng

ABSTRACT

This paper focuses on how immigrant activists interact with the host state in socio-political spheres where they exercise their citizenship. Located in Taiwan's New Southbound Policy (NSP), this paper adopts the concept of 'act of citizenship' to analyse Vietnamese activists' interactions with the NSP. This paper finds that the NSP appropriated immigrant women's motherhood and family relationships in order to boost tourism and facilitate Southeast Asian language acquisition in the short term and to enhance Taiwan's relationship with Southeast Asia in the long run. In response, immigrant activists utilised the NSP to build their own capacity and to realise their acts of empowerment, compassion and contestation in the family and public domains. They not only improved individuals' wellbeing but also made the Taiwanese state accountable for gender bias and inequality. These findings offer a much needed gender perspective into immigrant activists' dialectical relationship with the migration state of Taiwan.

Introduction

Since the mid-1990s, Taiwan has featured as a major destination in East Asia for Southeast Asian women seeking marriage with local citizens. When their number rose rapidly in the early 2000s, there were concerns that they would pose challenges to Taiwan's ethnic composition, as indicated by the National Security Report (National Security Council (NSC) 2006, 61-62). More than a decade later, with the launch of the New Southbound Policy (NSP) in August 2016, the women's relationship with the Taiwanese state was reframed. They are now not only encouraged to maintain close contact with their natal families in Southeast Asia but are also imagined as being able to pass down their cultural and linguistic heritage to their mixed children in Taiwan. Thus, instead of being dismissed as 'private', 'domestic', 'local', or 'trivial' (Enloe 2014, 3), relationships amongst the women, their natal families and their mixed children, particularly mother–child intimacy as experienced through language and cultures, become political economic assets to be exploited by the Taiwanese state. If migration policy is a sphere in which the structure of gender, ethnicity and class is institutionalised, then the NSP renders itself a fluid socio-political sphere where immigrant women's everyday practices are positively viewed by the state for their potential political utility.

Answering Piper's call to explore immigrant women's citizenship through their struggle in socio-political spheres (2008, 251), this paper explores how Southeast Asian women exercise their citizenship in the dynamic socio-political sphere constructed by the NSP. In the early 2000s, when the stigmatisation of marriage migration reached a new height, as reflected by the low public support for granting immigrant spouses citizenship (Chen and Yu 2005), immigrant activists participated in the campaign led by local activists to end the denunciation of immigrant women and reform the exclusionary citizenship legislation (Hsia 2009). More than a decade later, with most immigrant women who arrived in Taiwan in the early 2000s having acquired citizenship, the NSP's reframing opportunely facilitates a socio-political sphere in which immigrant activists may exercise their citizenship. Thus, this paper raises two questions. First, how does a host state appropriate immigrants' family – and particularly mother–child – relationships to implement its public policy? Second, how do immigrant activists interact with the state and enable the acts of empowerment, compassion and contestation? As the Taiwan–Vietnam relationship has grown considerably in three decades and Vietnamese women have become a major presence in the Southeast Asian community, this paper utilises the experiences of Vietnamese activists as a case study.

This paper presents rich findings to answer these two significant questions. For the first question, this paper shows that the NSP instrumentalises Southeast Asian women's roles as transnational daughter and mother. Specifically, by sponsoring children to visit their mothers' hometowns, the NSP seeks to use their family ties and motherhood to contribute, in the long run, to enhancing the relationship between Taiwan and Southeast Asia. Capitalising on immigrant women's cultural and linguistic heritage, the NSP uses these resources to raise Southeast Asian language proficiency in Taiwan and boost tourism from Southeast Asia. To answer the second question, this paper regards the activists' interactions with the NSP as their 'act of citizenship' (Isin 2007, 2009, 2017), a concept that conceptualises the exercise of citizenship as a dynamic enactment of citizenship in socio-political struggles wherein an immigrant becomes a rights claimant *in relation to* other actors. In this vein, this paper finds that Vietnamese activists utilised the NSP's funding and the legitimacy derived from its endorsement of Southeast Asian cultures to support the empowerment of and compassion for immigrant spouses, mixed children and migrant workers. In doing so, the private family domain became one of the sites of their act of citizenship. Beyond helping individuals in need on a personal scale, they not only contested the NSP's blindness to gender bias throughout the family domain and the labour market but also its lack of due diligence over migrant workers' rights. By examining their empowerment, compassion and contestation, this paper offers a critical and relational understanding of citizenship from a much needed gender perspective.

Marriage migration, gender and 'act of citizenship'

Marriage migration in East Asia is not only *feminised* because women outnumber men as migrant spouses, but the phenomenon is also *gendered* (Hugo 2005; Jones and Shen 2008; Bélanger and Linh 2011; Kim 2012). In particular, immigrant women's citizenship is gendered on many fronts, as revealed in the growing scholarship on the relationship between women's socio-biological reproduction and the host state's nation-building. Their foreignness is either the target of assimilation or the marker that contrasts the state's multicultural credibility (Bélanger 2007; Sheu 2007; Wang and Bélanger 2008; Kim 2009, 2013; Cheng 2013; Lan 2019). When citizenship stands for a group of rights that enables women to exercise agency, the notion of 'political motherhood' (Schirmer 1993; Werbner 1999) sheds light on the effect of women's caring, compassion and responsibility in the political domain. 'Political motherhood' becomes a *practice* undertaken by Indonesian mothers who assert their mixed children's right to inherit Indonesian nationality (Winarnita 2008), by foreign mothers in Malaysia who demand their right to citizenship in view of their parenting duties and thus contribution to Malaysian families (Chin 2017), and by immigrant women in Taiwan who vote and engage in community work in order to ensure their children's future (Cheng 2017). Scholarship on the effect of citizenship in facilitating integration has also given attention to immigrant women's participation in civil organisations, advocacy work and in rights-claim movements aimed at changing public discourse or reforming migration legislation (Lee 2003; Kim and Shin 2018; Choo 2016, 2017; Tsai and Hsiao 2006; Hsia 2009; Lin, J. H. Lin 2018a; Chang 2020). These studies also caution that when offering counselling or implementing integration programmes, service-providing organisations may deepen the internalisation of gender values amongst immigrant participants (Choo 2017; Lin 2018b; Chang 2020). Yet, such literature also points up the fact that immigrant women may become their own agents in negotiating the host state's gendering schemes (Kim and Shin 2018).

This reservoir of research on marriage migration linking gender and citizenship prompts us to explore how citizenship is experienced by women in the roles of daughters, wives, mothers and daughters-in-law at different levels: at the micro level through their daily experiences; at the community level with regard to their integration; and at the state level as part of a nation-building project. The convergence between their private family relationship and their public participation suggests that their exercise of citizenship is *relational* to their roles as mothers, wives, daughters-in-law and citizens vis-à-vis their in-laws and the host state.

To understand how immigrant women position themselves in relation to both the public and private spheres, this paper adopts the concept of 'act of citizenship' advocated by Isin (2007, 2009, 2017). In order to reposition the study of citizenship away from the dichotomy that regards citizenship as either status or habitus (Isin 2007, 16) (or status and practice, as in Isin 2009, 369), Isin proposes the concept of 'act of citizenship' to meet the growing interest in understanding citizenship. globalisation, colonialism, nationalism and the welfare state slot the subjects of citizenship into the silos of insiders (citizens), strangers (women and blacks who are seen as lacking capacity), outsiders (migrants and refugees who are disposable or deportable) and aliens (terrorists or enemy combatants who are rejected for citizenship). These silos are created by the state's measurement of their permissibility for citizenship (Isin 2007, 16, 2017, 503–505); that measurement results in the formation of a web of rights and responsibilities that are conferred on them or withdrawn from them (Isin 2007, 15). However, maintaining these silos presupposes the existence of citizenship as a fixed entity. Failing to view citizenship beyond the silos overlooks not only the subjects' challenge to the rights and responsibilities assigned to them by the state, but also their socio-political struggles that contest the thoughts and conduct habitually associated with citizenship (Isin 2017, 501–502). If viewed through their contestation of who is eligible for what kind of rights, we will not only see how the subjects of citizenship exercise their rights, but, more importantly, how, *across* the silos, different subjects make claims to these rights. Therefore, as urged by Isin, our focus should be on those 'acts through which subjects transform themselves into citizens' (Isin 2007, 18), whereby they define their relation to each other. That is, through these acts, they may offer solidarity with, or condone antagonism towards or alienation of, people in different silos. When focusing on their acts, Isin argues that it is necessary to also probe the 'site' (the fields where the contestation takes place and issues, interests and stakes congregate) and 'scale' (the scope appropriate to the contestation) whereby their acts may 'creatively transform' the meanings and functions of citizenship (Isin 2017, 501).

For this paper, applying 'act of citizenship' as proposed above will yield a fruitful investigation of immigrant activists' exercise of citizenship in the realm of the NSP. This investigation will elucidate what they *do* with their citizenship (their acts) in different 'sites', such as family, civil organisations, or elsewhere, as emerging from their interactions with the NSP. Focusing on their struggles will show how they conduct their acts of empowerment, compassion and contestation in their different roles *along their life course* (daughter, wife, mother, daughter-in-law, worker, citizens), across silos (immigrant spouses, migrant workers) and on different scales (individual, community, societal, state). It will highlight how they make claims to their rights and the rights denied to migrant workers. In all, this investigation will generate a dynamic and relational understanding of their exercise of citizenship.

Research methods

Using government briefs released between 2016 and 2017, this paper demonstrates how the NSP promoted 'people-centred' interactions between Taiwan and Southeast Asia in the realms of mixed children's 'root-seeking', language acquisition and tourism. These materials are published by the Executive Yuan, the Legislative Yuan, the Control Yuan, the Office of Trade Negotiation (OTN), the Ministry of Education (MoE) and the Ministry of Transport and Communication (MoTC).

In order to investigate how immigrant activists interacted with the NSP from the bottom up, this study draws on interviews with five Vietnamese activists between April 2017 and July 2020. These activists are Trinh Minh Ha, Ly Van Trang, Ngô Xuân Phuong, Nguyễn Thị Minh Thu and Hồ Minh Mai. I also include my interview with Phạm Thanh Van in 2009 for her experience as an interpreter employed by a service-providing civil organisation founded and staffed by local Taiwanese. I refer to them by Vietnamese pseudonyms not only to conceal their identity but more out of respect for their in-between identity that belongs to both Vietnam and Taiwan. Some contextual information is concealed to further protect their identity.

I have maintained a long standing relationship with them through in-person meetings, texting and emailing in spoken and written Chinese since 2009. During our long association, I observed how they exercised their agency and overcame structural constraints of hardship and stigmatisation. Fluent in Mandarin, and having acquired a public role, they became immigrant leaders in their respective localities, whilst remaining true to their identities as daughters, wives, mothers and daughters-in-law. This gender identity forms the basis of their public acts, whereas motherhood is their guiding morality. Humbled by their struggles and knowing the emotive power of their experiences to inspire others, this paper uses their experiences as a case study, which is grounded on the commonality between them and other Vietnamese activists as well as on their niche development trajectories. As detailed in the following pages, one commonality is their *rite of passage* from being young wives/mothers to becoming experienced activists, equipped with civic skills, Chinese language proficiency and social capital. Reflecting their networking and vision, their unique trajectories demonstrate how they utilised resources derived from the NSP for their acts to both empower and care for immigrant spouses, mixed children and migrant workers.

Stereotyping Southeast Asian women and their children

When the NSP was announced in August 2016, a total of 140,941 women from Southeast Asia resided in Taiwan with the status of local citizen's spouses. Constituting more than 93% of the population of all foreign wives residing in Taiwan, they included 94,477 Vietnamese, 28,338 Indonesian, 7,992 Filipino, 5,852 Thai, and 4,282 Cambodian (National Immigration Agency (NIA) 2016). Up to 2015, there were a total of 112,729 children born to foreign-born mothers (Department of Household Registration n.d.), the great majority of whom were Southeast Asian women, with the Vietnamese being the largest group, as shown above.

Public discourse surrounding marriage migration from Southeast Asia to Taiwan was typified by the stigmatisation of migrant women and their children. Stereotyped as 'Foreign Brides' who barter marriage via commercial matchmaking for escape from poverty (Wang and Chang 2002; Wang 2007, 715–716; cf. Tseng 2015), they were seen as young and rural virgins who not only lacked education but also embodied 'back-wardness' because of the lower level of development of Southeast Asia (Wang 2010). They were perceived as victims suffering human trafficking or domestic abuse (Hsia 2007; Sheu 2007; Tseng 2014; cf. Wang 2007; Tang and Wang 2011). Their children were alleged to be slow or late in their development (Keng 2016). Indicating that Southeast Asian women were not 'high quality' population Taiwan needed, the security apparatus cautioned against them and their children as posing 'challenges to Taiwan's economy, society, culture and politics' (National Security Council (NSC) 2006, 61), on top of the presumption of their incompetent motherhood and their children's poor academic performance (Chin and Yu 2009). Considered a remedy to such deficiency, Chinese language proficiency was added in 2005 to the prerequisites for naturalisation. Although this requirement applies to the naturalisation of all foreign nationals, it is particularly aimed at assimilating Southeast Asian women for nation-building (Wang and Bélanger 2008; Cheng 2013; Lan 2019). Assimilation is thought to be particularly important in the private family domain, where the speaking of Southeast Asian languages is discouraged, if not completely forbidden, by Taiwanese husbands or parents-in-law (Cheng 2021a). Public discourses surrounding 'New Children of Taiwan' (Yang 2004), a label given to their children, prioritised the children's patrilineal bond with Taiwan over their matrilineal link with Southeast Asia. As such, their children were expected to identify them-selves as being rooted in Taiwan and to discard their maternal ties with Southeast Asia

(Liao and Wang 2013). As a result of protests led by the immigrants' movement, the derogatory label of 'Foreign Brides', which was at the centre of the disparaging discourse outlined above, was replaced with 'New Residents' in references to immigrant women by the media and in government pronouncements (Hsia 2009). Nevertheless, as illustrated by interviewed activists, this sort of stereotyping has lingered on in their everyday lives. Against this backdrop, as explained below, the NSP and its policy briefs have brought about a new discourse *in parallel with* this lingering stereotype.

The New Southbound Policy: 'people-centred' interactions

Announced on 16 August 2016, the NSP aims to forge 'strategic partnerships' with 16 countries in Southeast Asia and South Asia, Australia and New Zealand, partly in the hope to ride on the tide of the US's promotion of a 'Free and Open Indo-Pacific Ocean' region (Hsiao and Borsoi-Kelly 2019). Attempting to make Taiwan a global actor of regional significance, in 2017 the NSP tasked the government to collaborate with the private sector in order to contribute to agricultural development, medical and public health, industrial talent development, green energy and innovation in information and communication industry, and smart machinery for the region (Office of Trade Negotiations (OTN) 2017). Amongst the NSP's target countries, Vietnam has become a focal point. In 1993, prior to the NSP's implementation, Vietnam was the most popular destination of Taiwanese investment in Southeast Asia (Chen 1996) and, during the 2010s, was frequently mentioned in the media for its rapid economic growth (e.g. Commonwealth 2016; Global Vision 2016). After the NSP's launch, in 2017, 383,329 Vietnamese visitors entered Taiwan, an increase of 94.9% compared to the previous year (New Taipei City Government (NTCG), n.d.; News 2021). In 2018, with 12,983 students in Taiwan, Vietnam became the third largest source country of overseas students (National Development Council (NDC) n.d.). Up to 2019, Taiwanese investment in Vietnam was more than US $32 billion, making Vietnam the largest recipient of Taiwanese investment in Southeast Asia (Bureau of Foreign Trade (BoFT) n.d.). Between 2017 and 2019, the bilateral trade generated the second largest surplus for Taiwan of all its Southeast Asian partners (BoFT n.d.).

Aspiring to enhance 'people-centred' interactions with the target countries, the NSP's ambitions extend beyond the economic arena. Criticising Taiwan's earlier attempts in the 1990s for narrowly focusing on profitability, the president vowed in her election manifesto to enhance 'people-centred' interactions between Taiwan and Southeast Asia (President Tsai Ing-wen Facebook, 6 December 2015). Soon after the President's inauguration in May 2016 and the NSP's initiation in August, the government announced in September the NSP Action Plan, which encouraged mixed children to become 'Southbound Seeds' and endorsed affirmative action to enable those mixed children who prove to have Southeast Asian language capability to go to university (Executive Yuan (EY) 2016). Related to this recognition of the importance of Southeast Asian languages, in December 2016 the MoE announced that, from the academic year of 2018 onwards, Southeast Asian languages were to be offered as a core subject in primary education and an optional subject in secondary education (Ministry of Education (MoE) 2016). In January 2017, under the heading of 'Natal Home Diplomacy' (*niangjia waijiao*), the MoE's Action Plan described the mixed children as 'Southbound Vanguards' and encouraged them to 'return home and seek their roots'. To materialise their 'root-seeking', the MoE now finances short stays of primary and secondary school pupils in their mothers' hometown, expecting them to 'increase [Taiwan's] friendly social capital' in its relationships with Southeast Asian countries (Ministry of Education (MoE) 2017, 14, 21).

To increase 'people-centred' interactions, in October 2017 the OTN announced its promotion of tourism from Southeast Asia and education of Southeast Asian students for tertiary degrees or vocational skills (Office of Trade Negotiations (OTN) 2017). The acquisition of Southeast Asian languages was seen by the OTN as critical for encouraging cultural appreciation and attracting Southeast Asian students to Taiwan (Office of Trade Negotiations (OTN) 2017, 9). The OTN's vision was in tandem with the NSP's pledges that it would assist immigrant women to use their 'cultural and linguistic advantages' to obtain employment in tourism and teaching languages (Executive Yuan (EY) 2016). To boost tourism from the NSP's target countries, in July 2016 the government announced a visa waiver for Southeast Asian tourists, with those from Thailand, Brunei and the Philippines prioritised for the trial of this programme (Control Yuan (CY) 2017). This focus on promoting tourism from Southeast Asia prompted legislators' criticism in February 2017 over the very small number of licenced tour guides speaking Southeast Asian languages (respectively, 27, 47 and 18 guides able to speak Indonesian, Thai and Vietnamese) (Legislative Yuan (LY) 2017, 1092). In response, in March, the MoTC reported that immigrant women could be trained to become tour guides (Legislative Yuan (LY) 2017, 1094–1095).

Southeast Asian mothers and their children are not only included in the NSP Action Plan but characterised as an asset. The old label 'New Children of Taiwan' given to mixed children has been discarded and their matrilineal ties with Southeast Asia are now highlighted. Valuing the women's natal family as 'home' and 'root', the NSP invests in maintaining the link between the women and their home via financing the children's visits. Dropping the stereotype of the women's perceived poor education, the NSP foresees the possibility of training them to become tour guides. Instead of dismissing them as a liability for Taiwan's competitiveness, the NSP reimagines the women as a pool of linguistic resources. Overlooking the fact that the women were restricted from speaking their own languages to their children in pubic and in private, it presumes the children to have linguistic advantages. In sum, the NSP instrumentalises the women's relationships with their natal families and children in order to realise its 'people-centred' aspiration (see Hsia in this special issue for how the NSP rescripted the women and their children from being 'social problems' to 'social assessts').

Having explained the re-scripting of the NSP as 'people-centred' aspiration, this paper now turns to focus on how the five interviewed activists enacted their citizenship in their interactions with the NSP.

Vietnamese activists' act of citizenship

Capacity-building

In enacting citizenship through participation in civil organisations, immigrants draw on civic skills, language proficiency and social capital to build capacity (Gittell, Ortega-Bustamante, and Steffy 2000; Yang, Lee, and Torneo 2012). Seeing capacity building as a strategic goal, Trinh Minh Ha's organisation utilised the NSP's funding and employed Vietnamese, Thai, and Indonesian staff. The goal, as explained by its Taiwanese head, was to equip the immigrant staff with civic skills, including drafting funding proposals, delivering projects, managing public speaking, bookkeeping and completing project reports (interview, 14 April 2017). Building capacity in these skills is critical, since drafting funding proposals is identified as a major challenge for immigrant activists who undertook leadership training (Han 2021).

Trinh Minh Ha is one of the trainees who demonstrated the benefits of acquiring these skills. Her experiences have to be juxtaposed with those of the women in other 'capacity-deficit' organisations. It is argued that Taiwanese-staffed, service-providing organisations are liable to run the risk of reinforcing immigrant women's gender stereotype in the name of their integration (Lin 2018b). This was acutely pointed out by Phạm Thanh Van in 2009, after she left such an organisation where she worked as an interpreter. Based on her own observations, she criticised these organisations because they 'described us as miserable victims and used this image for their funding applications. We're not stupid or incapable, it's just that we didn't understand *how it works*' (interview, 15 April 2009, emphasis added). Knowing 'how it works', Ha was able to exercise her citizenship on personal and community scales, as explained in the following pages.

The utility of capacity building is further demonstrated by Ly Van Trang and the Vietnamese culture workshop that she runs. Trang was a primary school dropout in Vietnam and obtained Chinese proficiency by attending language courses in Taiwan. The NSP's positive publicity about Southeast Asian cultures fed an expanding appetite for multicultural events, a demand she was able to meet, thanks to her accomplishments in the cultural industry, her organisational skills, and her network of contacts with Taiwanese activists and civil servants. The premises of her workshop function as a friendly social space for Vietnamese spouses and workers in her neighbourhood to meet. Her evident capability saw her assisting universities to deliver the latter's 'social responsibility' projects, aimed at helping migrant communities. She also advised businesses on providing Chinese-language training for their migrant workers, since lacking Chinese proficiency deepens migrant workers' vulnerability vis-à-vis their brokers, employers and the Taiwanese state.

In short, civil organisations and public engagement became a site in which immigrant activists exercised their citizenship. An illustrative example is a public seminar convened by a Vietnamese activist in August 2019. At this event, invited Taiwanese activists and officials gave brief opening remarks to the audience of immigrant women and their families. Both Trang and Hồ Minh Mai, a Vietnamese language teacher, were invited to give featured talks. Trang condemned the Taiwanese government's indifference towards the inhumanity suffered by migrant workers at the hands of brokers and employers. Mai defended the right of immigrant mothers and their children to speak the mother's language and updated her audience on the rollout of the teaching of Southeast Asian languages at different levels of education. The presence of Trang and Mai made visible their networking within and beyond the migrant community. Their advocacy for the rights of immigrant spouses and migrant workers underlined their capacity in public education and agenda-setting, integral to their socio-political struggles.

Motherhood motivation and empowerment

As mentioned above, the NSP promoted the acquisition of Southeast Asian language proficiency in Taiwan. This provided Hồ Minh Mai with critical resources for strengthening the self-esteem of mixed children. That is, although she was a university teacher, she offered to teach at her daughter's primary school, since commanding respect as a teacher in front of all pupils protected not only her daughter but also other mixed children at the same school from the discrimination experienced by mixed children (interview, 11 December 2017). In so doing, the school became a site of her motherhood-instantiated act in which she contested the stigmatisation of immigrant women as incompetent mothers. However, she also cautioned that the number of teaching hours was small hence it might not be a reliable source of income for immigrant women.

As discussed above, the mother–child relationship is at the centre of the NSP's re-scripted discourse. In response, the interviewed activists made this relationship a site of citizenship in which they transformed their motherhood from a private intimacy to an act of compassion for other women and their children. Critically, Mai reminded that 'grannies and granddads (parents-in-law) don't read those glossy business magazines [which reported the reframing of the women and their children]' (interview, 15 April 2017). This saw Ha organised immigrant mothers to read books to children at school and in the library. She also designed activities encouraging Taiwanese in-laws' appreciation of Southeast Asian cultures. Aiming to raise the sense of worth of the mothers and their children, Ha's outreach reduced their isolation and included them in the migrant community, whilst she offered herself not only as a trustworthy contact but also as a reputable role model for the women. In this way, the NSP's instrumentalisation of the mother–child relationship was proactively utilised by Ha to enact her care and empowerment as part of her exercise of citizenship at home, at school or in the community.

On the other hand, maintaining the relationship amongst immigrant women, their natal family and their mixed children is branded as 'Natal Home Diplomacy' by the NSP. The mechanism of this 'diplomacy' is to finance the children's visits to their mothers' hometowns. The announcement of such funding was a highlight at the aforementioned public seminar. Two primary school children and their mothers thanked the Vietnamese host and her organisation for helping them win the grant. To showcase the children's knowledge of Vietnamese culture acquired during their stay in Vietnam, one of the children recited *in Vietnamese* the 'five things Ho Chi Minh taught (Vietnamese) children': 'love your country, love your comrade, learn well, take really good care of your sanitation, and be modest, honest and brave'. This recital received enthusiastic applause from Vietnamese mothers, arguably, for its evocation of their childhood memories, whereas the two children were praised for their academic capability. Whether and how the child's familiarity with the content of Vietnam's civic education given to primary school pupils contributed to Taiwan's 'Natal Home Diplomacy' seemed to be side-lined, since neither the convenor nor the two invited activists commented on this 'diplomacy'. Therefore, although the interviewed activists engaged with the NSP's reframing of their motherhood in their acts of empowerment and compassion, they appeared evasive about the NSP's politicisation of their transnational family ties.

Beyond the NSP's instrumentalisation, Trang saw the publicity surrounding the children's potential as an opportunity to build capacity of mixed children. She recruited mixed children as volunteers helping at multicultural events organised by her. Her goal was to nurture the children's sense of mission, capability and skills (see Camino and Zeldin 2002 for the youth's civic engagement). She explained that '[my daughter] didn't like my absence from home, but I told her what we do is *meaningful*' (interview, 17 April 2017, emphasis added). Her only daughter (a university student) has joined her campaign to help migrant workers and, in the summer of 2020, another mixed child began to participate in their work (interview, 9 July 2020). Trang's act of empowerment was echoed by Trinh Minh Ha's organisation. The organisation mobilised mixed children to join the campaign to demand reform of decision-making in matters of migration (social media posts, 8, 10 September 2020). These socio-political struggles were intended to instil a sense of ownership of migration issues amongst the children and enabled them to continue the reform campaign initiated by their mothers' generation. In the socio-political sphere constituted by the NSP, the interviewed activists enacted their citizenship *in relation to* their children, fellow migrants and the Taiwanese state and laid claim to their cultural rights and their autonomous motherhood.

Contesting the exploitation of migrant workers

In the socio-political sphere constructed by the NSP, the interviewed activists also laid claim to labour rights on behalf of their fellow migrants. Perceived as transient, temporary and disposable *outsiders*, Southeast Asian workers, who numbered 605,935 (Ministry of Labour (MoL) n.d.) when the NSP was announced, form the largest group of foreign residents in Taiwan. Paying a high recruitment fee to their brokers for their employment in Taiwan, they fill the chronic labour shortage in the manufacturing, construction, fishing, agriculture and care industries. Although contributing to Taiwan's production and reproduction, they suffer discrimination, debt bondage and 'legal servitude' (Lan 2007), a plight contested domestically and internationally (e.g. documented in the Trafficking in Persons Report published by the U.S. State Department). Even though they constitute an existing 'people-centred' link between Taiwan and Southeast Asia, halting the violation of their human rights is not included in the pronouncement of the NSP's 'people-to-people' aspiration.

Also experiencing the *othering* of outsiders as imposed by the host society, the interviewed activists reached out to migrant workers out of compassion for their situation of suffering exploitation and injustice. Ha's organisation published a quarterly magazine in Chinese, Vietnamese, Indonesian and Thai languages for their Taiwanese and migrant readers. The magazine included sections on 'Know Your Rights' and news from their home countries. These were intended to keep the migrant spouses and workers informed of their rights and maintain their cultural links with their home countries. Ha and her organisation also assisted individual migrant workers to retrieve salaries withheld by their employers and helped sexually abused workers to return home.

Whilst these acts defended individual workers, Ly Van Trang's campaign was a fundamental challenge to migrant workers' recruitment and employment as regulated by the state. In April 2017, invited to give a talk to university students, Trang argued that the violation of migrant workers' rights has tarnished Taiwan's human rights record. Her audience asked what the Taiwanese government should do, citing the NSP's promotion of 'people-centred' interactions. She reminded the students that migrant workers '*do not have the right to vote*, therefore no Taiwanese politicians care about them' (17 April 2017, emphasis added). Mentioning that the Vietnamese government also did not respond to her petitions, she urged the two governments to cooperate to reform the exploitative brokerage system and combat corruption. At the abovementioned public seminar in August 2019, she called for the abolishment of recruitment fees. In sum, in the site of the labour market, the activists enacted their solidarity with migrant workers and, on their behalf, laid claim to the rights they had been deprived of. Trang's stress on migrant workers' ineligibility to vote specifically underlined the differentiation between citizens and non-citizens legalised by the Taiwanese state and the resultant socio-political and economic inequality exacerbated by exploitative brokerage and employment.

Contesting gender bias

As analysed above, the NSP's appropriation of the mother–child relationship rendered the family a site for the activists to empower and care for immigrant mothers and children and defend their cultural rights. Nevertheless, the same discourse also reiterates immigrant women's role as mother and increases pressures on their maternity (see Chien, Tai, and Yeh 2012). For Nguyễn Thị Minh Thu, a long-term volunteer at a local public health station, maternity and motherhood is the most difficult challenge encountered by immigrant women, who are often pressured by their in-laws into early childbirth and over their son preference (see Sheu 2007; Lan 2008 for women's repro- duction pressure). Therefore, her priority was to help Vietnamese women protect their health and ameliorate the tension between them and their in-laws. She accompanied social workers in their home visits to newly arrived women. Capitalising on the respect she enjoyed in the neighbourhood, she acted as a personal guarantor for these women and tried to persuade their in-laws to allow them to leave home and attend language training that was indispensable for their independence. In short, Thu assisted the women to protect their health and their mobility.

The NSP's gender bias is not only found in immigrant women's maternity but also in the labour market for tour guiding, as highlighted by Ngô Xuân Phoung's experiences. In addition to being an interpreter leading a self-help organisation, Phoung is also a licenced tour guide. Experiencing the physical, mental and financial constraints imposed by her in-laws on her spatial freedom and knowing the prevalence of such impositions amongst immigrant women, Phuong asked 'how many husbands or in-laws would allow their wives or daughters-in-law to leave home [to work as a tour guide]?' (interview, 13 April 2017). To answer her question, it is necessary to unpack women's gendered mobility (Martin and Dragojlovic 2019, 276).

Women's gendered mobility is derived from their role as home-bound carers. As mentioned above, when Trang's daughter was young, she reluctant to see her away from home for work, whereas Thu endeavoured to ensure that newly arrived women could leave home and attend language training. Gendered mobility is particularly pronounced in the tour-guiding profession. The tour-guiding market is globally known for its gender bias (World Tourism Organization (UNWTO) and United Nations Entity for Gender Equality and the Empowerment of Women (UN Women)

2011, 9). In Taiwan, restricted by their caring duties, licenced female guides do not necessarily enter the market and male guides outnumber female guides, mainly because tour operators prefer to employ male guides for their physical strength and lower lodging costs (sharing accommodation with male drivers) (NTCG n.d.). In addition to being expected to stay at home and look after their families (see Chuang, Hsieh, and Lin 2010, 520), immigrant women were also challenged by their level of Chinese language proficiency (NTCG n.d.), a disadvantage illustrated by the fact that in 2018, only 44 Vietnamese women passed the licence examination (Taiwan News 2018b). Thus, it is immigrant women like Phuong who are more likely to pass the written exam, become licenced and able to join the market, due to their higher level of acculturation and Chinese language proficiency, as well as having adult children and thus being free from daily childcare. In this light, Phuong's question echoes the assertion that women's access to citizenship rights is hampered by their role as home-bound carers (Walby 1994).

On the other hand, the extremely small number of licenced tour guides is also a reminder that immigrant women's absence from home is perceived to cast doubt on their chastity. That is, absence from home is derogatorily associated with 'running away' (Lin 2018b), a tell-tale sign of abandoning their marriages or fraudulent marriages associated with sex work (Tseng 2014). The public's intrusive curiosity in their intertwined mobility and chastity put them under the watchful gaze of their elderly neighbours. Mai recalled this kind of intrusion: 'I don't need to tell my husband where I'm going, but I'll have to tell them. If I dress up, they'd ask where I'm going, or what I'm doing today. If I leave home for work early or late, or return home from work early or late, they'd ask what I did today' (interview, 15 April 2017). Behaving like 'de facto parents-in-law', these elderly neighbours were in effect conducting a 'neighbourhood watch' over immigrant women's mobility and chastity. In sum, the experiences of Phuong and Mai foregrounded gender bias embedded in the labour market and gendered mobility in the women's everyday lives. They made the NSP's utilisation of immigrant women for tourism revenue a site of contestation against the bias whereby they laid claim to women's employment rights as well as their right to socio-economic and spatial mobility.

Conclusion

Regarding the NSP as a fluid socio-political space, this paper has examined how the five Vietnamese activists enacted their citizenship in the family domain and public sphere. This paper found that the NSP treated Southeast Asian women's family relationships and motherhood as political resources, through which a positive discourse towards the women and their children emerged. A manifestation of this purposeful reframing was the 'Natal Home Diplomacy' discourse and its financing of mixed children's 'root-seeking' politicised the private family domain as a public policy arena. The NSP aimed to use immigrant women to realise its goals in the acquisition of Southeast Asian languages and the increase in tourism from Southeast Asia. These political economic interests conflated the women's private role as daughters and mothers and their public roles as workers and immigrants of foreign culture. Taiwan is proposed as an example of a 'migration state' (Hollifield 2004) which opens its market for economic benefits but closes the political polity for the sake of cohesion (Cheng 2021b). However, the NSP's 'discovery' of the political usefulness of immigrant women and their children and the resultant positive reframing underlines its self-serving inclusion of them for political and economic gains.

Analysing the activists' exercise of citizenship as their 'acts of citizenship', this paper found that, aided by the NSP, their acts were enabled by building their capacity for participation in civil organisations and public engagement. The *meaningful* acts that were carried out by them not only improved individuals' wellbeing but also contested structural bias and differentiation that perpetuate gender inequality and the inequality between citizens and non-citizens. The former included their empowerment of and compassion for immigrant women, mixed children and migrant workers. The latter was manifested by their protest against the gender bias embedded in their daily life and the exploitation of migrant workers. Unfolding along the change of their life course from being a wife to being a mother, citizen and worker, their empowerment, compassion and contestation took place in the sites of family, civil organisation, school, library and labour market on individual, community, societal and state scale. In their socio-political struggles, they laid claim to their rights to speak their own languages, free themselves and their children from discrimination, assert their autonomous motherhood against politicisation by the state, and protect their health and their mobility. Out of compassion, they also promoted migrant workers' rights against exploitative brokerage and employment. Their rights-claim demonstrated their subjectivity and independence.

Being sensitive to the gendering of marriage migration, this paper contributes to offering insights into immigrant women's exercise of citizenship in their multiple roles as daughters, wives, mothers, citizens and workers (Piper and Roces 2004) along their changing life course. Answering the call to emphasise immigrant women's resistance (Choo 2018), this paper foregrounded their grassroots-level acts and demonstrated their potential for making differences. That is, equipped with their daily experiences and practices, they set an example of making the state accountable for its indifference to gender bias and its indifference towards human rights violations. Although publicised as exercising 'warm power' to advance 'human values' (Yang and Chiang 2019), the NSP's 'people-centred' aspiration is criticised for being vague and difficult to measure in terms of efficacy (Chen 2020). From the bottom up, the activists' advocacy for migrant workers further discredited the image as a 'human rights defender' carefully constructed by the Taiwanese state (Cheng and Momesso 2017). Mostly, their dynamic, complex and contentious interactions with the NSP underlined its hypocrisy and neoliberalism (Lan 2019) which is a 'terrain of struggle' (Stasiulis and Bakan 1997) for them to realise their act of citizenship.

Disclosure statement

No potential conflict of interest was reported by the author(s).

References

Bélanger, D. 2007. "The House and the Classroom: Vietnamese Immigrant Spouses in South Korea and Taiwan." *Population and Society* 3 (1): 39–59.

Bélanger, D., and T. G. Linh. 2011. "The Impact of Transnational Migration on Gender and Marriage in Sending Communities of Vietnam." *Current Sociology* 59 (1): 59–77. doi:10.1177/0011392110385970.

Bureau of Foreign Trade (BoFT). n.d. *New Southbound Policy: the Information of the 18 countries; statistics of individual countries* (in Chinese). Accessed 29 October 2020, https://newsouth boundpolicy.trade.gov.tw/#, https://newsouthboundpolicy.trade.gov.tw/PageDetail?pageID=2047&nodeID=27

Camino, L., and S. Zeldin. 2002. "From Periphery to Center: Pathways for Youth Civic Engagement in the Day-to-day Life of Communities." *Applied Developmental Science* 6 (4): 213–220. doi:10.1207/S1532480XADS0604_8.

Chang, H. C. 2020. "Do Gender Systems in the Origin and Destination Societies Affect Immigrant Integration? Vietnamese Marriage Migrants in Taiwan and South Korea." *Journal of Ethnic and Migration Studies* 46 (14): 2937–2955. doi:10.1080/1369183X.2019.1585014.

Chen, C. J., and T. L. Yu. 2005. "Public Attitudes Towards Taiwan's Immigration Policies." *Taiwanese Sociology* 10: 95–148.

Chen, P. K. 2020. "Taiwan's "People-centered" New Southbound Policy and Its Impact on US–Taiwan Relations." *The Pacific Review* 33 (5): 813–841. doi:10.1080/09512748.2019.1594349.

Chen, X. 1996. "Taiwan Investments in China and Southeast Asia: "Go West, but Also Go South"." *Asian Survey* 36 (5): 447–467. doi:10.2307/2645493.

Cheng, I. 2013. "Making Foreign Women the Mother of Our Nation: The excluding and Assimilating Immigrant Wives from Outside." *Asian Ethnicity* 14 (2): 157–179. doi:10.1080/14631369.2012.759749.

Cheng, I. 2017. "She Cares because She Is a Mother: The Intersection of Citizenship and Motherhood of Southeast Asian Immigrant Women in Taiwan." In *International Marriages and Martial Citizenship: Southeast Asian Women on the Move*, edited by A. Fresnoza-Flot and G. Ricordeau, 158–175. Abingdon: Routledge.

Cheng, I. 2021a. "Maneuvering in the Linguistic Borderland: Southeast Asian Migrant Women's Language Strategies in Taiwan'." In *Taiwan: Manipulation of Ideology and Struggle for Identity*, edited by C. Shei, 183–202. Abingdon: Routledge.

Cheng, I. 2021b. "Productivity, Cohesion and Dignity: The Contestation of Migration Policy under the First Tsai Ing-wen Administration." In *Navigating in Stormy Waters: Taiwan during the First Administration of Tsai Ing-wen*, edited by G. Shubert and C.-Y. Lee. Abgindon: Routledge.

Cheng, I., and L. Momesso. 2017. "Look, the World Is Watching How We Treat Migrants! the Making of the Anti-Trafficking Legislation during the Ma Administration." *Journal of Current Chinese Affairs* 46 (1): 61–99. doi:10.1177/186810261704600104.

Chien, L. Y., C. J. Tai, and M. C. Yeh. 2012. "Domestic Decision-making Power, Social Support, and Postpartum Depression Symptoms among Immigrant and Native Women in Taiwan." *Nursing Research* 61 (2): 103–110. doi:10.1097/NNR.0b013e31824482b6.

Chin, J., and S. Yu. 2009. "School Adjustment among Children of Immigrant Mothers in Taiwan." *Social Behavior and Personality* 36 (8): 1141–1150. doi:10.2224/sbp.2008.36.8.1141.

Chin, L. C. 2017. "Reconciling Marital Citizenship in Malaysia through Activism: Gender, Motherhood and Belongingness." In *International Marriages and Martial Citizenship: Southeast Asian Women on the Move*, edited by A. Fresnoza-Flot and G. Ricordeau, 59–78. Abingdon: Routledge.

Choo, H. Y. 2016. *Decentering Citizenship: Gender, Labor, and Migrant Rights in South Korea*. Stanford University Press.

Choo, H. Y. 2017. "Maternal Guardians: Intimate Labor and the Pursuit of Gendered Citizenship among South Korean Volunteers for Migrant Women." *Sexualities* 20 (4): 497–514. doi:10.1177/1363460716651416.

Chuang, H. L., N. Hsieh, and E. S. Lin. 2010. "Labour Market Activity of Foreign Spouses in Taiwan: Employment Status and Choice of Employment Sector." *Pacific Economic Review* 15 (4): 505–531. doi:10.1111/j.1468-0106.2009.00461.x.

Chung, C., K. Kim, and N. Piper. 2016. "Marriage Migration in Southeast and East Asia Revisited through a Migration-development Nexus Lens." *Critical Asian Studies* 48 (4): 463–472. doi:10.1080/14672715.2016.1226600.

Commonwealth. 2016. *Why Would Vietnamese Bank Open Branch in Taiwan?*, 24 November. Accessed 18 June 2018, https://www.cw.com.tw/article/article.action?id=5072629

Control Yuan (CY). 2017. *Investigation Report* (serial number: wai diao 009). 22 November. Taipei: CY.

Department of Household Registration (DoHR). n.d. *Population Statistics by County, by Legal Status and by Parents' Nationality.* Accessed 27 October 2020, https://www.ris.gov.tw/app/portal/346

Enloe, C. 2014. *Bananas, Beaches and Bases: Making Feminist Sense of International Politics.* Berkeley: University of California Press.

Executive Yuan (EY). 2016. *The New Southbound Policy Action Plan*, 26 September. Accessed 27 October 2020, www.ey.gov.tw (under the heading 'Important Policy').

Gittell, M., I. Ortega-Bustamante, and T. Steffy. 2000. "Social Capital and Social Change: Women's Community Activism." *Urban Affairs Review* 36 (2): 123–147. doi:10.1177/10780870022184804.

Global Vision. 2016. *Why Would Taiwan Increase Investment in Vietnam against All Odds?*, 27 October. Accessed 18 June 2018, https://www.gvm.com.tw/article.html?id=22288

Han, P. C. 2021. "A Blueprint of Leadership Development for Female Marriage Migrants: A Pilot Exploration in Taiwan." *Adult Learning* 20 (6). 1045159520981164.

Hollifield, J. F. 2004. "The Emerging Migration State." *International Migration Review* 38 (3): 885–912. doi:10.1111/j.1747-7379.2004.tb00223.x.

Hsia, H. C. 2007. "Imaged and Imagined Threat to the Nation: The Media Construction of the "Foreign Brides" Phenomenon as Social Problem in Taiwan." *Inter-Asia Cultural Studies* 8 (1): 55–85. doi:10.1080/14649370601119006.

Hsia, H. C. 2009. "Foreign Brides, Multiple Citizenship and the Immigrant Movement in Taiwan." *Asian and Pacific Migration Journal* 18 (1): 17–46. doi:10.1177/011719680901800102.

Hsiao, R., and M. Borsoi-Kelly 2019. "Taiwan's New Southbound Policy in the U.S. Free and Open Indo-Pacific", *Asia Pacific Bulletin* No. 470. 10 April. Accessed 13 January 2021, https://www.eastwestcenter.org/publications/taiwan%E2%80%99s-new-southbound-policy-in-the-us-free-and-open-indo-pacific

Isin, E. F. 2007. "Theorising Acts of Citizenship." In *Acts of Citizenship*, edited by E. F. Isin and G. M. Nielsen, 15–43. London: Zed Books.

Isin, E. F. 2009. "Citizenship in Flux: The Figure of the Activist Citizen." *Subjectivity* 29 (1): 367–388. doi:10.1057/sub.2009.25.

Isin, E. F. 2017. "Performative Citizenship." In *The Oxford Handbook of Citizenship*, edited by A. Shachar, R. Bauböck, I. Bloemraad, and M. Vink, 500–524. Oxford: Oxford University Press.

Jones, G., and H. H. Shen. 2008. "International Marriage in East and Southeast Asia: Trends and Research Emphases." *Citizenship Studies* 12 (1): 9–25. doi:10.1080/13621020701794091.

Jones, G. W. 2005. "The "Flight from Marriage" in South-East and East Asia." *Journal of Comparative Family Studies* 36 (1): 93–119. doi:10.3138/jcfs.36.1.93.

Keng, K. Y. 2016. *School Performance of Second Generation Southeast Asian Taiwanese Stigmatised and Undiscovered Potentials in Globalisation.* Doctoral dissertation, University of Hawaii.

Kim, A. E. 2009. "Demography, Migration and Multiculturalism in South Korea." *The Asia-Pacific Journal* 7 (6): 1–18.

Kim, H. K. 2012. "Marriage Migration between South Korea and Vietnam: A Gender Perspective." *Asian Perspective* 36 (3): 531–563. doi:10.1353/apr.2012.0020.

Kim, M. 2013. "Citizenship Projects for Marriage Migrants in South Korea: Intersecting Motherhood with Ethnicity and Class." *Social Politics* 20 (4): 455–481. doi:10.1093/sp/jxt015.

Kim, Y., and H. Shin. 2018. "Governing through Mobilities and the Expansion of Spatial Capability of Vietnamese Marriage Migrant Activist Women in South Korea." *Singapore Journal of Tropical Geography* 39 (3): 364–381. doi:10.1111/sjtg.12229.

Lan, P. C. 2007. "Legal Servitude and Free Illegality: Migrant "Guest" Workers in Taiwan." In *Asian Diasporas: New Formations, New Conceptions*, edited by L. Bailey, B. Harries, and S. Lok, 253–277. Stanford: Stanford University Press.

Lan, P. C. 2008. "Migrant Women's Bodies as Boundary Markers: Reproductive Crisis and Sexual Control in the Ethnic Frontiers of Taiwan." *Signs: Journal of Women in Culture and Society* 33 (4): 833–861. doi:10.1086/528876.

Lan, P. C. 2019. "From Reproductive Assimilation to Neoliberal Multiculturalism: Framing and Regulating Immigrant Mothers and Children in Taiwan." *Journal of Intercultural Studies* 40 (3): 318–333. doi:10.1080/07256868.2019.1598952.

Lee, H. K. 2003. "Gender, Migration and Civil Activism in South Korea." *Asian and Pacific Migration Journal* 12 (1–2): 127–153. doi:10.1177/011719680301200106.

Legislative Yuan (LY), 2017. "*Legislative Yuan Motion Brief*". Legislative Yuan No. 887, Executive Yuan Initiative No 15700–192. The Fifth Session of the Ninth Legislative Yan (立法院議案關係文書, 院總第887號政府提案第15700 號之192): 1091–1096. 15 March.

Liao, P. C., and Y. H. Wang. 2013. "Growing up in Taiwan: Cultural Adjustment and Challenges for Children of Foreign Brides." *Journal of Diversity Management* 8 (1): 15–22.

Lin, J. H. 2018a. ""Assisting You to Become a Local": NGOs and Constructed Foreign Spouses in Eastern Taiwan." *Gender, Place & Culture* 25 (1): 118–133. doi:10.1080/0966369X.2017.1395819.

Lin, S. M. 2018b. ""Then You Can Ride the Scooter to Run Away!" Gender Positioning of Marriage-migrants in Adult Mandarin Education in Taiwan." *International Journal of Bilingual Education and Bilingualism* 21 (6): 617–631. doi:10.1080/13670050.2016.1192102.

Martin, F., and A. Dragojlovic. 2019. "Gender, Mobility Regimes, and Social Transformation in Asia." *Journal of Intercultural Studies* 40 (3): 275–286. doi:10.1080/07256868.2019.1599166.

Ministry of Education (MoE). 2016. *Southeast Asian Languages Added to the Teaching of Indigenous Languages for Primary and Secondary Education Curriculum so as to Enhance Students' Understanding of Southeast Asian Cultures*, 10 December. Accessed 19 June 2018, https://www.edu.tw/News_Content.aspx?n=9E7AC85F1954DDA8&s=A776960664EFC953

Ministry of Education (MoE). 2017. *New Southbound Policy Talent Cultivation Plans*. Accessed 14 January 2021, http://ia.cku.edu.tw/ezfiles/28/1028/attach/46/pta_32781_8669520_47276.pdf

Ministry of Labour (MoL). n.d. *Numbers of Industrial and Social Welfare Workers by Industry*, August 2016. Accessed 27 October 2020, https://statdb.mol.gov.tw/evta/jspProxy.aspx?sys=100&kind=10&type=1&funid=wqrymenu2&cparm1=wq14&rdm=I4y9dcIi

National Development Council (NDC). n.d. *Numbers of Overseas Students in Higher Education; Numbers of Migrant Workers by Nationality*. Accessed 29 October 2020, https://www.ndc.gov.tw/Content_List.aspx?n=80C3A12901E1F481 and https://www.ndc.gov.tw/Content_List.aspx?n=421CC0712EC314BD

National Immigration Agency (NIA). 2016. *Numbers of Foreign Spouses and Mainland Spouses (Including Spouses from Hong Kong and Macao) by Certificate*. Accessed 27 October 2020, https://www.immigration.gov.tw/5385/7344/7350/8887/?alias=settledown

National Security Council (NSC). 2006. *National Security Report*. Taipei: National Security Council.

New Taipei City Government (NTCG). n.d. *A Plan to Improve the Training of Southeast Asian language-Speaking Tour Guides and Managers; A Follow-Up Plan* (both in Chinese). Accessed 4 April 2021, https://tour.ntpc.gov.tw/Content/Upload/ContentPageFile/5b63b284-3869-4a2c-af10-b7bb8665956f.pdf, and https://tour.ntpc.gov.tw/Content/Upload/ContentPageFile/a39c961b-a8da-4806-831f-53d3ae05fb29.pdf

Office of Trade Negotiations (OTN). 2017. *The New Southbound Policy – A Practical Approach Moving Full Steam Ahead*, 6 October. Accessed 18 June 2018, https://www.moea.gov.tw/Mns/otn_e/news/News_En.aspx?kind=6&menu_id=6193&news_id=72912

Piper, N. 2008. "Political Participation and Empowerment of Foreign Workers: Gendered Advocacy and Migrant Labour Organising in Southeast and East Asia." In *New Perspectives on Gender and Migration: Livelihood, Rights and Entitlements*, edited by N. Piper, 247–273. London: Routledge.

Piper, N., and M. Roces, eds. 2004. *Wife or Worker? Asian Women and Migration*. Lanham: Rowman & Littlefield.

Schirmer, J. 1993. "The Seeking of Truth and the Gendering of Consciousness: The COMADRES of El Salvador and the Conavigua Widows of Guatemala." In *'Viva': Women and Popular Protest in Latin America*, edited by S. A. Radcliffe and S. Westwood, 30–64. London: Routledge.

Sheu, Y. H. 2007. "Full Responsibility with Partial Citizenship: Immigrant Wives in Taiwan." *Social Policy & Administration* 41 (2): 179–196. doi:10.1111/j.1467-9515.2007.00546.x.

Stasiulis, D., and A. B. Bakan. 1997. "Negotiating Citizenship: The Case of Foreign Domestic Workers in Canada." *Feminist Review* 57 (1): 112–139. doi:10.1080/014177897339687.

Taiwan News. 2018a. *Tourism between Taiwan and Vietnam Surged in 2017*. 13 April. Accessed March 26 2021, https://www.taiwannews.com.tw/en/news/3404648

Taiwan News. 2018b. *Follow Me! More New Residents Passed Tour Guide and Manager Exams* (in Chinese). 20 July. Accessed 4 April 2021, https://www.taiwannews.com.tw/ch/news/3487173

Tang, W. H. A., and H. Z. Wang. 2011. "From Victims of Domestic Violence to Determined Independent Women: How Vietnamese Immigrant Spouses Negotiate Taiwan's Patriarchy Family System." *Women's Studies International Forum* 34 (5): 430–440. doi:10.1016/j.wsif.2011.06.005.

Tsai, Y. H., and H. M. Hsiao. 2006. "The Non-governmental Organizations (Ngos) for Foreign Workers and Foreign Spouses in Taiwan: A Portrayal." *Asia Pacific Forum* 33: 1–31.

Tseng, H. H. 2014. "Victims of Human Trafficking or Perpetrators of Fraudulent Marriage? Foreign Spouses Engaging in the Sex Industry in Taiwan." In *Human Trafficking in Asia: Forcing Issues*, edited by S. Yea, 49–63. London: Routledge.

Tseng, H. H. 2015. "Gender and Power Dynamics in Transnational Marriage Brokerage: The Ban on Commercial Matchmaking in Taiwan Reconsidered." *Cross-Currents: East Asian History and Culture Review* 4 (2): 519–545. doi:10.1353/ach.2015.0032.

Wang, H. Z. 2007. "Hidden Spaces of Resistance of the Subordinated: Case Studies from Vietnamese Female Migrant Partners in Taiwan." *International Migration Review* 41 (3): 706–727. doi:10.1111/j.1747-7379.2007.00091.x.

Wang, H. Z., and D. Bélanger. 2008. "Taiwanizing Female Immigrant Spouses and Materializing Differential Citizenship." *Citizenship Studies* 12 (1): 91–106. doi:10.1080/13621020701794224.

Wang, H. Z., and S. M. Chang. 2002. "The Commodification of International Marriages: Cross-border Marriage Business in Taiwan and Viet Nam." *International Migration* 40 (6): 93–116. doi:10.1111/1468-2435.00224.

Wang, Y. H. 2010. "From "Farming Daughters" to "Virgin Brides": Representation of Vietnamese Immigrant Wives in Taiwan." *Gender, Technology and Development* 14 (2): 217–239. doi:10.1177/097185241001400205.

Werbner, P. 1999. "Political Motherhood and the Feminisation of Citizenship: Women's Activism and the Transformation of the Public Sphere." In *Women, Citizenship and Difference*, edited by N. Yuval-Davis and P. Werbner, 221–245. London: Zed Books.

Winarnita, M. S. 2008. "Motherhood as Cultural Citizenship: Indonesian Women in Transnational Families." *The Asia Pacific Journal of Anthropology* 9 (4): 304–318. doi:10.1080/14442210802506412.

World Tourism Organization (UNWTO) and United Nations Entity for Gender Equality and the Empowerment of Women (UN Women). (2011). *Global Report on Women in Tourism 2010*. doi: 10.18111/9789284413737.

Yang, A. H., and J. H. Chiang. 2019. "Enabling Human Values in Foreign Policy: The Transformation of Taiwan's New Southbound Policy." *Journal of Human Values* 25 (2): 75–86. doi:10.1177/0971685819826707.

Yang, M. L., ed. 2004. *New Children of Taiwan: Taiwan's Competitiveness in the Next Hundred Years*. Taipei: Commonwealth Magazine.

Yang, S. B., Y. Lee, and A. R. Torneo. 2012. "Political Efficacy and Political Trust among Marriage Immigrants in South Korea." *Philippine Political Science Journal* 33 (2): 202–223. doi:10.1080/01154451.2012.734098.

Negotiating citizenship and reforging Muslim identities: the case of young women of Japanese-Pakistani Parentage

Masako Kudo

ABSTRACT

Drawing on longitudinal research, this article investigates the processes of citizenship negotiations by the daughters of Japanese mothers and Pakistani fathers. The respondents' narratives indicate a disjuncture between their full citizenship and their sense of belonging. While they are treated as others in schools and local communities in Japan, within the family, the daughters feel deprived of freedom due to their migrant fathers' patriarchal control. Yet they claim rights and freedom by reconfiguring their Muslim selves. By bringing the family to the fore of the analysis, I show that the daughters' religious journeys are interwoven with power dynamics between citizen mothers and migrant fathers who, as their life cycle progresses, reposition themselves in families, communities, and nation-states. In conclusion, I argue for the importance of combining a family lens and multi-tiered approach to conceptualize identity formation as an integral part of citizenship struggles.

Introduction

Drawing on longitudinal research among Japanese-Pakistani families, this article investigates how young women of Japanese mothers and Pakistani fathers negotiate their membership in families, communities, and nation-states and how family dynamics and processes are interwoven. The children of female Japanese citizens who marry foreign citizens have been granted citizenship upon birth ever since the nationality law was amended in 1984. Hitherto, Japanese citizenship was transmitted only through male citizens in the case of international marriages. The narratives of the children, however, suggest that there is a disjuncture between their full citizenship and their sense of belonging. They were treated as others in school and local communities in Japan because of differences in appearance, names, and their religious practices as Muslims, which, to the eyes of their peers, contradicted the homogenous image of the Japanese. Moreover, the daughters of Japanese-Pakistani families felt that, due to the ideals of Muslim femininity to which their fathers expected them to adhere, they did not receive the same rights and freedom to study, work, and marry as their male siblings and non-Muslim female friends.

This research reveals that the young women's struggles for rights and belonging involve acts of reconfiguring their Muslim selves, suggesting that citizenship is not only about the legal status granted by the state but also about identity and belonging (Werbner and Yuval-Davis 1999; Siim 2000; Modood 2008). Drawing on longitudinal research, I analyze how women's identity negotiations are affected by changes in citizen mother/migrant father families. This study takes a multi-scalar approach to shifts in power within the family and the positionings of citizen mothers, migrant fathers, and their daughters in their local and transnational communities, kin circles, and nation-states.

The present study fills the lacunae of citizenship studies on Muslim women in the context of migration in two ways. First, women's negotiations of citizenship and identity have been explored mostly in the contexts of Western nations, where a sizable Muslim diaspora has developed, while other national contexts are rarely studied. The present study offers an exploration of the negotiation of Muslim women's citizenship in the context of Japan, which is an emergent immigrant-receiving country. By so doing, it advances a more contextualized understanding of citizenship (Siim 2000; Chiu and Yeoh 2021). Second, while studies on young Muslims with migrant backgrounds have tended to focus on intergenerational conflicts between co-ethnic migrant parents and their children, the exercise of power between parents is often missing from the analysis. Through the case of Japanese-Pakistani Muslim couples and their daughters, this study investigates how gender, nationality, generation, and other power differences intersect within families formed by citizen wives and migrant husbands and how the power dynamics affect the ways their daughters negotiate citizenship.

In what follows, I situate my approach within the scholarship on citizenship. I then discuss the socio-economic conditions of Japanese-Pakistani couples at the early stages of their marriage. Next, I turn to the citizenship experiences of the daughters. After I demonstrate their social marginalization and struggles within the family, I present the women's narratives to reveal the complex processes through which they reconfigured their Muslim selves in their quest for rights and belonging. In conclusion, I discuss how these findings contribute to reconceptualizing the notion of citizenship.

Identity, Family Dynamics, and Multi-Tiered Approaches to Citizenship

While legal status and accompanying rights and duties are central pillars of what constitutes citizenship, identities associated with a specific nation-state have been part of the citizenship project that nation building entails. Globalization and an increased pace of migration transformed the complementary relationships between citizenship and identity as different ethnic groups began asserting their group identities (Joppke 2008). In this context, there is a tension between the universal aspirations of citizenship and particularistic claims of identity (Isin and Wood 1999). Isin and Wood (1999), however, argue that there is an affinity between citizenship and identity in that they are both 'group markers'. The former carries legal weight while the latter carries social and cultural weight. They elaborate the nature of affinities between the two by noting that the boundaries of 'groups' are never static. In other words, in both identity and citizenship, whether they are related to an ethnic group or the nation-state, group boundaries are fluid and contested by members and non-members (Isin and Wood 1999, 20–22). Such a view allows us to conceptualize identity as a process of political struggle, which forms an integral part of the ongoing negotiation of citizenship.

Following Isin and Wood's conceptualization of identity and citizenship, I view identity as an important dimension of citizenship and explore how these young women of Japanese-Pakistani parentage reformulate their identities as Muslims in their citizenship negotiations. In doing so, I bring the family to the fore of the analysis. This approach is informed by the writings of feminist scholars who have criticized the abstract notion of citizen (Lister 2003; Werbner and Yuval-Davis 1999; Siim 2000). As Siim (2000, 19) argues, the liberal model of citizenship based on individual autonomy does not apply to women, and we need to examine how people's citizenship struggles are mediated by gender. Further, feminist scholarship on citizenship calls for attending not only to gender but also to the family dimension of citizenship as women's positions within the family determine their social positions and resources (Werbner and Yuval-Davis 1999, 16). Empirical studies on marriage-migrant women have captured the complex processes of their citizenship struggles by bringing gender and family into their analysis (Ito 2005; Wang and Danièle 2008; Yeoh, Chee, and Vu 2013; Kim, Park, and Shukhertei 2017). While these women's citizenship experiences are shaped by state interventions over marriage and the reproduction of its citizens (Turner 2008, 50–51; Fresnoza-Flot and Ricordeau 2017), women's struggles for their rights and belonging involve everyday negotiations within the family (Chiu and Yeoh 2021). Through an analysis of Filipino marriage-migrant women in Japan, Ito (2005) demonstrates the intricacy of their struggles and argues that, for these women, family can alternately be a site of negotiation, resource for strengthening one's position in the citizenship regime, and an apparatus of gender and racial subordination. Through the family lens, her study moves the notion of citizenship beyond its exclusive relationship with the state.

Another, but interconnected, way to reconceptualize citizenship beyond state-centricity is to develop a multi-tiered construct of citizenship (Werbner and Yuval-Davis 1999; Lister 2008). Werbner and Yuval-Davis argue that T. H. Marshall's definition of citizenship as 'full membership in the community' (1950 quoted in Werbner and Yuval-Davis 1999, 5) opened up a way to view citizenship as a multi-layered concept because political subjects are often involved in varied political communities, be they local, ethnic, national, or global. More importantly, membership in one collectivity can have crucial effects on citizenship in others (Werbner and Yuval-Davis 1999, 5). This is not to say that the nation-state has ceased to play a central role in regulating the flow of people's movements across national boundaries. Rather, this exclusionary aspect of citizenship is what leads people to form communities beyond the nation-state. As Leitner and Ehrkamp (2006) demonstrated through their exploration of the migrant imaginings and practices of citizenship in Germany and the United States, migrants acknowledge the importance of national citizenship in their struggles for mobility across borders. Yet their everyday experiences of inequalities and discrimination have led them to participate in more than one national community, thus challenging the conceptions of bounded national citizenship.

Yeoh, Chee, and Vu (2013) further develop the multi-tiered construct of citizenship by bringing in gender and family perspectives. Through the case of Vietnamese women who married Singaporean men, their study reveals how gender, global inequalities, and state regulations over the reproduction of its citizens affect how women negotiate their multi-layered membership in both natal and marital families and nation-states. Erel and Reynolds (2018) highlight multi-tiered constructs of citizenship by focusing on migrant mothers' caring roles. Through their analysis, they demonstrate that these women's citizenship is constituted on familial, local, national, transnational, and supra-national scales of belonging and participation. These levels interactively shape how women actively involve themselves in producing notions of rights, community, and participation through childcaring (Erel and Reynolds 2018, 3).

While building on these approaches, the present study expands multi-tiered constructs of citizenship by bringing family dynamics and identity to the fore of the analysis. In the case of the young women in my study, their everyday struggles for rights and family and local community belonging are closely interrelated to the exercise of power between citizen mothers and migrant fathers. I illuminate the complexity of the daughters' citizenship and identities by showing how different members of the family reposition themselves within the multiple scales of their lives. Longitudinal research offers insights into how family power evolves through time and affects the ways in which daughters reconfigure their religious selves. This enables us to denaturalize the concept of 'collectivities' and 'communities' and see them as an outcome of 'constant processes of struggles and negotiations' (Anthias and Yuval-Davis 1992 quoted in Yuval-Davis 1997, 8).

Research Methodology and Participants

I base this discussion on longitudinal research that I conducted in two different phases. The first phase began in 1998 with ethnographic field research involving in-depth interviews and participant observation with 40 Japanese women married to Pakistani migrants. Although the research was conducted most intensively until 2001, I have conducted follow-up interviews with some key informants in Japan and abroad (Kudo 2017a).

The second phase of research was carried out between 2016 and 2018. This was part of a larger project in which I interviewed 35 young people from 24 families formed by marriages between Japanese women and Pakistani men. Twelve of the families I knew from the previous research. Of the 24 families, in seven families, parents were legally divorced. The overwhelming majority of the families (21 of 24 families) ran businesses exporting used cars from Japan. Of 35 youth, 12 were male and 23 female. This article draws on the narratives of female participants but uses data from male participants when relevant. The 23 women were between 18 and 30 years old. At the time of the first interviews, 11 resided in Japan, five in Pakistan, three in the United Arab Emirates (the U.A.E.), and four in other countries including the U.K. and Thailand. They received education until the age of 18 in various countries: six through high school solely in Japan; six studied at schools abroad, including Pakistan, at some point, but spent the rest of their childhood in Japan. The remaining 11 interviewees were educated almost solely in Pakistan or countries such as the U.A.E. and the U.K. Of the 23 respondents, 11 were students, at the time, seven of whom were university students. The remaining 12 interviewees included teachers, office workers, and one medical professional. Two held British citizenship, and 21 held Japanese citizenship.[1] In terms of language use, all respondents conversed in Japanese with their mothers. They also spoke Japanese with their Pakistani fathers in most cases except for those who relocated to Pakistan in their early childhood. Among those who spent their childhoods abroad, their competency in written Japanese varied. For this reason, when contacting them for the first time, I sent them a letter explaining my research both in Japanese and English. The interviews were conducted mostly in Japanese, except for two cases in which the respondents wished to be interviewed in English. Some of the interviewees corresponded with me through emails in English prior to the interview, but spoke mostly in Japanese when we met, sometimes switching to English during their interviews.

While these women shared a religion and had fathers with similar occupations, a variety of migratory trajectories imply that they experienced different forms of inclusion and exclusion during their childhood in schools and local communities. Further, their diverse familial, educational, and occupational backgrounds allowed me to investigate how they utilized different socio-cultural and linguistic resources to navigate national and transnational spaces.[2]

Forming Japanese-Pakistani Families in Japan

The marriages between Japanese women and Pakistani men emerged against the backdrop of a growing number of international marriages in Japan during the 1980s and the 1990s (Ministry of Health, Labour and Welfare 2020). While the majority of the international marriages were between Japanese men and foreign women, the number of Japanese women who married foreign citizens also rose. An increase in the number of international marriages between Japanese women and Pakistani men was part of this trend. Behind this increase was a flow of incoming migrants from Pakistan that soared in the late 1980s.[3] The number of Pakistani nationals who were registered under the visa category of Spouse or Child of Japanese National increased from 112 in 1984 to 1,630 in 2000 (Japan Immigration Association 1985-2001-2001). Drawing on the 2000 census, Kojima (2012) shows that 83.4% of Pakistani men living in Japan who married there married Japanese women. In 2020, those registered under Spouse of Japanese National and Permanent Resident visa categories accounted for 32% of the 18,296 Pakistani residents in Japan (Ministry of Justice 2020). Many of those who hold permanent residency apparently held spousal visas previously.

The majority of husbands in my sample were from middle- or lower-middle-class backgrounds and came from cities such as Karachi and Lahore or their surrounding areas. Upon arriving in Japan, they found employment mainly in factories or on construction sites. After marrying Japanese women, many started used car export businesses, an economic niche for Pakistani migrants in Japan. Starting businesses was one of the few ways in which these Pakistani migrants could overcome their socio-economic marginality in Japan. They were marginalized in Japanese society as 'racial others', 'foreign workers', and 'Muslims' and were subjected to an increased level of state surveillance after a series of incidents, including the terrorist attacks of 9/11.

Japanese wives faced challenges and difficulties in marrying Pakistani men. Their experiences echo the findings of López (2015), who demonstrated that US citizens who married illegal migrants in America had diminished rights. Kofman (2004) pointed to the marginalized position of women citizens marrying migrants in

Europe. Japanese wives likewise experienced downward social mobility within Japan. They encountered difficulties in obtaining spousal visas for their husbands, the majority of whom were overstaying their visas. The women had to undergo a long and challenging process of applying for a visa for their husbands as the state practiced stricter controls to prevent 'sham marriages', which authorities suspected were rising. In addition, some women I interviewed received negative comments about their marriages to Pakistani men from the immigration officers who dealt with their husbands' visa applications. Such difficulties experienced by the women indicated state attempts to regulate the reproduction of citizens as the number of international marriages increased in Japan (Toyota 2008). While marriages between Japanese men and foreign women were tolerated because the state expected foreign female spouses to contribute to the nation by biologically reproducing Japanese nationals (Chiu and Yeoh 2021), foreign male spouses and their children tended to be regarded as outside of the Japanese nation.

Citizen wives also met overt forms of discrimination including being denied housing despite having sufficient income to ensure the couple's economic stability. Behind this was not only xenophobia but also a gender biased assumption that the husband is the main provider for the family and that the status of a family is determined by the husband.

In my sample, state regulations in Japan proved to be a driving factor in Japanese wives' conversion to Islam. For foreign husbands to be granted a spousal visa in Japan, couples must certify that they have been married in accordance with the laws of both countries. Pakistan requires the submission of a religious marriage contract, a *nikāh nāma*. Prior to signing the contract, the women in my sample, except for one who was already a Muslim, converted to Islam because, according to the Muslim law of Pakistan, Muslim men can marry only Muslims or 'people of the Book', meaning generally Christians and Jews, but not others, without their fiancées converting. Because of this legal requirement, many Japanese wives regarded themselves as 'Muslim only in name', but their religious self-perceptions transformed as their lives progressed (Kudo 2015).

Starting in the 1990s, Pakistani Muslims contributed to an increase in the number of mosques in the Kanto region. In some cases, religiosity intertwined with a sense of marginality that they felt in Japan. One man remarked that his experiences of being discriminated against in his workplace made him reflect upon who he was, as a result of which he became religious. Pakistani male migrants who exported used cars formed close-knit networks through attending prayers at newly built mosques.

As children reached school age, some relocated with their mothers mostly to Pakistan or in many fewer cases, other countries, while migrant husbands remained based in Japan to continue working and sending remittances. Destinations included the U.A.E. and New Zealand where husbands established a business link. The main reason for splitting families across borders involved husbands' desires to raise children, especially daughters, in Islamic environments. In cases of migrating to non-Islamic countries such as New Zealand and the U.K., the families mobilized their Pakistani/ Muslim networks to settle in the new countries and give their children an Islamic education. Their migration trajectories evolved as their life course progressed (Kudo 2017a).

Being Marginalized as *Hāfu* within the National Discourse of Homogeneity

Having discussed how the respondents' parents established their lives in Japan and beyond, I turn to the children's experiences of citizenship. Many of the respondents who spent most of their childhood in Japan disclosed negative experiences of being labelled as foreigners or *hāfu*, a Japanese term taken from the English word 'half'. *Hāfu* basically refers to those who were born to a Japanese citizen and a foreigner, although what the term connotes and refers to has changed and can be contextual (Shimoji 2018). This contrasts with the experiences of the respondents who were raised abroad. Although they might have experienced discrimination against them as foreigners, East Asians, or Muslims, depending on the social contexts in which they lived, they did not feel that having parents with different nationalities had influenced how people perceived them. For example, a male respondent in his 20s who was raised in Pakistan stated that his school friends considered him Japanese not only because of his nationality but also because there was no such socially constructed category as *hāfu*, suggesting that the forms of otherization differed depending on national contexts. Other respondents who had studied in the U.A.E or New Zealand recollected that they felt accepted because they were just one of many who had multiple backgrounds.

According to Shimoji (2018), while children of international marriages were stigmatized as '*konketsu*' [mixed] through the 1960s (see also Hsia 2021), a positive image emerged from the 1970s to the 1980s. This change took place as popular media represented *hāfu* in entertainment industries and sports as being white, wealthy, and global, leaving issues related to discrimination and poverty untouched. While the positive images of *hāfu* empowered them to a certain extent, the stereotype marginalized those who did not fit the celebrated image (Shimoji 2018). Many of my respondents felt alienated because their physical appearances, language, names, and religious practices, such as avoiding *harām* (meaning 'prohibited' in Arabic) food at school, did not fit the stereotype of Western background *hāfu* that circulated through the media (Kudo 2017b). For example, many of those who were based in Japan during their childhood tended to feel marginalized because they did not fit the stereotype of multi-lingual *hāfu*. Although they were familiar with the native languages of their fathers, which included Urdu, Punjabi, and Pashto, their competence in those languages was often limited.

The children of Japanese-Pakistani marriages were also marginalized as *gaijin* or *gaikoku-jin*, which literally means a 'foreign national'. The term, however, does not only concern legal status but often bears a negative connotation of being outside of the homogenous Japanese nation (Chiu and Yeoh 2021).[4] Being asked where the border between *nihon-jin* [Japanese] and *gaikoku-jin* [foreigner] lies, a young male respondent of Japanese-Pakistani parentage first explained in terms of citizenship rights such as the right to vote and other basic rights. However, asked if those who naturalized, like some of the Pakistani fathers, can be considered Japanese, he commented that there were different degrees of Japanese-ness, elaborating that those who are naturalized are 'borderline Japanese [*giri-giri nihon-jin*]', while *hāfu* like himself are positioned between them and 'the perfect Japanese [*kanpeki nihon-*

jin]' (Kudo 2017b). His remark captures the hierarchical nature of Japanese-ness and how *hāfu and gaijin* constitute the spectrum of otherness in the narratives of Japanese nationhood.

Daughters' Struggles within the Family

Although both male and female respondents suffered discrimination, their experiences at home were starkly different. I now move on to the women's experiences within the family and investigate their struggles against patriarchal control. Salma, who spent her childhood in Japan and is now in her late 20s, recalled her childhood:

> My father tried to control my freedom in almost everything, including what I wore and whom I went out with. My non-Muslim female friends are allowed to go on overnight school trips and to take part in club activities at school without any issues, but these presented tremendous challenges to me. Even getting out of the house was a huge deal. My brother never had the same issues, though. He was free to do anything. Although I was rebellious from time to time, I always had to think twice before I did anything that my father might be against me doing. As a result, I gave up most of my wishes relating to study and work even before trying, just thinking that my father would intervene anyway.

Although the degrees to which fathers exerted control over daughters differed among respondents, Salma's story resonated with many other respondents' narratives of struggles within their families. Salma observed that her father's attempts to control her were not necessarily borne of his Islamic ideals of femininity but followed from 'his pride'. The majority of respondents, whether they lived in Japan or abroad, also understood that their fathers tried to control their sexuality mainly because they valued maintaining their honor vis-à-vis the communities of Pakistani males in Japan and abroad and extended kin in Pakistan. Behind this was the idea of honor [*izzat*], which in the context of Pakistani society depends most importantly on the sexual modesty of female kin, daughters especially. Sexual modesty was closely associated with the ideals of *purdah*, according to which females should be segregated either physically or symbolically (through veiling) from unrelated males once they have reached puberty. The practice of *purdah* varies according to class, region, and other factors, and it is observed most strictly by the middle- and lower-middle-classes in urban areas from which many Pakistanis in Japan originate. Becoming migrants is likely to be another factor contributing to the fathers' patriarchal control over daughters. Aisha, who relocated to Pakistan in her early childhood, discussed the control that her father in Japan had exerted over her. She noted differences in attitudes between the parents of her Pakistani friends and her father who left the country as a young man:

> Pakistan is changing and boys and girls mingle more with each other than they used to. While many Pakistani parents with few connections to foreign countries are now quite open, my father does not see the changes in Pakistan, which is transforming so rapidly.

Further, I argue that Pakistani men's economic activities in Japan factor into the ways they controlled their daughters. After becoming engaged in used car exports the men forged close-knit networks among themselves. They expanded their diasporic networks globally through their transnational businesses. Under such circumstances, controlling women in accordance with shared codes of honor among Pakistani men not only maintained male authority within their domestic sphere but also served to elevate their status vis-à-vis other male compatriots within their diasporic spaces. A respondent, Farida, who spent her childhood in Japan, except for short trips to Pakistan and other countries, remarked that her father, who became pious after he became involved in Muslim networks abroad through the expansion of his business, wanted her to marry a Muslim because he wished to maintain his honor among his circle of Pakistani Muslims in Japan and other countries. As Kandiyoti (2017) observed, the reproduction of patriarchal relations involves relations not only between but also within genders.

The Roles of Citizen Mothers in Daughters' Citizenship Struggles

Having discussed daughters' relationships with their fathers, I now focus on what it meant for those who resided in Japan to have citizen mothers. My findings suggest that while some thought their citizen mothers unlikely to understand their harsh reality of being discriminated against in their native country, many appreciated that their mothers helped them navigate difficult childhoods. Their mothers could mobilize citizen resources to help alleviate the marginality of their mixed children. First, citizen mothers could provide them with cultural resources. Saera, who spent her childhood in Japan and felt marginalized in the local community, valued staying with her maternal grandmother because it allowed her, like her peers, to experience 'normal' ways of living, which included *oshōgatu* (the New Year celebration) and *shichi-go-san* (a major traditional rite de passage for young children). Those events gave her a sense of inclusion in Japanese society.[5]

Second, the social capital of citizen mothers helped daughters navigate school life. Sadia, who returned to Japan after spending her early childhood in Pakistan and the U.A. E., remarked that she could utilize information provided by a network of Japanese mothers that her mother cultivated through her role in the Parent and Teacher Association. She could also learn social skills and norms by observing how her mother interacted with other Japanese mothers.

Third, citizen mothers' linguistic ability and knowledge about the social system helped them participate in Japanese society through education and work, while they could not rely on their migrant fathers in those respects. Sadia's mother searched online and found a women's university that both suited her aspiration and her father's expectation that she would observe Islamic norms of sexual segregation.

Imaan's relationship with her mother was more ambivalent. Imaan was raised in Japan and presently works in an entertainment industry. She remarked that she was able to start her career because of moral and practical support from her mother. She added that because her mother grew up in Japan, she understood what being a Muslim minority woman meant to her. She, however, recalled her difficult childhood during which her father tried to control her freedom, and her mother could not always support her. Her and other respondents' narratives strongly indicated that power relations between their parents mediated how much freedom was allowed for daughters. Hina, who spent her teens in Japan after returning from Pakistan, noted:

Much of what we are allowed and not allowed to do is actually not stated in the religion itself. Rather, that is more or less up to our fathers. In our family, the father has the authority. .... Although I am aware that it is basically laid out in the tenets of Islam, the limit of what we can wear so much depends on the fathers. ... My father, however, is not really strict compared to others. As I see it, it depends on how much the mother can say to the father. My mother has more say than perhaps some other mothers in Japanese-Pakistani families as she is older than my father and she knows much more about how to do things in Japanese society. That may be why my mother can support me to contest some of the restrictions imposed by my father who would be quite domineering otherwise.

My longitudinal research reveals that the power relations between Pakistani men and their citizen spouses shifted as the family cycle progressed. In the early stages of their marriages, Pakistani husbands had to depend on their citizen wives to apply for visas for themselves and for kin to travel to Japan. Power dynamics shifted as wives left full-time jobs to care for their children, a commonly observed work trajectory of Japanese married women.[6] Leaving the workforce increased their economic dependence on their husbands, and at the same time their husbands' Japanese immigration status stabilized. Forming transnational families in which wives relocated abroad with their children was another factor affecting such power dynamics (Kudo 2017a). These complex dynamics, shaped by gender, nationality, and mobility, determined wives' negotiating power, affecting the degree to which they could support their daughters' freedom vis-à-vis their husbands.

Reforging Muslim Selves

As daughters grew into early adulthood, they began negotiating their rights by reformulating Islam, which they felt had been imposed on them by their fathers. The next two stories exemplify the complex interrelations between struggles for freedom and the processes of reforging Muslim selves.

The Case of Mariam[7]

Mariam, in her late 20s, finished a two-year college program in Japan and was working in another country in Asia. She lived mostly in Japan until age 20, although she had attended school in Pakistan for a few years. As a child, she hated being treated as a foreigner because she considered herself Japanese. When interacting with strangers, who considered her a foreigner, she showed her Japanese nativity by exhibiting her Japanese language skills, accents, and meticulous Japanese manners and etiquette. In this way, she tried to redefine what constitutes being a legitimate member of the nation, although her name and appearance deviated from the homogenous Japanese image. At the same time, however, she felt guilty because she thought that she was excluding her father and other foreigners by doing so.

Her father was strict with her. She felt that her freedom was curtailed in many aspects, including clothes, education, and part-time work after school. She noted that as she approached her late teens, 'My father used to say that he wanted to marry me off when I turned 20'. Although she was not always obedient to her father, she did not want to cause serious family trouble by confronting him, and so she abandoned her plans for a four-year university and attended a two-year college instead. She faced a challenge when she found an opportunity to work abroad:

> When I received my present job offer, my father did not like it because it was in a non-Islamic country. He then suggested I instead go to the U.K. to study at a university. He thought that, because there are large Muslim communities there, the chances for me to meet a prospective marriage partner would increase. Studying at a British university was an attractive option for me, but my mother advised that because I may have to marry soon any way, it would be perhaps better for me if I gained life experiences by working abroad instead of studying further for nothing. I followed her advice.

Thus, she carefully avoided her father's intention to control her education and career trajectory. While her father was not entirely happy, he allowed her to relocate abroad to work on a fixed-term contract.

While she used to feel that Islam was imposed upon her family by her father, after Mariam relocated abroad to work, her perception of the religion changed:

> In terms of Islam, I used to follow only what my father told me to do. After I relocated abroad, I started to study the religion myself. This is because I saw Islamophobia growing worldwide and feared the possibility of being harassed because of my religion. When I heard what so-called 'radical Islamists' said in the media, I began checking on the internet whether what they said was actually stated in Islam.

Her views on other Muslims also evolved. She continued:

> I used to think that, outside Islamic countries such as Pakistan, it was only me and a few other [Japanese-Pakistani] minority Muslims I personally knew who struggled to be a Muslim among the non-Muslim majority. After I moved abroad, I realized that there were in fact many minority Muslims like myself. Moreover, I came to learn that there can be many different ways of being a Muslim. For example, I saw that female Muslims who do not wear a hijab, just like myself, confidently assert their Muslim identity. This was a revelation to me, and I began searching for my own way of being a Muslim.

In articulating how she reconfigured her Muslim self, she compared her position as a Muslim with that of her father and her extended kin in Pakistan:

> In Pakistan, religion and culture merge with each other. Since my father was born and raised in Pakistan, he had been influenced by the Islam practiced in Pakistan. The encounters with many different forms of Islam abroad made it possible for me to distance myself from the ways in which Islam is practiced in Pakistan.

Thus, Mariam started to reconstruct Islam in a way that was distinct from her father. In our interview, she added that her father's religiosity also underwent transformation as he aged away from home. Elaborating on this point, she said:

> Before, it was unthinkable that he would allow me to work abroad on my own. Also, his views on Islam began changing. He now says, 'People in Pakistan may do that, but you do not have to do it because it has nothing to do with Islam'.

Mariam observed that his attitudes changed as he became exposed to different views of Islam through lectures he accessed on the internet and by meeting religious leaders who had been invited to his local mosque in Japan from various countries. Amplifying this point, a male respondent stated that 'there are two types of Pakistani fathers in Japan;

some change as they age in Japan while others do not', meaning that some fathers' religious perceptions and practices transform and become more reflective of what 'true' Islamic teachings are. Japanese wives support his remark. Saima, who relocated to Pakistan with her children, recalled that while her husband used to wear a black thread around his neck, believing that it would protect him, he stopped doing so after studying Islam on his own in Japan and realizing that not all practices in Pakistan accorded with Islamic teachings.

The Case of Nabila

Nabila, a university student in her early 20s, moved to the U.A.E. with her mother while her father remained in Japan. In her interview, she discussed difficulties that she was undergoing with her parents:

> My father is really strict. I am not allowed to choose clothes I really want to wear. I used to wear a hijab before, but I do not do that anymore. Even if you wear a hijab, men will harass you no matter what you wear. I still believe in Islam, but I have my own perspective on it. I still listen to what my parents tell me, but we fight a lot. We fight over a piece of cloth.

After observing how men treated unrelated women in public, Nabila started to reflect on the meaning of veiling. As a result, she changed her perspective on Islam and decided to remove her scarf.[8] Her father, who lives in Japan, tried to exert his control over her attire from afar by pressuring her mother, who acted as a moral guardian to the daughters in his absence. When she discussed her lack of freedom, she, too, associated it with the asymmetrical power balance between her parents:

> I see a lot of women being controlled by their husbands, both in the Pakistani community here and in my family. My father has a lot of say about my clothing and what I should be doing. And my mother, being a good wife, she has to listen to him. So, I think it is really unfair.

However, she appreciated support from her mother with regards to her future career and compared her to other mothers in Pakistani communities in the U.A.E.

> I am very grateful to my Mum for being open-minded in some aspects. For example, regarding occupations, if you go to a Pakistani family, usually girls do not work. They will study, they will have certificates for everything, but as soon as they pass those levels of education, they will get married because they cannot be independent. Then in Japan, like, even you are high schooler, you can work after school. My mother says that I should work, but my father is like, 'No'!

Observing patriarchal relationships at home and in Pakistani communities, Nabila was determined to develop her career after graduating from university and contest her father's opposition to her developing a career:

> I am sure it is not Islamic teaching. Our prophet's first wife was a businesswoman. So, I think that it is not the religion, but the culture of Pakistan. I also think it has something to do with men's pride.

Thus, she asserted her right to work by mobilizing Islamic knowledge that she had acquired through formal and informal religious education available within the U.A.E. Further, she did so by separating Islam from 'the culture' of Pakistan.

Mariam's and Nabila's religious journeys echoed other respondents' experiences, although the contexts in which they reformulated Islam differed depending on the resources for doing so, family circumstances, migratory trajectories, and other factors. For example, in the case of Mariam, her English language skills were essential for gathering information from the internet to construct her own way of being a Muslim. In the case of Nabila, being brought up in an Islamic environment enabled her to access diverse models of Muslim womanhood. Her transnational experiences travelling between Japan and the U.A.E. and familiarity with Pakistani communities in the U.A.E. gave her additional reference points. Her situation was in sharp contrast to the respondents who had been raised in Japan and whose reference points for negotiating their Muslim-ness were often limited because they usually knew only a handful of Muslims.

While the respondents tended to distance themselves from the culture of Pakistan when constructing narratives of 'true Islam' by drawing on the *Qur'an*, some respondents – including Mariam – who spent periods of their childhood in Pakistan, sustained fond memories of the country. Another respondent, Mumtaz, who was raised and had studied in several countries including Japan, Pakistan, and the U.A.E., valued her memories of Pakistan from her early childhood and added that 'while I am aware that Pakistani culture is not always in line with the true teachings of Islam, I am emotionally attached to it and feel that Pakistan is at the core of who I am'. Two respondents who had been based in Japan started to learn their fathers' languages only recently because they felt that it was part of their identities. This reconnection to Pakistan also served to reconstruct their self-images as they navigated early adulthood.

Discussion

This study has explored the ways young women of Japanese-Pakistani parentage negotiate citizenship in families, communities, and nation-states by focusing on families and on the young women's (re)configuration of their Muslim identities.

First, the findings unveil the ambivalent positions of citizen mothers as they raise future citizens. On the one hand, citizen women and their children tend to be socio-culturally marginalized in the Japanese nationhood despite their formal citizenship. Sana, a citizen mother, told me that her children's schoolteacher did not expect them to learn *kanji* (Chinese characters, one of three components of the Japanese writing system) because their father was foreign, and therefore they would not need them. This suggests that despite the amendment of the nationality law, the reproduction of the nation through male lineage is still presupposed in people's imaginings of citizenship.[9]

On the other hand, citizen women play a significant role in how their daughters cope with their experiences of being marginalized as *hāfu* or *gaijin*. Mothers do so by mobilizing various citizen resources. This contrasts with the experiences of marriage-migrant mothers who lack those resources. In her study on Filipinas married to male Japanese, Takahata (2009) reports that their inability to read and write Japanese well, together with their stigmatized images as 'entertainers' working in sex industries in Japan, made it difficult for them to win the respect and trust of their children. Filipino mothers negotiate their positionings in Japan by leaving night work and taking up more 'respectful' daytime jobs such as English teaching and care work to reduce stigma and build confidence in their children (Takahata 2009). In addition, these migrant mothers respond to their marginal positions by other means such as organizing associational activities and transmitting their language and culture to their children (Ito 2005). The comparison between citizen and migrant mothers elucidates distinct ways in which they are engaged in citizenship practices through caring and cultural work (Erel 2011; Chiu and Yeoh 2021) and devising mothering techniques (Fresnoza-Flot 2018).

In contrast to migrant mothers, citizen mothers appear to be better equipped to help their mixed children alleviate feelings of marginalization. The extent to which they can do so is, however, negatively affected by shifts in the balance of power in their families. Economic dependence on husbands is likely to reduce their ability to challenge their husbands' control over their daughters' freedom. Importantly, citizen women's economic positions are shaped not only by the religio-cultural gender norms that their husbands expect wives to observe, but also by these women's transnational mobility and by the gender inequalities in the Japanese labor market. Although an increasing number of middle-age Japanese women are returning to the workforce, the majority are engaged in part-time work (Gender Equality Bureau Cabinet Office 2018). Working in the care industry, which is low-paid and labor-intensive, is one of the few skilled employment options open to both Filipino and Japanese women, after completing relatively minimal training when they return to the workforce in middle age (Takahata 2009). While Japanese women's citizen resources remain essential to the sustenance of their husbands' businesses, the structural gender inequalities prevalent in Japanese society affect citizen mothers' ability to contest their migrant husbands' patriarchal control over daughters.

Second, migrant fathers' domestic patriarchal control should be understood in relation to their positionings in the wider socio-economic contexts. As the narratives of the daughters suggest, migrant fathers restrict their daughters' freedom not merely because of the Islamic norm of female modesty that fathers hold, but also because they hope to maintain their membership and status vis-à-vis other Pakistani men who run the same types of businesses. Engaging in transnational businesses to escape from their socio-economic marginalities in Japan has repercussions for their daughters' freedom. Relationships between migrant fathers' citizenship and their exercise of patriarchal control are complex and shifting, affected by multiple factors such as the socio-economic positions of citizen mothers and migrant fathers' desires to elevate their status in Pakistani communities in Japan and beyond.

Third, the daughters' narratives highlight a new form of Muslim selves emerging through rights-claiming struggles. Mariam and Nabila's stories demonstrate that their religious journeys have varied depending on the resources they cultivated in their migratory trajectories. They both construct the discourse of 'true Islam', through which they contested their fathers' notions of Islamic female modesty as rooted in the culture of Pakistan but not necessarily in accord with the *Qur'an*. In addition, in Mariam's case, the complex emotions she holds toward her migrant father have shaped her journey. While she resents the patriarchal control her father exerts, she has a sense of unity and sympathy toward him because they share the painful experiences of being racialized and discriminated against within Japanese society. Thus, her experiences of patriarchal control within the home interact with her sense of being marginalized in local communities, which shapes the intricate ways she reworks her Muslim self.

The transformation of religious selves enables my respondents to reposition themselves within the family and in relation to non-Muslims. The majority of the respondents who spent most of their childhoods in Japan felt pressure to conform to the national discourse of homogeneity and suppressed their religious identity at school. As they grew into early adulthood, reformulating Islam allowed some to redefine their positions vis-à-vis their non-Muslim peers and claim their Muslim identities. Thus, their struggles in their families are part and parcel of citizenship negotiation that take place in multiple overlapping spheres of life. Further, Mariam's case indicates that her father's perceptions and practices of Islam are fluid and have evolved as he grew older. Her father has also undertaken his own religious journey, through which he has reworked his positions vis-à-vis extended kin in Pakistan and male circles of Pakistanis in Japan and transnational spaces.

Concluding Remarks

The literature on citizenship points to the importance of moving beyond the state-centric view of citizenship by investigating people's positionings in multiple collectivities. I advance this multi-tiered approach further by bringing the family to the fore of the analysis. By so doing, I unveil not only how the daughters' membership in multiple collectivities relates to each other but also how their citizenship negotiations interact on multiple fronts with the ways their citizen mothers and migrant fathers reposition themselves in families, communities, and nation-states. Further, by employing a longitudinal method, this study reveals the evolution of citizenship practices. Through the processes of reconfiguring Muslim selves in a way different from their fathers, daughters create autonomous spaces that allow them to study and work. Their everyday struggles within the family call for decoupling citizenship from the legal status endowed by the state (Chiu and Yeoh 2021) and conceptualizing identity formation as an integral part of citizenship struggles. Finally, the newly emerging selves of young women of Japanese-Pakistani parentage stand in tension with the national discourse of homogeneity that continues to be reproduced on multiple levels, including state-led discourses (Shimoji 2018). There is a need to further investigate how the women's identity negotiations will evolve and interact with the on-going processes of nation building. Research should attend to how such processes are mediated by shifting family dynamics and citizenship negotiations by other family members. Examining women's relentless reforging of Muslim selves through a familial lens refocuses the concept of citizenship. It reveals a wider vista that looks beyond citizenship's exclusive relationship to the state, illuminating its multi-tiered and transformative nature.

Notes

1 Among the Japanese citizens, five once held Pakistani nationality but renounced it by the age of 22. According to the current (August 2021) Japanese nationality law, those who have acquired multiple nationalities before becoming 20 years old are required to choose their nationality before reaching 22 years of age. For details, see Ministry of Justice (2021).
2 To maintain the anonymity of research participants, I use pseudonyms, and some personal data have been changed.

3 The number of entrants from Pakistan to Japan declined after a 1989 suspension of the mutual visa exemption between the two countries and a 1990 amendment of Japanese immigration law. Unable to renew their visas, many decided to overstay in Japan.

4 Policy level discourse by local administrators and the state further reinforces the dichotomous notion of the Japanese and the foreign as discussed by Kashiwazaki (2013). She demonstrates that both advocacy efforts and policy discourses on 'multicultural co-living' by local and central governments ignores ethnic and cultural diversity among immigrants, which does not readily overlap the Japanese/foreign axis (Kashiwazaki 2013, 43).

5 Shimoji's interviews with *hāfu* reveal, however, that they encountered discriminatory remarks against *hāfu* and foreigners within the maternal family, showing that the family is not an unbreachable sanctuary that escapes narratives of Japanese national homogeneity (Shimoji 2018, 362-363).

6 Some became involved in their husbands' businesses. For its implications on negotiating power vis-à-vis their husbands, see Kudo (2017a).

7 Mariam's story is an updated version of her story that I included in my paper 'Negotiating identities, constructing cultural forms: A case of Muslim youth born to Japanese mothers and Pakistani fathers' presented at the 1st Asian Consortium for South Asian Studies 'South Asian Diaspora and Popular Cultures in Asia' organized by NIHU Project Integrated Area Studies on South Asia (INDAS-South Asia), Hankuk University of Foreign Studies, National University of Singapore, Vietnam Academy of Social Sciences, and Indian Studies Center of Chulalongkorn University held at Chulalongkorn University, Bangkok, on November 14, 2017.

8 In the cases of the participants who began their quests to reconfigure their Muslimness, the ways they expressed their religious identities through attire varied greatly. While some wore hijabs, others did not but considered choosing modest clothes an important part of their Muslim selves.

9 Although children's Islamic practices can become a marker of difference at school, my findings suggest that such practices are often interpreted by their teachers not as their religious identities but as deriving from the foreignness of their fathers.

Acknowledgments

My sincere gratitude goes to those who participated in this research. I am also indebted to Tuen Yi Chiu, Brenda S. A. Yeoh, and two anonymous reviewers for their insightful comments and suggestions. This research was made possible by the financial support provided by JSPS KAKENHI Grant Numbers JP23251006, JP16K03244, and JP20H05828.

Disclosure statement

No potential conflict of interest was reported by the author(s).

References

Association, J. I. 1985-2001. *Zairyū Gaikokujin Tōkei [Statistics on Foreigners Registered in Japan].* editions. Tokyo: Japan Immigration Association.

Chiu, T. Y. and B. S. A. Yeoh. 2021. "Introduction" in "Marriage Migration, Family and Citizenship in Asia," Special Issue, Citizenship Studies.

Erel, U. 2011. "Reframing Migrant Mothers as Citizens." *Citizenship Studies* 15 (607): 695–709.

Erel, U., and T. Reynolds. 2018. "Introduction: Migrant Mothers Challenging Racialized Citizenship." *Ethnic and Racial Studies* 41 (1): 1–16.

Fresnoza-Flot, A. 2018. "Raising Citizens in 'Mixed' Family Setting: Mothering Techniques of Filipino and Thai Migrants in Belgium." *Citizenship Studies* 22 (3): 278–293.

Fresnoza-Flot, A., and G. Ricordeau, eds. 2017. *International Marriages and Marital Citizenship: Southeast Asian Women on the Move.* London: Routledge.

Gender Equality Bureau Cabinet Office. 2018. *Danjo Kyōdō Sankaku Hakusho: Heisei 30 nen ban* [White Paper on Gender Equality 2018] accessed 1 May 2021. https://www.gender.go.jp/about_danjo/whitepaper/h30/zentai/index.html

Hsia, H-C. 2021. "From 'Social Problems' to 'Social Assets': Geopolitics, Discursive Shifts in Children of Southeast Asian Marriage Migrants, and the Mother-Child Dyadic Citizenship in Taiwan" in "Marriage Migration, Family and Citizenship in Asia," Special Issue, *Citizenship Studies.*

Isin, E. F., and P. K. Wood. 1999. *Citizenship and Identity.* London: Sage Publications.

Ito, R. 2005. "Crafting Migrant Women's Citizenship in Japan: Taking 'Family' as a Vantage Point." *International Journal of Japanese Sociology* 14: 52–69.

Joppke, C. 2008. "Transformation of Citizenship: Status, Rights, Identity." In *Citizenship between past and Future,* edited by E. F. Isin, P. Nyers, and B. S. Turner, 36–47. London: Routledge.

Kandiyoti, D. 2017. "The Paradoxes of Masculinity: Some Thoughts on Segregated Societies." In *Dislocating Masculinity: Comparative Ethnographies,* edited by A. Cornwall and N. Lindisfarne, 185–200. London: Routledge.

Kashiwazaki, C. 2013. "Incorporating Immigrants as Foreigners: Multicultural Politics in Japan." *Citizenship Studies* 17 (1): 31–47.

Kim, H. M., S. Park, and A. Shukhertei. 2017. "Returning Home: Marriage Migrants' Legal Precarity and the Experience of Divorce." *Critical Asian Studies* 49 (1): 38–53.

Kofman, E. 2004. "Family-related Migration: A Critical Review of European Studies." *Journal of Ethnic and Migration Studies* 30 (2): 243–262.

Kojima, H. 2012. "Correlates of Cross-Border Marriages among Muslim Migrants in Tokyo Metropolitan Area: A Comparison with Seoul Metropolitan Area." *Waseda Studies in Social Sciences* 13 (1): 1–17.

Kudo, M. 2015. "Crafting Religious Selves in a Transnational Space: Japanese Women Who Converted to Islam upon Marrying Pakistani Migrants." In *Rethinking Representations of Asian Women: Changes, Continuity, and Everyday Life,* edited by N. Ijichi, A. Kato, and R. Sakurada, 105–121. New York: Palgrave MacMillan.

Kudo, M. 2017a. "The Evolution of Transnational Families: Bi-national Marriages between Japanese Women and Pakistani Men." *Critical Asian Studies* 49 (1): 18–37.

Kudo, M. 2017b. "Negotiating the Meanings of Being Hafu: The Case of Japanese-Pakistani Mixed Children." In *Hapa Japan: Identities & Representations,* edited by D. R. Williams, 73–86. Los Angeles: USC Shinso Ito Center for Japanese Religions and Culture/Kaya Press.

Leitner, H., and P. Ehrkamp. 2006. "Transnationalism and Migrants' Imaginings of Citizenship." *Environment & Planning A* 38: 1615–1632.

Lister, R. 2003. *Citizenship: Feminist Perspectives.* [1997]. New York: New York University Press.

Lister, R. 2008. "Inclusive Citizenship: Realizing the Potential." In *Citizenship between past and Future,* edited by E. F. Isin, P. Nyers, and B. S. Turner, 48–60. London: Routledge.

López, J. L. 2015. "'Impossible Families': Mixed-Citizenship Status Couples and the Law." *Law & Policy* 37 (1–2): 93–118.

Ministry of Health, Labour and Welfare. 2020. *Jinkō dōtai tōkei* [Vital Statistics of Japan]. accessed 10 October 2020. https://www.e-stat.go.jp/dbview?sid=0003411850

Ministry of Justice. 2020. *Zairyū gaikokujin tōkei* [Statistics on Foreigners Registered in Japan]. accessed 15 March 2021. https://www.e-stat.go.jp/stat-search/files?page=1&layout=datalist&toukei= 00250012&tstat=000001018034&cycle=1&year=20200&month=12040606&tclass1=000001060399

Ministry of Justice. 2021. *Choice of Nationality*. accessed May 2 2021. http://www.moj.go.jp/EN/ MINJI/minji06.html

Modood, T. 2008. "Multiculturalism, Citizenship and National Identity." In *Citizenship between past and Future*, edited by E. F. Isin, P. Nyers, and B. S. Turner, 113–122. London: Routledge.

Shimoji, L. Y. 2018. *'Konketsu' to 'Nihon-jin': 'Hāfu', 'Double', 'Mikkusu' No Shakaishi [Mixed Blood and the Japanese: A Social History of 'Halfs', 'Doubles', and 'Mixes']*. Tokyo: Seido-sha.

Siim, B. 2000. *Gender and Citizenship: Politics and Agency in France, Britain and Denmark*. Cambridge: Cambridge University Press.

Takahata, S. 2009. ""Zainichi Filipin-jin Kaigosha: Hitoashi Sakini Yattekita 'Gaikoku-jin Kaigo Rōdōsha'" [Filipino Care Workers in Japan: 'Foreign Care Workers' Who Came First]." *Gendai Shiso [Contemporary Philosophy]* 37 (2): 106–118.

Toyota, M. 2008. "Editorial Introduction: International Marriage, Rights and the State in East and Southeast Asia." *Citizenship Studies* 12 (1): 1–7.

Turner, B. S. 2008. "Citizenship, Reproduction and the State: International Marriage and Human Rights." *Citizenship Studies* 12 (1): 45–54.

Wang, H.-Z., and B. Danièle. 2008. "Taiwanizing Female Immigrant Spouses and Materializing Differential Citizenship." *Citizenship Studies* 12 (1): 91–106.

Werbner, P., and N. Yuval-Davis. 1999. "Introduction: Women and the New Discourse of Citizenship." In *Women, Citizenship and Difference*, edited by N. Yuval-Davis and P. Werbner, 1–38. London: Zed Books.

Yeoh, B. S. A., L. H Chee, and T. K. D. Vu. 2013. "Commercially Arranged Marriage and the Negotiation of Citizenship Rights among Vietnamese Marriage Migrants in Multiracial Singapore." *Asian Ethnicity* 14 (2): 139–156. doi:10.1080/14631369.2012.759746

Yuval-Davis, N. 1997. "Women, Citizenship and Difference." *Feminist Review* 57: 4–27.

Afterword

Katharine Charsley

ABSTRACT
This Afterword to the Special Issue on 'Marriage Migration, Family and Citizenship in Asia' seeks to foreground some key themes from the six articles it contains. Drawing on some old conceptual friends of the field – including Appadurai's model of disjunctive global 'scapes' and flows, and Plummer's notion of 'Intimate Citizenship' – it highlights particularly significant contributions to understanding processes and practices of citizenship connected to marriage migration, through attention to diversity, continuity, and disjuncture. The disjunctures documented here encompass tensions between processes not just at the level of family and the nation, but between national and inter- or transnational dynamics – highlighting inequalities in intimate citizenship, but also providing potential spaces for change and agency. This rich collection therefore represents a substantial contribution to a foundational issue in the literature on marriage migration – the question of how to conceptualise the agency of marriage migrants, who paradoxically manage the agentic leap of migration at the same time as being profoundly dependent on their citizen spouses, with the well documented potential for victimisation this dependency contains.

Introduction

In 2008, Mika Toyota and colleagues published a Special Issue in this journal on the topic of 'International marriage, rights and the state in East and Southeast Asia'. Rates of transnational marriage in several countries in the region had been rising rapidly but it was as yet, they noted, a relatively understudied phenomenon. Their focus on rights and the state featured issues of citizenship as a central concern. As Toyota set out in the Introduction:

> International marriage has become an arena of contention over rights, privileges and access to citizenship. While the reasons and opportunities for individuals to contract marriages with partners of other nationalities have increased in the current globalizing processes, state sovereignty rests on the assumption that its citizens and their family units belong to just one nation. In this regard, international marriages by their very existence challenge the state and the boundaries of its sovereignty. The contemporary conception of marriage has evolved within the context of the construction of the modern nation-state and marriages involve not only the relationship between one individual and another, but also between the state and the individual. (2008, 3)

At that point in time, research on marriage-related migration was gaining pace. Two agenda setting edited collections with an Asian focus – Constable's (2005) *Cross-border Marriages: Gender and Mobility in Transnational Asia* and Piper and Roces (2003) *Wife or Worker? Asian Women and Migration* had been published a few years earlier. Both volumes critiqued stereotypical representations of marriage-migrant women as simply passive or victims, replacing them with more nuanced understandings of gendered and embedded agency in local and transnational contexts. Piper and Roces (2003) volume in particular draws connections with access to citizenship as a crucial frame for understanding such women's choices – as wives and mothers, but also workers, thus laying important groundwork for Toyota's (2008) Special Issue, and for this new collection which updates and expands our understanding of 'Marriage Migration, Family and Citizenship in Asia'.

Whilst scholarship on the topic of marriage-related migration in other parts of the world exists (e.g. Johnson 2007), Europe and Asia emerged early on as particular foci for research on the topic – in Asia because of the increasing numbers of cross-border marriages, but in Europe more likely stimulated by a resurgence in attempts to limit this form of immigration.

In the early 2000s, European research on marriage-related migration was often subsumed within the broader and longer-established field of family migration, in which a focus on issues such as 'trailing wives' and migration as a family strategy, had developed as part of the dominant economistic approaches characteristic of much of 20th Century migration studies (Cooke 2008; Kofman 1999). But with increasing recognition of the centrality of gender for understanding migration and a growing focus on women's migration developing through the 1980s and 1990s (Kofman 1999), the importance of marriage as a source of women's mobility became more apparent (Charsley 2012). Marriage-related migration or cross-border marriage is now an established and diverse area of research in its own right, spanning areas of scholarship including policy, integration, and gendered dynamics of power. An informal scan of google scholar for publications on 'marriage migration' suggests over 50 articles on the topic were published in 2020 alone.

In Europe, much academic interest in marriage migration has been stimulated by increasingly restrictive spousal immigration regimes. There had been earlier attempts to control such immigration (such as the UK's introduction of the 'Primary Purpose Rule' in the 1980s, under which would-be spousal immigrants had to prove that immigration was not the primary purpose of their marriage) but from around the turn of the 21st century, Denmark pioneered a new wave of curbs on the rights of citizens and long term residents to be joined by foreign partners. Restrictions subsequently increased in other Western European countries, with regulations across Europe developing a 'family resemblance' (Wray, Agoston, and Hutton 2014) amidst concerns to limit or 'manage' immigration (particularly that involving migrants considered 'low-' or 'un-skilled'). Marriage has long been a significant source of settlement migration to many European countries, but the renewed policy attention on spousal immigration was not stimulated by a dramatic increase in overall numbers. Rather, the focus was on particular types of marriage migration – the intra-ethnic marriages of former labour migrants and their descendants – often viewed as a kind of 'chain migration' at odds with the goals of a selective 'managed migration' regime. Hence, in the UK, early policy discourse saw restrictions to spousal immigration justified with reference to forced marriage, often portrayed as primarily a South Asian issue (Wilson 2007), whilst in Denmark, the 'Combined Attachment' rule made it harder for those with familial connections to their spouse's home country to achieve reunification in Denmark (Jorgensen 2012).

In East and Southeast Asia, the scale of the phenomenon of international marriage commanded the attention of both politicians and social science researchers. Many of these marriages were inter-ethnic, commercially brokered, and in some countries such as South Korea promoted by the government as a solution to perceived demographic challenges of reduced fertility or rural bride shortages. Although some of the major Asian marriage migration receiving countries featuring in this Special Issue appear to have passed the peak in terms of volumes of marriage migrants and proportions of citizen marriages involving migrants, such marriages appear to have stabilised at often quite a high level – around a third of marriages in Singapore and Hong Kong (2021, and 2021) – becoming an established part of the demographic, political and social landscape.

For a scholar of marriage migration to Europe, it is exciting not only to read new research illuminating the differences and parallels between issues surrounding cross-border marriage and its regulation in these differing geographical contexts, but also see how this Special Issue develops the conversation started in the pages of this journal over a decade ago. Whilst Toyota's Introduction to the 2008 Special Issue is concerned primarily with citizenship in a formal sense, Turner's (2008) contribution on 'Citizenship, reproduction and the State' advocated the concept of 'reproductive citizenship' in the sense of gaining rights and claims on the state through reproduction, viewing citizenship as a process. This new Special Issue not only updates the discussion to encompass recent developments, but builds on these insights to explore more diverse conceptualisations of citizenship.

In this Afterword, I seek to foreground some key themes from the six articles contained in this Special Issue, drawing on some old conceptual friends of the field – including Appadurai's model of disjunctive global 'scapes' and flows, and Plummer's notion of 'Intimate Citizenship' (2001, cf. Bonjour and De Hart 2020) – to highlight what I see as some particularly significant contributions which can be drawn from this collection.

Intimate citizenship

The articles in this volume address citizenship in its formal sense, but also practices and experiences of citizenship, particularly but not only within families. The marriage migrants described here are incorporated into their citizen spouses' societies not simply as individuals, but through families, as wives, mothers and affines. In some Asian societies, marriage to a citizen on its own is often insufficient as a route to formal citizenship, but giving birth to a citizen child appears to enhance a migrant wife's chances of success in long-term residency or citizenship applications. Hence Hsia (2021) writes of Taiwanese citizenship as constructed through the 'mother-child dyad', Yeoh et al (2021) of 'reproductive citizenship' in Singapore, and Chiu (2021) of 'maternal citizenship' in

Hong Kong – although in this latter case, Chiu shows that for divorced or separated marriage migrant women, being a mother to citizen child is insufficient to ensure even long-term visiting rights, and that such women may seek out opaque possibilities for 'discretionary citizenship'.

In Hong Kong, moreover, widowed marriage migrant women are reported to have better chances of success in securing residency rights than those who are divorced or separated – suggesting a 'marrytocracy' (2021) in which migrant wives' motives for and commitments to their marriages are under suspicion. 'In the public discourse of many [Asian] host countries', Chiu (2021) writes, 'marriage migrants are often depicted as materialistic gold diggers who take advantage of local men for money, employment opportunities, and citizenship'. In the UK and Europe, amidst more general negative stereotypes of racialised minority and Muslim men, such suspicions are more commonly held about migrant husbands (Charsley and Wray 2015; Bonjour and De Hart 2020), although some nationalities of migrant wives are also sometimes portrayed as ruthlessly instrumental (e.g. Sims 2012 on Thai women). Evidently, a 'marrytocracy' therefore not only connotes the significance of marriage as potentially providing a route to incorporation, but also differentiation within the category of marriage migrants, with some viewed as more acceptable as potential members of the national community than others.

In other words, these are questions of 'intimate citizenship' (Plummer 2001) – of what practices of intimacy denote the boundaries of insiders and outsiders. The contributors to this volume repeatedly demonstrate that the family is a crucial site for the negotiation of citizenship, and a location from which marriage migrants may be incorporated but also excluded. In Taiwan, Hsia (2021) notes that spousal immigrants granted citizenship may be stripped of that status if the marriage is retrospectively judged to have been fraudulent. Interestingly, the possibility of a similar power to strip such spouses of residency rights was also raised in a UK Home Office immigration policy public consultation – along with the suggestion that British ex-partners could be consulted as part of such processes (Home Office 2007). The State's 'moral gatekeeping' (Wray 2006) of these boundaries includes not just the questions of immigration motivations or commitment to marriages, but compliance with expected marital forms and behaviours, such that the Japanese women married to migrant men described by Kudo (2021) (in this volume) found expectations that heads of households would be male citizens could lead to them being denied housing (cf. Kwak 2019 on South Korea), and legal discourses on 'runaway brides' in South Korea reveal the expectation that marriage migrant women will not abandon their 'home' even if it is a location for abuse and confinement (2021).

As Plummer outlines, however, 'intimate citizenship' is not just a question of national inclusion and belonging, but rather 'about a plurality of rights and obligations shaped through participatory, *differentiated social worlds (and communities), each with contested status and continuing tensions that need resolving*' (Plummer 2001, 241, emphasis added). In other words, that negotiations of 'intimate citizenship' take place at various scales – bringing to mind Pessar and Mahler's formulation of the 'gendered geographies of power' operating at different scales and social locations (2003) – but also that the processes within these different dimensions may be disjunctive.

Disjuncture between family and nation-state

The concept of disjuncture appears, explicitly or implicitly, in each of the papers in this collection. They encompass tensions between processes not just at the level of family and the nation, but between national and inter- or transnational dynamics.

The role of the state, as Yeoh et al (2021) observe, is not monolithic, but rather can be riven with multiple and sometimes conflicting objectives. Hence, Hsia (2021) describes how tensions between regional geo-political goals and domestic objectives for which these 'unselected' marriage migrants were seen as undesirable meant that: 'As the wives of Taiwanese citizens, the Taiwan government could not reject their access to Taiwanese citizenship and consequently adopted a "dual exclusion-assimilation scheme" (Cheng 2013) that aimed at increasing barriers for marriage migrants to acquire citizenship and initiated programs to assimilate them into Taiwanese culture and "improve" their "population qualities"'.

In Yeoh et al's (2021) article on the family as a site of mediation and negotiation of citizenship for marriage migrants in Singapore, the authors describe the 'disjuncture between intimate incorporation of marriage migrants into the work of reproducing the family on the one hand, and their enforced partial citizenship vis-à-vis the nation-state on the other'. Whilst their pathway to formal citizenship might rest on motherhood, as members of Singaporean families such women negotiate reproductive roles against their desires, and sometimes the families' need, that they would undertake paid employment. Full membership of a family here contrasts with partial membership of the nation, with consequences in terms of the 'patriarchal bargains' (Kandiyoti 1988) that women may strike or be forced into accepting.

In the papers by Hsia (2021) and Cheng (2013), both on the Taiwanese context, we again see disjunctures between the national and the familial, this time in the context of changing discourses about migrant wives and their offspring. First perceived as a problem of 'population quality' (2021) to be remedied by targeted education interventions, 'New Taiwan's Children' were presented as problematic others to be incorporated into the national community. In the context of geopolitical competition with China, they have been reframed in official discourse as the 'seeds' for the 'New Southbound Policy' of South East Asian economic expansion, their transnational ties and language abilities revalued as a nation building resource. Their mothers, in turn, are reframed as potential language tutors and tour guides for visitors from the region. This positive reframing, however, is shown in disjunction with the lived realities of migrant wives' existing roles – the limited teaching hours (Cheng 2013) or flexible mobility required of tour guides are a poor match for the obligations of women who have been incorporated as reproductive labour, whilst also often acting as breadwinners. An interesting echo of these assumptions is found in the UK Migration Advisory Committee's 2018 suggestion that family migrants in the UK could be used to fill the low-skilled labour deficit created by Britain's departure from the European Union's free-movement arrangements – overlooking the possibility that such migrants' family responsibilities and locations may undermine their reconceptualization as a flexible labour force.

The re-evaluation of marriage migrants and their children in the Taiwanese political discourse may present opportunities for some such women and their families (Cheng 2013) but sits uneasily alongside the contingency and fragility of their citizenship status.

Cheng's (2013) description of the Taiwanese case resonates with Chiu's (2021) account of the Hong Kong state accessing migrant wives' reproductive labour, without accepting responsibility through provision of full citizenship rights. And as with Kudo's (2021) discussion of 'hafu' ('half' or 'mixed') children of one citizen and one migrant parent in Japan, the new valuation of their identity in some contexts sits alongside continued experiences of exclusion and discrimination (2021). As one of Cheng's (2013) participants commented, 'grannies and granddads don't read those glossy business magazines' – in other words, the new representations reach only certain audiences. For Kudo's (2021) Japanese-Pakistani young women participants, their secure citizenship status belies their struggles of belonging both within families and a society in which ethnic 'purity' remains normalised. These accounts of disjunction, and the endurance of logics of reproductive labour, 'quality' and 'purity' provide a rather pessimistic response to Bonjour and de Hart's recent challenge (2020) for researchers to examine the lived consequences of changing discourses around transnational marriage.

Finally, Yi's (2021) article situates discourses surrounding 'runaway wives' in South Korea in the disjuncture between the state's use of marriage migrants to address a perceived demographic crisis in birth rate, and recognising them as agentic beings beyond the role of 'wife' or 'mother'. It is to this issue of agency, and its relationship with disjuncture that I now turn.

Disjuncture as a site for change and agency

Appadurai's (1990) influential model of globalisation suggests multiple disjunctive and interacting 'scapes' of globality (of people, finance, media, ideology and technology). These 'scapes' are, like landscapes, perspectival – appearing from different perspectives for various global audiences, so that the 'ethnoscapes' of marriage migrants may appear both as an integration challenge for a receiving country, and a high-stakes migration route risking citizen women's exploitation for some bride-sending states. This model of 'scapes' was picked up early on in the development of research on cross-border marriages, with Nicole Constable (2005) echoing the typology in her coining of the notion of 'marriagescapes' in which not just spouses but ideas and images about marriage circulate.

For Heyman and Campbell (2009), Appadurai's depiction of chaotic unpredictability in disjuncture and flow suggests a false equality of influence of the various scapes, and would be enhanced by recognising the particular weight carried by economic factors. We could see this in the logics by which, in many of the national contexts described in the articles of this Special Issue, 'elite' or high skilled migrants are given paths to citizenship whilst work permit holders or 'guest workers' are viewed as labour resources from whom access to settlement is withheld. Amidst this logic, marriage migrants hold an ambiguous position – for Turner (2008) the 'profound contradiction between the economic requirements of flexibility and fluidity in the labour market and the states' goal of defending its territorial sovereignty' means that 'international marriages can be regarded as a site where these contradictions between state and market are condensed'.

State responses to marriage migration can be seen as reactions to these disjunctures. For Appadurai (1990), it is in disjuncture that flow and change occurs. I would argue that this perspective provides theoretical context for a range of (sometimes apparently contradictory) developments described in the contributions to this volume: the South Korean state's initial encouragement of marriage migration to address the economic challenges of declining birth rates, despite concerns over the 'quality' of the resulting migrants and their parenting; or the ramping up of restrictions to citizenship for marriage migrants to restrict them to a position more akin to labour migrants (2021), particularly in Singapore where the opaque requirements for migrant spouses to obtain citizenship seem to include issues of socio-economic status. Once more, this is a situation which finds echoes in the European context where several countries have imposed minimum income requirements for citizens and residents sponsoring the immigration of a spouse. In the UK, these were set in 2012 at significantly above the subsistence level suggested by welfare payments, and above the level of income of over 40% of the working population (Sumption and Vargas-Silva 2019).

We can also apply this insight of disjuncture as encouraging change to the discourses surrounding marriage migrants and their children in Taiwan (Cheng, 2021). Neither classified as a high 'quality' elite to enhance the national economic body, nor purely labour migrants with few claims to become insiders, the Taiwanese reconceptualization of marriage migrants and the 'second generation' as economic resources in the 'New Southbound' policy seeks to make use (or sense) of a category of migrant not selected by the state for their economic utility. A similar logic can be found in the UK Migration Advisory Committee's (2018) suggestion, noted earlier, that family migrants could be used to back-fill the shortfall of low-skilled EU migrant workers lost through Brexit. As we see above, however, these initiatives themselves create further points of tension and disjuncture, not least between old and new logics and discourses.

If disjuncture encourages change at the state level, the articles in this collection show that the same can be true at the level of individuals and families. We can envision these as gaps creating spaces for agency, or at least points of leverage from which to attempt to open up such spaces. Hence, in Singapore, Yeoh et al (2021) describe marriage migrant women's struggles over childbearing and employment as attempts to negotiate not just their positions within families but the meaning of citizenship. For Japanese-Pakistani young women (2021), disjunctures between new valorisations of mixed ethnicity and lived experiences of racism, and the tensions between gendered positions within families and society, and between local and transnational experiences, produce a space in which they may negotiate new identities and trajectories. The tension between rhetoric and actual policies and practices on the ground can also constitute a space for activism. In Hong Kong (2021), NGOs assist women who have been widowed, divorced or separated from their citizen husbands in seeking out opportunities for 'discretionary citizenship' – concealed points at which they might find purchase for leverage, whilst Cheng (2013) and Hsia (2021) describe situations in which marriage migrants themselves become activists, seeking new opportunities within the ambiguities of their status as marriage migrants.

Interestingly, in the article by Cheng (2013), we also hear of a marriage migrant activist campaigning for migrants' rights in a broader sense, challenging the rigid categorical thinking which underpins so much of the regulation of international marriages, and indeed migration scholarship (Dahinden 2016; Moret, Andrikopoulos, and Dahinden 2019; Anderson 2013) and which divides migrants into categories of 'labour' and 'family'.

This volume's exploration of disjunction and agency therefore represents a substantial contribution to a foundational issue in the literature on marriage migration – the question of how to conceptualise the agency of marriage migrants, who paradoxically manage the agentic leap of migration at the same time as being pro-foundly dependent on their citizen spouses, with the well documented potential for victimisation this dependency contains (e.g. Williams and Yu 2006). In the articles making up this Special Issue, we see not only the tensions and disjunctures which characterise the field of marriage migration on so many levels, but also that these can emerge as potential sites of agency for marriage migrants. Taken as a whole, therefore, this collection of articles develops a consideration of 'Marriage Migration, Family and Citizenship in Asia' providing new insights into process not just of citizenship but also of disjuncture, change and agency, reaching into the heart of debates surrounding transnational marriage.

Future directions

This Special Issue also points to several areas ripe for further exploration. The processes of 'reproductive' or 'maternal' citizenship explored in these pages are deeply gendered, and of course women make up the clear majority of marriage migrants in the national contexts considered in these pages. Men, however, form a growing minority of foreign spouses married to citizens in many countries, so the continued relative neglect of migrant husbands in research in this area is notable. Indeed, only one paper (2021) in this collection deals with migrant husbands, and even then is focussed on their female offspring. By pointing this out, I do not mean to criticise the contributors to this Special Issue – the articles clearly demonstrate the utility of exploring the politics and experiences of female marriage migration. But research in other geographical and cultural contexts suggests that male marriage migrants also provide fertile ground for gendered analyses (Charsley 2005, Charsley and Ersanilli 2019; Gallo 2006; George 2005). In the field of citizenship which forms the focus of this volume, work has begun to address dynamics of national belonging for such couples, as such men tend not to be valued for their reproductive capa-cities; indeed, their fathering of citizens can present particular challenges in the context of enduring patrilineal ideologies of nationhood (Kwak 2019 on South Korea).

If female marriage migration is the implicit norm in marriage migration policy and research, the same can be said of the heterosexual family (Manalansan 2006). In drawing connections between this volume and the concept of 'intimate citizenship', it would be difficult to avoid the issue of queer and non-normative relationships which have been central to the development of the concept (Plummer 2001; Roseneil 2010). Chiu (2021) deals with single mothers (cf. Constable 2018 on transient relationships and failed transna-tional marriages), but what other non-normative relationship configurations might be ripe for examination for their connotations for citizenship, belonging and agency? Such work is underway elsewhere (e.g. https://www.nwo.nl/en/projects/vividi195013, Luibheid and Chavez 2020), but given the diversity of legal regimes governing homosexuality in Asia, the recent partial legalisation of same-sex marriage in Taiwan, the strongly heteronormative bent of immigration regulations, and the potential for these 'intimate mobilities' (Groes and Fernandez 2018) to pursue channels other than official spousal immigration, this might be particularly interesting territory for further exploration (Chang 2019; Yi 2020).

Woven throughout this collection are also illustrations of the importance of temporality – an area of recent interest in migration studies (Griffiths, Rogers, and Anderson 2013; Charsley 2020). Process of citizenship are inherently temporal, whilst national belongings are constructed through shared temporalities (Golden 2002). The articles in this Special Issue explore the implication of time limited spousal visas, the extended and sometimes indefinite temporalities of gaining citizenship, and the ways in which lifecourse issues such as childbearing are intertwined with temporal processes of immigration status and integration (Charsley et al. 2020). What further insights could be developed by following these connections between time, cross-border marriage, and citizenship?

This rich collection therefore both adds to our understandings of international marriage, particularly but not only in relation to processes and practices of citizenship, and whets the appetite for further research in this fascinating area of diversity, continuity and disjuncture.

Disclosure statement

No potential conflict of interest was reported by the author(s).

References

Anderson, B. 2013. *Us and Them? The Dangerous Politics of Immigration Control*. Oxford: Oxford University Press.

Appadurai, A. 1990. "Disjuncture and Difference in the Global Cultural Economy." *Theory, Culture and Society* 7 (2–3): 295–310. doi:10.1177/026327690007002017.

Bonjour, S., and B. De Hart. 2020. "Intimate Citizenship: Introduction to the Special Issue on Citizenship, Membership and Belonging in Mixed-Status Families." *Identities* 28 (1): 1–17. doi:10.1080/1070289X.2020.1737404.

Chang, H.-C. 2019. "Marriage Migration in Asia: The Migration of LGBTQ Persons for Reasons of Marriage between Asian Countries." In *Global Encyclopedia of Lesbian, Gay, Bisexual, Transgender and Queer History*, edited by H. Chiang, 997–1000. New York: Charles Scribner's Sons.

Charsley. 2020. "Covid 19 and Integration: A Research Agenda." Keynote Lecture, RUNOMI Annual Conference: Migrant Inclusion Studies in Times of Covid-19 Global Pandemic, Nijmegen, The Netherlands: Radboud University, October 28.

Charsley, K. 2005. "Unhappy Husbands: Masculinity and Migration in Transnational Pakistani Marriages." *Journal of the Royal Anthropological Institute* 11 (1): 85–105. doi:10.1111/j.1467-9655.2005.00227.x.

Charsley, K., ed. 2012. *Transnational Marriage: New Perspectives from Europe and Beyond*. London: Routledge.

Charsley, K., and E. Ersanilli. 2019. "The "Mangetar Trap"? Work, Family and Pakistani Migrant Husbands." *NORMA* 14 (2): 128–145. doi:10.1080/18902138.2018.1533272.

Charsley, K., and H. Wray. 2015. "Introduction: The Invisible (Migrant) Man." *Men and Masculinities* 18 (4): 403–423. doi:10.1177/1097184X15575109.

Charsley, K., M. Bolognani, E. Ersanilli, and S. Spencer. 2020. *Marriage Migration and Integration.* London: Palgrave MacMillan.

Cheng, I. 2013. "Motherhood, Empowerment and the New Southbound Policy: The Act of Citizenship of Vietnamese Immigrant Activists in Taiwan' in 'Marriage Migration, Family and Citizenship in Asia." Special Issue, *Citizenship Studies.*

Chiu, T. Y. 2021. "Discretionary Maternal Citizenship: State Hegemony and Bottom-up Resistance of Single Marriage Migrant Mothers from Mainland China to Hong Kong' in 'Marriage Migration, Family and Citizenship in Asia." Special Issue, *Citizenship Studies.*

Constable, N. 2005. *Cross-Border Marriage: Gender and Mobility in Transnational Asia.* Philadelphia: University of Pennsylvania Press.

Constable, N. 2018. "Temporary Intimacies, Incipient Transnationalism and Failed Cross-Border Marriages." In *Intimate Mobilities,* edited by C. Groes and N. Fernandez, 52–73. New York: Berghahn Books.

Cooke, T. 2008. "Migration in a Family Way." *Population, Place and Space* 14: 255–265. doi:10.1002/psp.500.

Dahinden, J. 2016. "A Plea for the "De-migranticization" of Research on Migration and Integration." *Ethnic and Racial Studies* 39 (13): 2207–2225. doi:10.1080/01419870.2015.1124129.

Gallo, E. 2006. "Italy Is Not a Good Place for Men: Narratives of Places, Marriages and Masculinity among Malayali Migrants." *Global Networks* 6 (4): 357–372. doi:10.1080/01419870.2015.1124129.

George, S. 2005. *When Women Come First: Gender and Class in Transnational Migration.* Berkeley: University of California Press.

Golden, D. 2002. "Belonging through Time: Nurturing National Identity among Newcomers to Isreal from the Former Soviet Union." *Time and Society* 11 (1): 5–24. doi:10.1177/0961463X02011001001.

Griffiths, M., A. Rogers, and B. Anderson. 2013. "Migration, Time and Temporalities: Review and Prospect." (*COMPAS Research Resources Paper*). https://www.compas.ox.ac.uk/wp-content/uploads/RR-2013-Migration_Time_Temporalities.pdf

Groes, C., and N. Fernandez. 2018. *Intimate Mobilities: Sexual Economies, Marriage and Migration in A Disparate World.* New York: Berghahn.

Heyman, J. M., and H. Campbell. 2009. "The Anthropology of Global Flows: A Critical Reading of Appadurai's 'Disjuncture and Difference in Yhe Global Cultural Economy." *Anthropological Theory* 9 (2): 131–148. doi:10.1177/1463499609105474.

Home Office. 2007. "Marriage to Partners from Overseas: A Consultation Paper." https://webarchive.nationalarchives.gov.uk/20091207122842/http://bia.homeoffice.gov.uk/sitecontent/documents/aboutus/consultations/closedconsultations/marriagetopartnersfromoverseas/marriagepartnersfromoverseas.pdf?view=Binary

Hsia, H.-C. 2021. "From 'Social Problems' to 'Social Assets': Geopolitics, Discursive Shifts in Children of Southeast Asian Marriage Migrants, and the Mother-Child Dyadic Citizenship in Taiwan' in 'Marriage Migration, Family and Citizenship in Asia'." Special Issue, *Citizenship Studies.*

Johnson, E. 2007. *Dreaming of a Mail-Order Husband: Russian-American Internet Romance.* Durham, NC: Duke University Press.

Jorgensen, M. B. 2012. "Danish Regulations on Marriage Migration: Policy Understandings of Transnational Marriages." In *Transnational Marriage,* edited by K. Charsley, 60–80. London: Routledge.

Kandiyoti, D. 1988. "Bargaining with Patriarchy." *Gender and Society* 2 (3): 274–290. doi:10.1177/089124388002003004.

Kofman, E. 1999. "Female "Birds of Passage" a Decade Later: Gender and Immigration in the European Union." *International Migration Review* 33 (2): 269–299.

Kudo, M. 2021. "Negotiating Citizenship and Reforging Muslim Identities: The Case of Young Women of Japanese-Pakistani Parentage in 'Marriage Migration, Family and Citizenship in Asia." Special Issue, *Citizenship Studies.*

Kwak, Y. 2019. "Pushing Away from Their Own Country? South Korean Women Married to Husbands from Developing Countries." *Ethnic and Racial Studies* 42 (7): 1186–1203. doi:10.1080/01419870.2018.1473620.

Luibheid, E., and K. R. Chavez, eds. 2020. *Queer and Trans Migrations: Dynamics of Illegalization, Detention and Deportation.* Illinois: University of Illinois Press.

MAC (Migration Advisory Committee). 2018. "EEA Migration in the UK: Final Report." https://assets.publishing.service.gov.uk/government/uploads/system/uploads/attachment_data/file/741926/Final_EEA_report.PDF

Manalansan, M. F., IV. 2006. "Queer Intersections: Sexuality and Gender in Migration Studies." *The International Migration Review* 40 (1): 224–249. doi:10.1111/j.1747-7379.2006.00009.x.

Moret, J., A. Andrikopoulos, and J. Dahinden. 2019. "Contesting Categories: Cross-Border Marriages from the Perspectives of the State, Spouses and Researchers." *Journal of Ethnic and Migration Studies* 47 (2): 325–342. doi:10.1080/1369183X.2019.1625124.

Pessar, P. R., and S. J. Mahler. 2003. "Transnational Migration: Bringing Gender In." *The International Migration Review* 37 (3): 812–846. doi:10.1111/j.1747-7379.2003.tb00159.x.

Piper, N., and M. Roces. 2003. *Wife or Worker: Asian Women and Migration.* Washington: Rowman and Littlefield.

Plummer, K. 2001. "The Square of Intimate Citizenship: Some Preliminary Proposals." *Citizenship Studies* 5 (3): 237–253. doi:10.1080/13621020120085225.

Roseneil, S. 2010. "Intimate Citizenship: A Pragmatic, yet Radical, Proposal for A Politics of Personal Life." *European Journal of Women's Studies* 17 (1): 77–82. doi:10.1177/1350506810017001060.

Sims, J. M. 2012. "Beyond the Stereotype of the "Thai-bride": Visibility, Invisibility and Community." In *Transnational Marriage: New Perspectives from Europe and Beyond*, edited by K. Charsley, 161–174. London and New York: Routledge.

Sumption, M., and C. Vargas-Silva. 2019. "Love Is Not All You Need: Income Requirement for Visa Sponsorship of Foreign Family Members." *Journal of Economics, Race and Policy* 2: 67–76. doi:10.1007/s41996-018-0022-8.

Toyota, M. 2008. "Editorial Introduction: International Marriage, Rights and the State in East and Southeast Asia." *Citizenship Studies* 12 (1): 1–7. doi:10.1080/13621020701794083.

Turner, B. S. 2008. "Citizenship, Reproduction and the State: International Marriage and Human Rights." *Citizenship Studies* 12 (1): 45–54. doi:10.1080/13621020701794166.

Williams, L., and M.-K. Yu. 2006. "Domestic Violence in Cross-Border Marriage: A Case Study from Taiwan." *International Journal of Migration, Health and Social Care* 2 (3/4): 58–69. doi:10.1108/17479894200600032.

Wilson, A. 2007. "The Forced Marriage Debate and the British State." *Race & Class* 49 (1): 25–38. doi:10.1177/0306396807080065.

Wray, H. 2006. "An Ideal Husband? Marriages of Convenience, Moral Gate-Keeping and Immigration to the UK." *European Journal of Migration and Law* 8 (3–4): 303–320. doi:10.1163/157181606778882582.

Wray, H., A. Agoston, and J. Hutton. 2014. "A Family Resemblance? The Regulation of Marriage Migration in Europe." *European Journal of Migration and Law* 16 (2): 209–247. doi:10.1163/15718166-12342054.

Yeoh, B. S. A., H. L. Chee, R. Anant, and T. Lam. 2021. "Transnational Marriage Migration and the Negotiation of Precarious Pathways beyond Partial Citizenship in Singapore' in 'Marriage Migration, Family and Citizenship in Asia." Special Issue, *Citizenship Studies.*

Yi, B. L. 2020. "'Happily Ever After' Eludes Taiwan, a Year after Asia's First Gay Marriages". https://uk.reuters.com/article/us-taiwan-lgbt-rights-feature-trfn/happily-ever-after-eludes-taiwan-a-year-after-asias-first-gay-marriages-idUSKBN22X03A

Yi, S. 2021. "Penalizing "Runaway" Migrant Wives: Commercial Cross-Border Marriages and Home Space as Confinement' in 'Marriage Migration, Family and Citizenship in Asia." Special Issue, *Citizenship Studies.*

Index

Note: Figures are indicated by *italics*. Tables are indicated by **bold**. Endnotes are indicated by the page number followed by 'n' and the endnote number e.g., 20n1 refers to endnote 1 on page 20.